Horses From History
By
Janice M. Ladendorf

Volume 2
Searching for the Real Frank T. Hopkins

Frank T. Hopkins at 65

Photo courtesy of Green Mountain Horse Association

Horses from History
Volume 2: Searching for the Real Frank T. Hopkins

Printed by CreateSpace.

Available from Amazon.com, CreateSpace.com, and other retail outlets.

Available on Kindle and other devices.

Searching for the Real Frank T. Hopkins

Preface

Frank Hopkins was born in 1865 near Fort Laramie, Wyoming. He was the son of a white scout and his Indian wife. Frank carried dispatches for the army during the Indian Wars, did specialty riding for Buffalo Bill's Wild West, and won 402 endurance races, one of which covered 3,000 miles in Arabia. In the 1930's, he was accepted by the eastern equestrian community as an experienced endurance rider and knowledgeable horseman.

Articles about his exploits and opinions appeared in reputable magazines like Western Horseman and in books by authors such as Frank Dobie. In an obscure Vermont magazine, he published a series of articles about horsemanship and his experiences on the frontier and with Bill's Show. Since he almost always competed in endurance races with mustangs, he was particularly popular with those who fought to save and maintain what Frank called American mustangs or Indian ponies.

Frank T. Hopkins married Gertrude Nehler in 1929 and died in 1951. In 1968, Robert Easton contacted her because he was interested in writing a biography of Frank. At that time, he was already well established as an author. His book, Lord of Beasts: The Saga of Buffalo Jones was published in 1961. Buffalo Jones was a great supporter of western mustangs and Easton's book about him may well be what introduced him to Frank Hopkins and his story.

He and Gertrude carried on a lengthy correspondence and she sent him what material she could, but Mr. Easton eventually decided he could not create a conventional biography because there were too many information gaps in what was available at that time. Fortunately, he donated what he had gathered to the American Heritage Center at the University of Wyoming. Unfortunately, some of these gaps still exist.

The movie, Hidalgo, is a fictional story based on one of Frank's exploits. In 1892, he took his mustang, Hidalgo, to Arabia to compete in a 3,000 mile race. Before the movie was released in 2004, a storm of controversy broke out over Frank's credibility. Was he or wasn't he a Western hero and a real horseman? Some say he was a liar, a fraud, a bigamist, or a psychopath. Attackers and defenders expressed their opinions in print and on the internet. From an historical perspective, opinions are not verifiable facts, especially when they are expressed in such a highly emotional tone.

In my opinion, Frank's published and unpublished material on horsemanship, endurance riding, and horses contains invaluable information, but validation required an extensive search to discover verifiable information about the real Frank T. Hopkins.

The results of my search are reported in this book. It begins with biographical information. Parts I and II are linked together with an outline format. Part I summarizes what little is known about Frank's life. It is meant for those who are not interested in bibliographical verification. Part II covers his life in detail and utilizes extensive quotations from both published and unpublished material. It contains and evaluates the evidence for each statement in the summary. Part III publishes or republishes Frank's articles or comments on horses, horsemanship, and endurance riding.

Bibliographic Verification for the Interested Reader:

The farther back in history a researcher goes, the more the results will be affected by the general and special factors described below.

General Factors:

1) Frank was born and bred on the western frontier. The public records maintained in such societies vary from fragmentary to non-existent.

2) Like most westerners, Frank said little about his personal history.

3) Frank spent most of his time traveling both here and abroad. Such people are often under represented in public records.

4) In 1870, only thirty percent of the populace was literate and this percentage was lower on the frontier. For example, the 1940 census says Frank never completed fourth grade, but his wife, Gertrude, came from New York and had completed eighth grade.

5) As time passes, memory is increasingly unreliable and the more people who pass on verbal information, the less accurate it will be.

6) Until the 1930's, employers had no legal incentive to maintain accurate records and did not have to take any action if an employee was accidentally killed or injured.

7) Real research into the history of the west did not begin until after Frank's death in 1951. Before that time and long afterwards, what most people knew about the West came from melodramatic dime novels, biased newspaper articles, and early movies.

8) In their search for heroes, Americans romanticized frontier life and cowboys.

Special Factors:

1) Frank has been misrepresented as the sole author of material that had been extensively edited and included misleading information. Provenance for every item quoted in this book has been carefully established. Where multiple or conflicting stories exist, the one with the most verifiable detail was used.

2) Except for the signature on Frank's marriage certificate, no other verifiable record of his handwriting has been found. His published articles were all submitted as drafts in his wife's handwriting. The material found at the University of Wyoming was also in her handwriting. Fortunately their personal voices were reflected in completely different styles of writing. One of Frank's critics claimed the differences in these styles proved Frank was psychotic.

When Gertrude was taking down dictation, her handwriting turned into a scribble and she added notes to it. Two valuable collections of material turned up in Frank's style and in this format. One was Frank's authentic memoir and the other his answers to letters from readers. When the unpublished material has been used, punctuation and spelling errors have been corrected to improve readability.

Table of Contents

Introduction: What did Frank T. Hopkins look like?

Frank T. Hopkins was a slim, lean, man who was about six feet tall and had black hair and hazel eyes. When he was competing in endurance rides, he weighed 152 pounds, all solid muscle without one ounce of fat. Unfortunately, not many photographs of him or his horses have survived. The photograph below was taken in 1905 when he was with Buffalo Bill's Wild West.

The first photograph below shows three of Frank's horses at Buffalo Bill's Wild West. The second one shows Frank on Gypsy Boy, one of the horses he bred for endurance racing. He has just won a race and is shaking hands with Bud Tobel.

Frank married Gertrude Nehler in 1929 when he was sixty-four years old. The first photograph on the next page shows him at age sixty-five. He is wearing one of his ten gallon hats and his custom made boots. This photograph was used with some of the articles he wrote for the Vermont Horse and Bridle Trail Bulletin.

The second photograph below shows some of the things Frank used when he was with Buffalo Bill's Wild West. Frank always wore a ten gallon hat and, like most cowboys of his day, he put special creases in his felt hats. This photograph shows one of Frank's special hats.

Like many of the old timers, Frank created a lot of his own gear. He made the bridle shown in the photograph below for parades and decorated it with mother-of-pearl and silver in intricate designs. The Wyoming State Museum still has this bridle. The donor states he made and used it with Buffalo Bill's Wild West from 1900-1915.

The last item in the photograph is his hand tooled boots. They were custom made for him by Shipley out of walrus hide. For trick riding, the heels were lined with baby kangaroo fur.

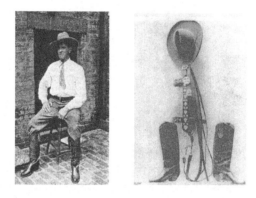

The photographs below were taken in 1948 or 1949 by Edith Pyle at Pocantico Farms, New York. At that time, Frank was eighty three years old. In the first photograph, his wife Gertrude is on his left and his friend, Ned Wehrman, on his right. He is holding Bluebird, a Canadian mustang owned by the Pyle family. In the second photograph, Frank is riding Bluebird.

Acknowledgements:

Photos 1, 2 and 7 courtesy of the American Heritage Museum, University of Wyoming. Photo 3 courtesy of the Horse, March-April, 1935. Photos 4 and 5 courtesy of the Pyle family. Photo 6 courtesy of the Green Mountain Horse Association.

Editor's Note: The few photographs we have of Frank were found in historical or personal files and mostly in sepia. As the above photos show, they varied considerably in quality. One had even been nibbled on by mice.

Part I - Summary of Biographical Information

Chapter 1: Early Life

1) Frank's parents

Frank's father, Charles Hopkins, was employed as civilian packer who led or guided pack strings and wagon trains when they delivered equipment and supplies to western Army posts and expeditions. Frank described him as a great plainsman who was always pleasant, but spoke very little. He was ninety-seven years old when he died in 1919.

The name of Frank's mother was Vallez Nauqua or Valley Naugra. With those names, she could not have been an Anglo Saxon and probably was an Oglala Sioux. Frank described her as a large woman over six feet tall who was always carefree and happy. She was born in 1848 and died in 1920.

2) Frank was born on August 11, 1865 and died on Nov. 5, 1951.

3) Fort Laramie had been built on a plateau in a bend of the Laramie River. South of the Fort and the River, there was a large flood plain where the Indians, half Indians, and transients were allowed to camp. Frank was born there in a teepee or possibly a small log cabin.

4) Frank's middle name was Tezolph and he refused to explain what it meant. His mother's relatives probably gave him an Indian name, but nobody remembers what it was.

5) Frank's maternal grandfather gave him his first pony. He described how Oglala Chief Sadheart taught him carving and helped him train his first wild horse.

6) Frank probably attended one of the two schools at Fort Laramie. One was for the children of enlisted men and civilian employees and the other for half Indian children.

7) Frank's father brought Morgan horses to establish a ranch near Fort Laramie. The Hopkins family probably relocated there sometime between 1868 and 1874. Frank described how he saved orphan foals.

8) The brand records indicate their ranch was located about twenty three miles northwest of Fort Laramie near the Goshen County border with Platte County.

Chapter 2: Carrying Dispatches, Hunting Buffalo, and Catching Wild Horses

1) Frank began carrying dispatches for the Army on his birthday, Aug. 11, 1877. He carried them for nine years until the spring of 1886. He traveled from the Sonora Mountains of old Mexico to the Canadian Northwest.

2) Franks described three dramatic incidents that occurred during his years of dispatch riding. In one, he was almost downed in a river crossing. In two, he was badly wounded and his horse carried him to safety. In three, he survived a bad blizzard.

3) Frank rode and won his first endurance race in 1877. During his years as a dispatch rider, Frank won 181 endurance races and bought the foundation mare and stallion for his own breeding program.

4) When he was not needed to carry dispatches, Frank worked as a dropper for the buffalo hunters (runners). Like the Indians, droppers selected individual buffalo to shoot from horseback.

5) Frank described two incidents that occurred on buffalo hunts in the winter of 1887-8. In one, he struggled to catch a white buffalo. In two, he is trapped in the middle of a stampeding herd and to stay alive, he had to ride on a bull buffalo.

6) During this time, Frank also caught wild horses. He liked to work on his own and described how he once caught a herd of 39 horses.

Chapter 3 - Race from Texas to Vermont (1800 miles)

1) The horse Frank rode in this race was named Joe. He described how he found him and what he was like.

2) Frank heard about the race and Buffalo Jones encouraged him to enter, paid his entry fee and backed him to win. Frank described what he did to get Joe ready for the race.

3) Frank described the rules and how the race was managed. He also mentioned some of his competitors. He and Joe reached Rutland in 31 days with an average of 57.7 miles per day. He waited thirteen days before the next horse to arrive. They had to wait a few more days for the third and last horse. Frank weighed 152 pounds while his saddle, pad, and slicker weighed 32 pounds. Joe had to carry one hundred and eight-four pounds on the ride, but he gained eight pounds.

4) Frank described how he cared for Joe during the race and some of his experiences along the way.

5) There are still some unanswered questions about exactly where the race ended in Rutland.

Chapter 4: Traveling with Buffalo Bill's Wild West

1) Frank described the difficult time he had adjusting to performing in an enclosed arena with cheering crowds.

2) In England, Frank's trick riding act with Black Elk was a great success. He described their first performance and the special show they put on for Queen Victoria. When Bill's show sponsored a race from Earls Court to Lands Edge, Frank got permission to ride in it and won. Uney, the horse he rode was the sire of Hidalgo.

3) Frank had soon figured out he had made a poor bargain with Cody and Salisbury. When the show closed at Richmond in Oct. of 1889, he refused to sign another contract.

Chapter 5: Riding with Buffalo Bills Wild West, 1889-1893.

1) Frank negotiated a new contract and went to Europe with the show. He described the results of the World Horseman Contest at the World's Fair in Paris, France, as well as the races he won in Italy, Germany, and England.

2) When Frank returned home in the fall of 1890, he described the one race he lost and the two he won in Oklahoma. Just before the Massacre of Wounded Knee, Frank arrived at Pine Ridge Reservation to visit friends, but he was not involved in the Massacre.

3) In 1892, Bill's Show spent the last six months at Earls Court in London, England. The death of Long Wolf, one of the Lakota Indians, is described.

4) Frank described his race to the Chicago World's Fair in 1893. He commented on Buffalo Bill as a marksman.

Chapter 6: Riding with Buffalo Bill's Wild West, 1894-1906

1) In 1894, Bill's show played the season at Ambrose Park, South Brooklyn.

Frank told the story of two races he won in New England.

Frank visited the Arapahoe Agency to buy horses.

2) In 1895, Bill's show was re-organized by James Bailey and began playing at many one night stands.

Frank told the story of two races he won, one in Canada and one in Vermont.

One of the charro ropers from Mexico told Frank about races along their border and he went south in the winter with Frank and his ponies. Frank won eleven races.

Frank got a chance to ride Hightower, the champion bucker of Bill's show. He rode him to a standstill.

Frank told the story of a old fashioned race in Idaho Falls. He loaned 17 of his ponies to other riders and won by eight minutes.

Frank told the story of Gypsy Boy, an orphan foal brought up by his mother. When Bill's show played in Cheyenne, Wyoming, she came to see them and he let his horse go home with her.

3) In 1903-6, the show tours Europe again.

Frank resolved a problem with a trotting horse owned by a Belgian with his trotting horse.

Chapter 7: Staying with Buffalo Bill's Wild West, 1907-1917

1) In 1907, Buffalo Bill got rid of the circus elements in his show and set up a new program of events.

2) Frank described how he felt about Buffalo Bill's show joining up with the one run by Pawnee Bill (Major Gordon Lillie).

The market for carriage horses died and Frank took on the responsibility of selling the old type Morgans bred by his father. His friend, Bud Tobel, advised him to turn them into polo ponies and he sold many to Argentina. He took some of his endurance ponies down there and won 68 races.

3) In 1913, Bill's show went bankrupt.

Frank lost some of his horses and all of his photographs in a bad fire.

4) In 1914 and 1915, Bill's show joined up with the Sells-Floto Circus.

Frank described what he felt about this new joint show.

Frank sold the rest of his father's horses to a Japanese army officer and took four of his endurance ponies to Japan where he won 38 races.

5) In 1916, Bill's show joined with the 101 Ranch Show.

Buffalo Bill died on Jan. 10, 1917. Several members kept the show going for the 1917 season.

Frank was asked to undertake confidential work for the government.

Chapter 8: Race in Arabia (3,000 miles)

1) Hidalgo's pedigree is described.

2) Information in Frank's memoir was compared to the route listings of the show's travels. The only time when this race could have occurred was the winter of 1892-1893.

3) In 1892, the race was politically feasible because the route went through areas controlled by the British, Oman, and the Ottoman Empires. It had to cross tribal boundaries, but not today's national ones.

4) The horses of Arabia are described. Frank's description identifies ones from North Yemen and the Ottoman province of Syria.

5) In 1892, the route of the race was geographically feasible because it occurred before the discovery of oil on the western coast of the Persian Gulf. Providing water and food to the contestants was probably done by dhows and camels. In the last phase, only camels could be used and water was scarce.

6) What Hidalgo ate was barley and vetches. This diet is used all through the Middle East and in California.

Frank states Hidalgo did lose condition. Considerable loss in flesh is common when horses are regularly ridden longer distances. He may also have suffered from some dehydration in the last phase of the race, but Frank reports he never faltered.

Chapter 9: Last Years

1) In 1919, Frank was devastated by the death of his parents. He describes the two years he spent training trotters in Belgium. Frank

returns home and enjoys his reunion with his five remaining mustangs. He accepts another training job.

2) Frank describes how he defended his reputation by winning his two final races. In 1926, an interview with a fraudulent Hopkins was published in a Philadelphia newspaper. A detailed analysis of this article is in the appendix to this chapter.

3) Frank finds a new career as a deep sea diver. In 1929, he marries Gertrude Nehler. The marriage certificate shows he lived at the boarding house run by Gertrude's mother and his mother's name was Vallez Nauqua. Gertrude's family history is traced through census records. Gertrude describes Frank and entertains his friends at their home. For the first time, the real Frank T. Hopkins appears in the 1940 census. His age and birthplace are correctly identified and he identifies his race as Indian.

Chapter 10: A Growing Reputation

1) When Frank lost his last mustang in 1928, he may have thought his riding days were over, but in 1926 the Green Mountain Association had been formed to build trails and promote trail riding in Vermont. In 1937, they sponsored an annual 100 mile ride on Labor Day weekend and it is still held every year. Frank had much to offer these people and three articles by Charles B. Roth, let them know he existed and now lived in Long Island City, NY.

2) Frank drew on his hard earned expertise and freely offered them information, as well as help to anyone who asked for it. He wrote a series of articles for their magazine, the Vermont Horse and Bridle Trail Bulletin. The articles are listed in Appendix A to this chapter. In one of them, Frank describes his experience as one of the judges at their sixth annual hundred mile ride.

3) Charles B. Roth sent Albert W. Harris one of his articles about Frank. Mr. Harris owned, rode, drove, and bred both Arabs and Mustangs. He was intrigued by the article and sent Mr. Roth many questions. He asked Frank to reply. His letters describe his breeding

program and his two longest races. Mr. Harris published the article and both letters in his classic book, The Blood of the Arab.

Mr. Harris was highly respected and his book well known. The information on Frank was accepted and used by such authorities as Frank Dobie, Jack Schaefer, and John Richard Young.

4) After Frank's death in 1951, many other authors utilized the information in Roth's articles, Frank's articles, and the Harris book.

5) The Pyle family knew Frank well. Tom Pyle had known him for years and valued him both as a horseman and naturalist. Edith Colgate had competed in five of the annual rides before she married his son, Walt. Frank often drove up to visit them and to ride on the trails of the nearby Rockefeller estate. In the late 1940's, every Sunday Ned Wehrman picked him up and drove him up to their home, Pocantico Farms. In 1948, Edith took a photograph of Frank riding one of their mustangs.

6) The Conroy family were professional horseman who knew Frank well and valued his knowledge of horsemanship.

7) Describes deaths of Lisette Nehler in 1949, Frank Hopkins in 1951, and Gertrude Hopkins in 1971.

Chapter 11: Conclusion

1) Positive and negative editing is discussed, as it relates to Gertrude's impact on Frank's manuscripts.

2) Frank never claimed to be any type of romantic western hero. His career is correctly defined as a dispatch rider, specialty rider with Bill's show, and endurance rider.

3) Many factors contributed to Frank's success as a great horseman. They are reviewed as an introduction to Part III.

Part II - Detailed Biographical Information

Chapter 1 - Early Life

Background Information: Public Records on the Wyoming Frontier

Frontier societies rarely maintained any public records and when they did, they could be inaccurate. Fort Laramie was eventually assigned to Goshen County and their public records did not begin until 1915. In Wyoming, this situation was aggravated by two factors. First, it contained the South Pass, which was the easiest way to cross the Continental Divide and reach Oregon, California, and Utah. People traveled through Wyoming, but did not stay there. Most of the first settlers lived by serving thousands of emigrants as they traveled west. Second, parts of the modern state had been originally assigned to the territories of Nebraska, Dakota, Oregon, Washington, Idaho, and Utah. This bureaucratic muddle complicated the maintenance of any public records. To become a territory, Wyoming had to prove it had a population of at least 5,000 inhabitants. It became a territory in 1869 and a state in 1890. As compared to other states, it still has a low population level.

1) Frank's Parents

They lived on the frontier and the only public record of their names is on Frank's marriage certificate.[1]

a) His father, Charles Hopkins, is usually described as a scout, but the Army used Indians as scouts and only occasionally hired an especially knowledgeable white man for that job. Charles Hopkins was described as a packer in the two items described below. These men led or guided the pack strings and wagon trains who delivered equipment and goods to Army posts and expeditions. To do their dangerous job, they had to know the geography of unmapped country and the Indian tribes on every route they had to take to get their cargos delivered.

John G. Bourke mentions Charles Hopkins twice in his book, *On the Border with Crook.* He described packers as a group of men who been forty-niners in the California Gold Rush and who had faced all the perils of frontier life, endured all the necessary privations, and survived.[2]

Charles Hopkins is also mentioned in an article about Thomas Moore, "Prince of the Packers".[3]

In his memoir, Frank describes him as a great plainsman who was always pleasant, but spoke very little. He was ninety-seven when he died in 1919.[5]

b) Frank's mother was identified on his marriage certificate. Her name could be read as Vallez Nauqua or Valley Naugria.[1] The minister probably had to write down phonetically what he heard Frank say. With those names, his mother could not have been Anglo Saxon [white]. She was probably an Oglala Sioux, but no records have yet been found to verify her tribal identity.

In his memoir, Frank described his mother as a large woman whose height was 6 feet and two inches. She was always happy and carefree. She was born seventeen years before him, probably in 1848 and died five months after his father in 1920.[5]

Frank's wife, Gertrude, stated "F.T. [Frank] did lots of things somebody else took the credit for - being of Indian blood."[4]

On his marriage certificate, Frank was described as white[1], but the minister could simply have assumed he looked like a white man. In the 1940 census, he identifies himself as Indian.[6]

2) Frank's Birth Date

a) According to the 1940 census, Frank T. Hopkins was born in Wyoming. At the time of the census was taken, he was 74 years old. His birth year was listed as about 1866.[6]

b) According to Frank's wife, Gertrude, his actual birth date 8-11-65 and he was born at sunrise. He died on Nov. 5, 1951.[7]

c) According to the Index of Find a Grave, Frank was born in 1865 at Fort Laramie, Goshen County, Wyoming.[8]

d)) Frank's wife, Gertrude, states he was 64 when they were married in 1929.[4]

e) According to his marriage certificate, Frank was 44 in 1929 and born in Laremie, Wyoming.[1]

Evaluation (a above):

When the Census Bureau hired people to collect information in a specified area, they went from door to door and wrote down information about every person who was in that location at that time. Given the interplay between birth dates, the date of data collection, and human error; birth years were often off by one or two years. Since census data was collected in April, Frank would have been 74 at that time and 75 after his birthday.

Evaluation (e above):

The information on the certificate was hastily written down by the presiding minister. Frank probably would have had a hard time explaining where his birth place to anyone who was unfamiliar with Wyoming geography and history. When Wyoming became a territory in 1869, Laramie County included both the city of Laramie and Fort Laramie. In 1911, historic Fort Laramie became part of Goshen County and since 1925, there has also been a town of Fort Laramie.

The town of Laramie is located on the Laramie River in Albany County on the route of the Transcontinental Railroad. It is one hundred miles southwest of Fort Laramie. From the town of Laramie, the Laramie River flows north through the Laramie Mountain Range before it reaches Fort Laramie. Along with the misspelled name and location, the incorrect age on the certificate may been a misunderstanding or a simple error made by the minister.

Background Information: Fort Laramie

Many frontier forts were built during the Indian Wars, but Fort Laramie had a different and longer history. In 1834, it was built by William Sublette to service the fur trade and he called it Fort William. The picture below shows it 1837. In 1841, it was purchased by the American Fur Company and renamed Fort John. In 1849, it was purchased by the Army and renamed Fort Laramie. All three forts were built near where the Laramie River flowed from the west into the North Platte River. This was strategic location and a crucial stopping point on the trail leading to South Pass.

This site was a desirable one. The Laramie River flowed down from the mountains so it contained good water and there was excellent grazing along its banks. The photograph below shows the River just before it reached the Fort.

By 1865, two settlements existed at the Fort. One was the military post which had been built on a plateau just north of the Laramie River. During the Civil War, the garrison was reduced to one hundred and thirty-two men.[9] The other settlement was on the flood plain south of the Laramie River. In 1865, three groups of people lived in the south settlement.

Group a) The wives, widows, and children of white men who had married Indian women. When the fur traders and mountain men went west, they found no white woman so they often married Indians. A common pattern was to maintain a white legal wife in St. Louis and to marry one or more Indian wives by tribal rituals. When they worked for the military, their children would have been categorized as Indians or half-breeds.

Group b) The second group was the Laramie Loafers. This band of the Oglala Sioux was led by Chief Big Mouth and hung around the Fort looking for handouts.[10]

Group c) The third group was visiting Indians who had come to the Fort to trade at the sutler's store.[11]

3) Frank's Birthplace

At Fort Laramie, the guides and wagon masters reported to the Quartermaster because they were civilian employees.[12] Frank's father probably lived with his Indian wife south of the River. The military paid little attention to what happened in that encampment and Fort Laramie has no records on any of the names of the Indian woman, children, or half-breeds who lived there.[13] Since Frank was half Indian, he would have been born there in a tepee or possibly a small log cabin.

4) Frank's Names

Frank probably had several names.

When searching public records for names as common as Frank Hopkins or Frank T. Hopkins, other information must be used to verify the individual has been correctly identified. The real Frank T. Hopkins describes his status as single on his marriage certificate.[1] The bigamy claim first came from a misidentification in the 1910 census records.

That Frank T. Hopkins had a wife and two children, was born in Texas in 1878, and drafted into the Army in 1918.[14]

According to his first and only wife, Gertrude, Frank's middle name was Tezolph and he consistently refused to explain what it meant.[4]

When Frank visited his mother's relatives, he probably would have been given an Indian name. Although stories of his exploits live on in Indian legends,[15] nobody remembers what it was.

5) Frank's Indian Relatives

The Hopkins papers at the University of Wyoming include answers to letters Frank had received from readers. In one of them, he states,

"I started riding when I was very young and I recall riding without stirrups a little squaw pony my grandfather brought to me for my birthday. My father would not allow me to use stirrups for a long time until I had learned to keep balanced and 'go with the horse' as he called it."[16]

One of Frank's published articles included a picture of one of his cravings of bison. The picture is shown below.

He says, "These buffalo were carved, with a common pocket knife, out of genuine mahogany, and I carved them at odd intervals during spare moments over a period of about two months. The 'bull' in the foreground stands about 6 inches high at shoulders and his body is 8 inches long. Two cows behind him with baby calves, are a bit smaller. The last year calves, or 'spikehorns' as we call 'em, are in the rear.

Carving is hobby of mine learned from old Chief 'Sadheart', a Dakota Indian of the Olgalala band of the Sioux Nation."[17]

In another one of his published articles, Frank tells a story about Chief Sadheart and one of his mustangs. He states,

"I recall a little stallion, the meanest bunch of muscles and bone ever wrapped in horse hide, who had been caught as a wild mustang and sold from the Trading Post at Fort Laramie, Wyo. The horse breakers tried to take the rough edge off him by choking him down and throwing him every day. This game little horse fought without giving an inch of ground. He was finally classed as a 'killer' and outlaw. He was run into a small corral and left alone. I watched this little feller fight the burning ropes that choked him, but every time, the horse 'won the round'.

I could not forebear telling those breakers they might learn something from that mustang if they hung 'round long enough. They said he was mine if I wanted to feed him in the corral, so every day I cut grass and fed the horse, by holding the feed in my hands. At first, he would not come near the bars. After a few days, he was hungry enough to make a grab at the grass and jump away. Later, learning there was nothing to harm him, he would poke his muzzle through the bars. Finally, I got him to eat grain from a wooden measure held in my hand. As I was only a boy then, it seemed to me I'd accomplished something and I ran over to Chief Sadheart's tepee to tell him about a wild horse eating out of my hand.

'Hi-w-in', he said, and started out for the corral with me in tow. There the old Chief told me of many wild horses he had tamed. He said to me, 'this horse is not bad - just afraid of man' and added that I should look though the skin and see the real horse who was all good, not mean. He then called my attention to the stallion's markings - a black roan, the white of his face spreading down the sides of the jaws. Both front legs were white nearly up to the chest. There was a white spot on the hips that reminded me of a bootjack and from this mark the pony got his name of Bootjack.

Within a few months, under Sadheart's tuition, I trained the first wild horse which I owned and which was my true friend until he died - full of arrows - five years later. The remains of this brave little animal rest not far where he fought those burning ropes of the horse breakers. I

24

always recall old Sadheart's words - 'when you can see through the skin, you will find the real horse.'"[18]

Evaluation:

In my opinion, the above stories indicate Frank had established a good relationship with some of his Indian relatives.

6) Frank's Education

In the 1940 census, Frank said he had never completed fourth grade.[6]

Schools were rare on the frontier and children were usually taught at home if they had a literate parent, but Fort Laramie did have two schools. One was started in 1864 for the children of enlisted men and civilian employees. Officers refused to send their children to this school. In 1968, it was taught by the post chaplain, in 1871-2 by Mrs. Ella DeWoolf, and in 1877 by the post surgeon. These teachers were exceptions, classes were normally taught by an enlisted man who hated his job and had trouble controlling the unruly children. School ran for three hours in the morning and three in the afternoon, but only in the winter months. There was a post library, but probably it would not have contained any reading material children would enjoy. Materials for the school were funded through a license tax for dogs. In 1878, it paid for twenty-five dollarrs of spelling, reading, and penmanship texts.[19]

The post also ran a special school for the half-breed Indian children from the encampment south of the River. It started in 1866 and began with thirty-five students.[20] Frank could have gone to either school and learned to read, but he may never have been taught how to prepare written documents. His minimal education may explain why he dictated all of his articles, letters, and memoirs to his wife.

Background Information: Wyoming Range

In the early days, most of Wyoming was open range. Even today some cattle roam loose on unfenced public land. Ranchers picked out a spot they liked, settled down on it, used it, and claimed it, but it was still public land. In the earlier 1900's, ranchers began homesteading the lands they had already claimed. The Wyoming Livestock Growers'

Association initially recorded cattle brands for its members by county. This function was taken over by the state in 1909.

7) Leaving Fort Laramie

Charles Hopkins had selected a good spot near Fort Laramie for a horse ranch. In one of his articles, Frank states,

"Next to the Mustang for hardiness, I believe are those oldtime Morgans, so hard to find today. I well remember those shortlegged chunks - much like the small horse of Holland. My father was probably the first man to bring those horses into the Northwest. I can recall when he went East and bought a number of mares and stallions although I was only a small shaver at the time and recall it only as one waking from a pleasant dream. Father had been wounded at the wagon-box fight [in 1867] and laid up for a long time but when he got well enough he went to New England and brought those horses back with him. They came by rail to North Platte, then were driven overland to Laramie. The first winter, all of them lived on the range without housing which is unusual for stable raised stock. In a few years he had a large herd and every cowboy in that part of the country was proud to ride of those C.H. horses and would say 'this yere one is a Morgan and the best cow hoss in these parts.' And they were top stock horses; many of them had a great burst of speed from a standing start; they could handle those old moss-horned cattle that weighed twice as much as they did. It was a pretty sight to see one of those horses come to a square stop with sixteen hundred pounds of beef at the other end of the rope. Those horses weighed between nine and ten hundred pounds and they could bust any bull or steer on the range and do it right. Father liked the straight blood in all his stock so the Morgan blood remained clear as long as he lived."[21]

The use of Laramie, rather than Fort Laramie, in this article was probably simply an informal abbreviation. By 1868, the town of Laramie and Fort Laramie were already in separate counties.

The above information suggests the Hopkins family moved from Fort Laramie to the C.H. Ranch sometime between 1868 and 1879. Before the move, Frank's father would had to have built buildings, corrals, etc. at the ranch. Initially they may have spent summers at the ranch and winters at Fort Laramie. The date of their final move may well have been 1879 when Frank's schooling was interrupted.

Frank gives us a glimpse of his boyhood on the ranch when he describes how he cared for orphan foals.

"As a child, my mother encouraged me in caring for motherless colts that I brought in off the range. Every spring I had many to care for - some were chilled to the point of stiffness. Mother let me bring them right into the kitchen beside the old big cook stove and helped me rub them till they were able get on their feet. Many times I stayed up all night caring for them - seldom one died. I'd rob the milk from cows that had calves to feed these colts, and I'd milk gentle mares with colts by their sides. I got bowled over often by these old mares - some of them would chase me right out of the feed corral. I did not always escape without a few blood blisters where they nipped me in the seat of my pants as I crawled through the rails of the corral."[22]

8) The C. H. Ranch?

The exact location of this ranch has not yet been identified, but the Hopkins brand is listed in the 1916 Brand Book.[23] The Wyoming Livestock Board sent me some information showing Frank Hopkins bought a brand on July 24, 1915 and held it until 1925. The location specified was Frederick, Goshen and Platte Counties.[24]

Frederick was a Post Office from 1894-1923 and near the Goshen/Platte county line. At one time, it had a population of seventy people. It was five and one half miles from Sunrise, the nearest railroad point. Sunrise is about eighteen miles northwest of Fort Laramie. Frederick and Sunrise are both located on the Hartville uplift, a rugged area with ravines, forest, and grassy basins.

Evaluation (Chapter 1):

In a letter to Robert Easton, one of Frank's friends states,

"Like most all of the 'Old Timers", he was chary, of those who were inclined to question, anything which smacked of doubt, as to his utterance. Perhaps this trait stems from the fact that in the early days, anyone who was inclined to delve into a matter of a personal nature, was taken as an insult. What was told was accepted. If a man was inclined to withhold details, such as small details, that was his business. Regardless of what name he might give, upon reaching a town, and asked his name, for instance, it was accepted. The rule prevailing that what he gave was his own affair, and further questioning resented."[25]

Gertrude married Frank in 1929, but Robert Easton found she knew little about his life before their marriage probably because he choose not to tell her about it. This is one of the first gaps in his biographical records. There is much we don't know about Frank's early life, especially as it related to the names of his Indian relatives and their heritage. His mother may have always spoken Sioux with him and he was fluent in that language. He probably learned trick riding and archery from his Indian relatives, but we do not know when and where this could have happened. Later, he does mention Indians who were boyhood friends and he may have learned trick riding with them.

As the photograph below shows, all his life he practised archery. This photograph was published an article, "The Toughest Race", by Charles B. Roth, Horse and Horseman, Jan. 1937, p. 31.

Acknowlegments:

Photos 1 and 2 courtsey of Wikepedia. Photo 3 courtsey of Green Mountain Horse Association. Photo 4 courtsey of The Horse and Horseman, Jan. 1937.

Footnotes:

[1]State of New York, The City of New York, Dept. of Health, Certificate and Record of Marriage, #3220.

[2]Bourke, John G. On the Border with Crook. Skyhorse Publishing, 2014, pp. 154, 210.

[3]Spring, Agnes Wright, "Prince of the Packers", True West, Sept.-Oct., 1970, p. 48.

[4]Gertrude Hopkins to Robert Easton, April 25, 1970, p. 4 and 1. Hopkins Papers, Robert Olney Easton Collection, American Heritage Center, University of Wyoming. It is also in their digital collection.

[5]Hopkins, Frank T. Memoir, Letter 1, p. 50. Hopkins Papers, Robert Olney Easton Collection, American Heritage Center, University of Wyoming.

[6]US Census Bureau. Records of the 1940 Census for Long Island City, New York.

[7]Gertrude Hopkins to Robert Easton, Election Day, 1968, p. 1. Hopkins Papers, Robert Olney Easton Collection, American Heritage Center, University of Wyoming.

[8]US Find a Grave Index, 1600's-Current, Memorial #10331690.

[9]Hafen, LeRoy R. and Young, Francis Marian. Fort Laramie and the Pageant of the West, 1834-1890. University of Nebraska Press, 1938, p. 303.

[10]Lavender, David. Fort Laramie and the Changing Frontier. Handbook 118, National Park Service, 1983, p. 67.

[11]Hafen, LeRoy R. and Young, Francis Marian. Fort Laramie and the Pageant of the West, 1834-1890. University of Nebraska Press, 1938, pp. 346-350.

[12]Hafen, LeRoy R. and Young, Francis Marian. Fort Laramie and the Pageant of the West, 1834-1890. University of Nebraska Pres, 1938, p. 254.

[13]Lowry, Sandy to Author, e-mails 1-4-16 NS 1-6-16.

[14]US Census Bureau. Records of the 1910 Census for Hudson, New York.

U.S., World War I Draft Registration Cards, 1917-1918.

[15]"The Legend of Hidalgo", recorded by Angelique Midthunder. www.frankhopkins.com.

[16]Frank Hopkins. "Sitting in the Saddle", Answers, Letter 6, p. 4. Hopkins Papers, Robert Olney Easton Collection, American Heritage Center, University of Wyoming.

[17]Hopkins, Frank T. "Hunting Buffalo", Vermont Horse and Bridle Trail Bulletin, January, 1942, p. 3.

[18]Hopkins, Frank T. "Horses and Horsemen", Vermont Horse and Bridle Trail Bulletin, July, 1943, p. 73.

[19]Lavender, David. Fort Laramie and the Changing Frontier. Handbook 118, National Park Service, 1983, pp. 136-7, 142.

[20]Excerpts of school records from the Fort Laramie Historical Archives.

[21]Hopkins, Frank. "Endurance Horses as I Know Them", Vermont Horse and Rider Trail Bulletin, July, 1941, p. 81.

[22]Hopkins, Frank T. "Trail Horses", Vermont Horse and Rider Trail Bulletin, Oct. 1946, p. 154.

[23]Wyoming Livestock Board, Wyoming Brand History (Frank Hopkins 7OL Brand).

Wyoming Livestock Board, Brand Book, 1916, p. 241. It can be found in the digital collection at the American Heritage Center, University of Wyoming.

[24]Wyoming Livestock Board, Frank Hopkins 7OL Brand, 1909-1925.

[25]Undated letter from Nevada Dick (Dickey, E. M.) to Robert Easton, p. 1. Hopkins Papers, Robert Olney Easton Collection, American Heritage Center, University of Wyoming.

Chapter 2: Carrying Dispatches, Hunting Buffalo, and Catching Wild Horses

Background Information: Dispatch Riding

The US Army normally used soldiers for delivering dispatches. When they had to move out to the western prairies and mountains, this practice no longer worked. They had an enormous area to cover and no maps of it existed. It was also filled hostile, semi-hostile, or semi-friendly Indians. To maintain communication among the frontier posts, they hired civilians as needed. These riders had to know the country, the trails, and the Indians well enough to get their messages delivered. On most rides they rode one horse, but when speed was required, they had several options. They could ride one horse and lead one, then regularly switch horses. They could also keep changing to a new horse, just as the Pony Express had done. Many of the dispatch riders were adolescent boys who rode light in the saddle. At that time in history, children were expected to do chores and adolescents to find a paying job.

1) Dispatch Rider

On Frank's thirteenth birthday, Aug. 11, 1877, he set out for the first time with dispatches for the Army. He comments,

"I was dispatch rider, riding from one fort to another to outpost Army camps and often to distant stations where those messages were telegraphed to the War Department in Washington. My trails led across north and south west, far down into the Sonora Mountains of old Mexico and up to the Canadian Northwest."[1]

"As a dispatch rider for nine years during the Indian troubles on the Western Plains, I tried out many different strains of horse. That kind of riding was hard on the horse and if he didn't have the stuff in him you'd soon find it out. Two or three hundred miles on a single trip was not unusual. The horse had to get his feed from the ground - all the care he got was to have his back rubbed off with a handful of buffalo grass. There were times when I had to race my horse for hours in order to save my life. Again, I would have a running fight with Indian scouts who were always lurking in the hills; the luckiest rider and best horse went on - the other generally stayed on the spot. Sometimes, there were rivers, good and bad, you had to swim your horse across. The winters back in those days were a good colder than they are now and the storms more severe - driving blizzards, cutting winds, deep snow and only a trail to follow - no shelter of any sort to put into. In the winter I broke the limbs from cottonwood to feed my mounts and dug down into the snow where I slept in the blankets. Plenty of that kind of work and hardship will surely test out a horse. During those nine years -1877 to 1886 - I had lots of time to find that comfortable spot on the old pigskin covered McClelland saddle and to learn which type of horse could best stand up under real hardship. I rode the best of the Kentucky Whips owned by the Army; the more life and style they had at the start the more miles I had carry messages on foot!"[2]

"I rode in more long rides than these (not contest rides) while carrying messages for the Army that kept me in the saddle day and night when there was trouble on the Plains. Since I was familiar with the country and knew every Pass even if I had to run the trails on foot which I often did when the horse could not make good and I never failed to deliver the messages. I was often so tired I lay down on the trail to rest then got up and run till I either got a horse or delivered the message."[3]

"I've met many great horsemen in my day and I also started to do a man's job when just a boy and had friends red men and white. Officers used to feel bad to see me start out on those long rides in severe winters we had. Their men sent with messages never returned - sometimes the horse came back with evidence of dried blood on the saddle. Tho I've been shot 7 times, clawed by a mountain lion, (bitten over the pulse by a 6' diamond back rattler) none of them hit just right and I'm here to tell about it."[4]

2) Incidents

a) "In the spring [of 1878], I was sent [east] over to Pine Ridge, across the Snake and Powder Rivers. When I came to the Powder, the banks were full; when more than 1/2 way across, my horse stopped swimming and tried to sound the bottom - the mad, rushing current caught his hips as he lowered to sound and turned him over backward; as his shoulders raised above the water I left the saddle, only to be shoved down beneath the horse as he turned over.

I was under long enough to come up partly filled with water; I could swim fairly well but there seemed to be something holding my left foot. The horse was close behind me; I fought hard to swim to one side to escape his hoofs, but had a hard time of it. Both of us swung to one side as there was a sharp bend in the stream which brought us close to the shore. The horse stood on the bottom. Then I found that the rein had caught around my boot above the spur. I used an army bridle and buckle at the end of the reins - from that day until the present, I have never tied or buckled the reins. If I used a bridle with a buckle at the end of the reins I cut the buckle off."[5]

b) "I'd delivered a message to one of the outpost camps. On my return to the Red Cloud Agency, I had to swim the Grand River - there wasn't any living thing in sight when I put the hoss into the water, but as I neared the other bank something struck me in the hip with such force I swung over in the saddle and the hip burned like fire. Then, I saw four Rees [Arikara Indians] ride out of the alders. I levelled my rifle at the one in the lead - when the smoke cleared he lay on the ground. I aimed steady at the next rider and he slid back over the horse's hips; the third one pitched forward to the ground.

Then I heard that familiar yelp, 'Hy kee ho' and from the alder brush rode several Rees. They rode to a small knoll and fired. I tried to make my pony go over there and had to roll the spurs along his sides as the little feller reared and plunged at the sound of the shots. He was willing to go the other way and I have often since thought that was good. Had that horse gone over there where I wanted him to I'd never have lived to tell about it. I was wounded and felt the pain. I wished I could wipe them out; they rode after me but my hoss was too fast so they gave it up. I was getting weak, the trail was getting darker; I dropped my arms down each side of the pony's shoulders. For over twenty miles that pony carried me. The next thing I remember was voices and then the face of General Terry bending over me. I had been shot through the hips and it was some time before I was polishing saddles again."[5]

Frank gives more detail on this incident in one of his answers to letters. He said,

"I came into the soldiers' town so badly shot I nearly bled to death. I was very near blued from loss of blood and high fever and my faithful mount brought me in. Soldiers' Town was where Standing Rock Agency is today. I was fourteen then."[6]

c) On Dec. 1, 1880, Frank set out on a ride of about one hundred and eighty miles to deliver a message to Fort Bridger. He probably started from Fort Steele. The weather was fine when he left, but the next day a terrible blizzard blew up.

"At midday, it began to snow and the wind howled through the ledges. I turned off my course and made for a pine and cottonwood grove in a large gulch. There I worked with my axe in a blinding storm until I had finished the shelter for the pony and myself. I cut light poles and wove cedar boughs through them. With a pile of cottonwood at one end of the lean-to we were out of the worst storm I can recall. It snowed three days and nights.

Every night, after the storm, the large grey wolves came. I kept a fire burning at the entrance of the lean-to and sat there with my rifle across my knee - now and then I shot one of those prowlers and then there was a fight. In the morning I could see where they had torn the wounded wolves apart, leaving only the bones and tufts of hair. During the day I could sleep safely, but at night I guarded my horse.

On the fourth day the food ran out and I dared not eat wolf because of the rabies germs they carry. There was not even a rabbit to shoot -the snow was too deep. About the eight day, I was feeling mighty weak and my lips were parched. On the following morning, I was forced to shoot my pony, skin his hip and slice off a piece of meat and eat it - warm and raw - I was really hungry.

I stayed there for five long weeks - the horse meat froze solid and kept, and I ate it again, but roasted on a stick. Right there I learned that money isn't everything in a man's life, for I had four hundred dollars of good American money in my pocket - and would have starved to death but for the horse!

The weather suddenly got warmer and then came a drizzling rain which froze, making a heavy crust on the snow. I made a pair of snowshoes out of the horse's hide, and with a number of extra rawhide strings and a chuck of horsemeat lashed to my back, I started out for Fort Bridger. ... In six days I delivered my message."[7]

Evaluation: Dispatch Riding (1 and 2 above)

During the Indian wars in the west, the Army did use civilian dispatch riders. The white scouts who rode with the Army, like Buffalo Bill Cody, received lots of recognition, but not the Indian scouts, the packers or the dispatch riders.

In 1942, Colonel R. Parker did write an article about the dispatch riders for the Vermont Horse and Bridle Trail Bulletin. He stated Frank T. Hopkins and King Stanley were two of the best, but did get into trouble for playing practical jokes. Due to the lack of accurate maps, he explained the distances they rode were typically understated or overstated. The authorship of this article has been questioned and could not be verified.[12]

Frank probably dictated the material above from memory some time in the 1930's. When he told the same story in more than one place, the details sometimes varied. Probably he could best remember dramatic incidents and easily create stories from what he remembered. Since he rode thousands of miles cross country without encountering any serious problems, he probably would not remember enough detail about these rides to turn them into interesting stories. In my opinion, he took the risks involved in his job for granted, as did his father, and he never saw himself as hero.

3) Endurance Racing

Background Information:

Horse racing had always been popular on the frontier and it was usually a major sport at all of the western frontier forts or outposts. According to Colonel Richard Irving Dodge, it was also a popular sport with the Plains Indians. Prizes and bets could be in ponies, various types of merchandise, or money. He describes one incident where an Indian pony was matched in three races with one of the three best racers in the garrison and he beat every one the blooded horses.[8]

a) Frank's first race.

"I rode my first endurance race back in 1877 - a ride of 350 miles on rough trails which had been marked so every rider had to cover the ground; I rode a dun colored Indian pony who weighed less than 800 pounds. General Alfred Terry was the judge. All of the other nine riders were mounted on Army horses weighting from 1000 to 1200 pounds. My pony came in eight hours ahead of the rest."[9]

b) Race Record

In his years as a dispatch rider, Frank rode "many endurance races with the troops. With the Sioux and the soldiers I rode 181 races in a few years. I won 12 ponies besides other articles (including pay). I always had a race in view, either with the cavalry or the Indians."[1]

4) Building His Own Herd

While Frank was still a dispatch rider, he began picking up horses he could use to breed his own line of endurance horses on the C.H. ranch.

a) In 1877, Frank bought a mare who was the foundation of his breed of endurance horses. He said,

"The White-y family, as I call them, started with a small white mare - even her eyes were white. This little 700-pound mare belonged to one of the Sioux Indians, Red Calf by name. The Indians had been put on Pine Ridge Reservation, their droves of ponies were taken away, leaving only two ponies to each teepee. This Indian, Red Calf, asked me to buy the little White-y, as he thought a lot of her, and Red Calf also told me that the mare could lope along all day without tiring. Red Calf and I had played together as small boys (his father was a Government scout at Fort Laramie, Wyoming where I was born) and we were still the best of friends. The following morning after I had talked with Red Calf I bought White-y from General George Crook (I was dispatch rider for him) for three silver dollars. This mare raised five colts for me - four of them were dark cream in color with white manes and tails and the fifth colt was spotted cream and white. That spotted mare was the dam of Hidalgo, the stallion that weighed 950 pounds. It is my personal opinion that Hidalgo was the greatest endurance horse that ever carried a rider."[10]

b) When Frank was in Arizona, he said

"I had bought a good spotted stallion from the White Mountain [Apache] Band; this pony had just what I wanted - a tough souled horse. I used him on long rides and knew he was worth taking home: I would breed him with my little albino mare, White-y, the mare I had bought from the Army and I rode her ninety miles from sunrise to sunset and knew she had all the staying qualities that could go with any horse. This mare was also an Indian pony. ... That stallion afterwards was the daddy of some of the best endurance horses I ever expect to see or hear of."[11]

5) Buffalo Hunting

Background Information:

There is more than one way to hunt buffalo. As soon as the Indians got horses, they developed a method that suited their goals. When a herd was found, no one was allowed to disturb it until the hunt was ready. When the hunters were all in place, the hunt began. Individual buffalo were lanced or shot with arrows. The rest of the tribe followed behind the hunt to begin skinning and butchering the carcasses. This method allowed them to select the animals with the best hides and meat. They used every bit of the carcasses.

When white men developed another method, they got most of their ammunition from the Army. When the buffalo runner [hunter] found a herd, he went back to camp to bring the skinners to the herd. When they were near enough to it, he set up a stand for his powerful gun and shot the lead cow. While the rest of the herd milled around the carcass, he shot the rest of the buffalo. When they had all been skinned, the meat was left to rot. The tongues were considered delicacies so sometimes they were removed. All of the skins were not of high quality and some were spoiled before they could be sold and shipped. This method succeeded in destroying all of the buffalo herds.[13]

a) Riding for Buffalo Jones

Whenever Frank was not employed as a dispatch rider, he would find a temporary job as a buffalo runner. He states,

"The following winter [1877-8] things were quiet on the plains - not a fight to get into or a message to carry, so I hired out with that great old plainsman, Buffalo Jones: he gave me the job of dropping Bison for the skinners: I had a nice string of ponies, all gun broke; they were the toughest bunch I ever expect to find - none of them weighed over 850 pounds, and they'd rather let you walk than ride. Jones told me one cold evening when I had come into camp, 'Boy, those nags you ride are wilder than a wild cat and you are wilder than the nags.' They were all Indian ponies, of as many colors as there is in a crazy quilt.

That spring, I rode 7 races against the cattlemen down Kansas way - Jones backed me; he often said he could never lose a dollar when I had a pony between my knees. But the racing was brought to a halt when General Terry sent for me."[14]

b) Learning His Job

In one of his published articles, Frank explains how he learned his job from one of the old skinners who worked for Buffalo Jones. He advised him,

"Let me tell you a thing or two about dropping these 'buffs'. Look for the spikehorns two years old or maybe three. Shoot them in the neck, close to the head - that will drop them until the skinners come along for they will only be paralyzed. Hides bring good money and skinning a frozen buffalo means a slashed hide that won't fetch much money."[15]

Frank listened to him and seldom gave the skinners an old bull or cow to skin. This procedure produced quality hides and may explain why Buffalo Jones made so much more money than most of the other outfits who hunted buffalo.

Later in the same article, Frank commented a mustang could be bought for three dollars, but a trained buffalo pony could be sold for three to five hundred dollars.[15]

6) Incidents

a) "Now, there was a rule among the buffalo runners, that if the 'dropper' shot an off-colored buffalo, the skin went to the dropper. One morning, I sighted something white moving among the bunch just as I started them into the wind. As the sun came up I could plainly see it was a cream-colored spikehorn - too far ahead for me to shoot. ... When I came up to Bob Rice, I told him about the spikehorn and he said, 'I'll go out in the morning and rope that calf for you.' ... Bob took great pride in being slick with his rope and he sure twisted a mean loop!

He and I rode out before daybreak. There, on the level plains were our buffalo standing, chewing their cuds. Beyond were two huge buttes not more than thirty feet apart at the base. As we encircled the herd at a safe distance, waiting for daylight, Bob saw the light-colored buffalo moving at the upper end of the draw, between the buttes. I rode out to the far end of the draw, while Bob stayed at the other end. We waited there until we could see clearer. Bob shouted, 'Run them down this way.'

The sound of his voice started the 'buffs' on a stampede. I turned the few that were in the draw and ran them Bob's way and as I drew nearer to them I could plainly see that the cream-colored one was not a calf but a large spikehorn - maybe in his third year. They were under full speed when Bob threw his rope, which fell true, catching our 'buff' around the neck, close to the shoulders. When the horse tried to hold, both cinches parted. Bob sailed over the horse's head and landed in a sitting position on the ground while he watch his rope and saddle go bounding down the valley.

Late that afternoon, I came to my prize all tangled up with the rope and greasewood brush. To make sure, I made a few more hitches and left my riding jacket tied to him so the wolves would be sure to smell the human scent which they fear, knowing they would not dare close in on my prey. It was after dark when I rode into camp with Bob's saddle. Jones inquired why I stayed out so late, warned me not to make a practice of it. When I told him about tying my prize however, he ordered the driver of our hide wagon to hitch up the mules and all hands went along. If anyone thinks it's easy to load a buffalo into a wagon, he is surely mistaken. We finally dragged this one into it with the aid of the lead mules. This 'buff' sold for $300."[15]

b) "I once took the ride of my life on a big 'bull' buffalo. Some of my rides on bad bucking horses have grown dim in my memory, but that ride on an old bowback will always remain fresh. I had been running that herd for two months, so they were getting cross. ... I could see a number of spikehorns and was waiting for them to raise their heads so I could get a shot at them. Soon, I felt my pony zig-zagging under me.

There I was - surrounded by hundreds of buffalo. Many had come in on the other side of the butte, catching my pony in the middle of the herd. Now he was getting badly squeezed for they were bumping that little horse from both sides. I dropped the rifle and grabbed both hands full of buffalo wool and pulled myself up onto that old bull's hump. It was always considered a disgrace in my part of the country to pull leather and I can honestly say I have never grabbed the saddle horn when riding broncs. But I will admit pulling wool out of that old bull's shoulders and I got my spurs so tangled it was hard to get them loose.

I was fourteen years old at the time; the only way I can describe that ride is like a man on a log going through a rough rapids. There were buffalo ahead of me and on both sides of me and behind me, running close together, their horns cracking as they ran. I must have been up there three or four hours for they had tired and were pacing, their tongues hanging out. Soon he [the old bull] came to a standstill, not paying any attention to me up there on his hump. I watched a few tired buffs pass, then slid down from my wooly seat and made my way to the alders beside the River. There I stayed until till the buffs had passed and then I started back afoot. ... the one [pony] I left, to ride on that bull, ... was trampled so badly I could only distinguish what was left by the hoofs, mane and tail hair."[15]

Editor's comment: Frank Meyer describes a similar incident.[13] They were rare, but sometimes a rider had to leave his pony and make that leap to save his life.

7) Catching Wild Horses

Frank not only carried dispatches for the Army and worked as a buffalo dropper, he also caught wild horses. His description of one such hunt is given below.

"There were many wild horses in all parts of the northwest then. They were Indian and army horses mixed together and you could sell anything in the shape of a horse that had four legs. I had run wild horses with old time hunters, so it was not new to me.

I found where a large band grazed and came for water, built a trap with the shape of a V, fenced off about eighteen feet at the narrow end and there I put Andy, a stallion that had been caught when a young colt. For three week I fed him grain and hay in this enclosure. The wild horses smelled him; at first they didn't come nearer but day by day they grew bolder and went into the trap and around the fence.

Every morning, I went to see their tracks. At sundown one evening, I let Andy out: he wandered down to the grazing ground. I had made a place where I could stay near the entrance of the trap without being seen. This was not strange to the horses for they had seen it every night. So I hid in this dugout. I heard the horses calling as they came out to feed. As morning dawned, Andy started for the trap to get his oats and the others followed him.

When they were at the lower end, I hung pieces of old clothes on the posts across the entrance: these posts were about eighteen feet apart): this held the horses while I put up the fence. They were afraid of those rags flying in the wind: all of them huddled in the far end of the trap. I had all the rails lying flat on the ground, so it was easy spiking them to the posts. I had thirty ponies and nine army horses. I returned these horses to the army and the ponies I gentled in the trap and took them out with Andy as the lead horse.

The gentling was easy: every day I went into the corral, moving around slowly, not paying any attention to the horses. Soon they came around to me. Some became real friendly. When I started out with them, I saw they had plenty of eat before I started. I led Andy out on a long rope and everyone of them followed.

This was one man's job from start to finish. I've been with other horse hunters who tried to run horses into their traps with a large force of riders. They got some horses, but the best ones they don't get. I caught a number of wild horses with honest old Andy. He never failed in bringing them in and he didn't care much about fighting. When he was twenty-two years old, I got the last family of ponies with him and Andy died shortly after."[16]

Evaluation (Chapter 2):

Frank was born and bred on the frontier. As an adolescent, he rode light and spent nine years of his life delivering dispatches, hunting buffalo, and catching wild horses. He accepted the challenges and risks these jobs entailed and survived. With every endurance race he organized or entered; he challenged himself to win. Most of these races were probably informal matches. At this time, he also began building his foundation herd.

In his real memoir, answers to letters, and published articles, he gives us some detailed descriptions of what he did during these years. To enhance readability, some punctuation has been added to the unpublished material. From his published articles, material has to be carefully selected. Unfortunately, some of them contained material presumably added by his wife Gertrude. Fortunately, Frank's style was concise and forthright while hers was rambling and romantic.

By the time Frank had become an adult, the frontier was gone. The buffalo had been destroyed and the Indians locked into reservations. He could continue to catch wild horses, break horses, and race, but would these activities satisfy him? As an adult, could he find a way to challenge death where he could still use his skills to survive?

Footnotes:

[1]Hopkins, Frank T., Memoir, Letter 1, page 1. Hopkins Papers, Robert Olney Easton Collection, American Heritage Center, University of Wyoming.
[2]Hopkins, Frank T.,"Mustangs", The Vermont Horse and Bridle Trail Bulletin, Jan. 1941, page 2.
[3]Hopkins, Frank T., Answers, Letter 6, page 21. Hopkins Papers, Robert Olney Easton Collection, American Heritage Center, University of Wyoming.
[4]Hopkins, Frank T., Answers, Letter 6, page 19. Hopkins Papers, Robert Olney Easton Collection, American Heritage Center, University of Wyoming.

[5]Hopkins, Frank T., Memoir, Letter 1, pages 3-4. Hopkins Papers, Robert Olney Easton Collection, American Heritage Center, University of Wyoming.

[6]Hopkins, Frank T., Answers, Letter 6, page 19. Hopkins Papers, Robert Olney Easton Collection, American Heritage Center, University of Wyoming.

[7]Hopkins, Frank T., "Mustangs", Vermont Horse and Bridle Trail Bulletin, Jan., 1941, pages 2-3.

[8]Dodge, Colonel Richard Irving. Our Wild Indians: 33 years of Personal Experience Among the Red Men of the Great West, NY, Archer House, 1959 (1st edition 1884), pages 337, 341-2.

[9]Hopkins, Frank T. As told to Charles B. Roth. Letter 4, Unpublished manuscript, dated August, 1940, pages 10-11. Hopkins Papers, Robert Olney Easton Collection, American Heritage Center, University of Wyoming.

[10]Harris, Albert W. The Blood of the Arab, Chicago, The Arabian Horse Club of America, 1941, p. 49.

[11]Hopkins, Frank T., Memoir, Letter 1, pages 5-6. Hopkins Papers, Robert Olney Easton Collection, American Heritage Center, University of Wyoming.

[12]Parker, Colonel R., "Riders and their Records", Vermont Horse and Bridle Trail Bulletin, July, 1942, pp. 105-7.

[13]Meyer, Frank H. with Charles B. Roth. The Buffalo Harvest, Pioneer Press, 1995 (1st published in 1958). Available on the Internet.

[14]Hopkins, Frank T., Memoir, Letter 1, pages 2-3. Hopkins Papers, Robert Olney Easton Collection, American Heritage Center, University of Wyoming.

[15]Hopkins, Frank T., "Hunting Buffalo", Vermont Horse and Rider Bridle Bulletin, Jan., 1942, p. 2-4, 20.

[16]Hopkins, Frank T. Memoir, Letter 1, pages 7-8 Hopkins Papers, Robert Olney Easton Collection, American Heritage Center, University of Wyoming.

Chapter 3 - Race from Texas to Vermont (1800 miles)

Background Information: Endurance Racing:

The winner of this race took thirty one days and averaged fifty-eight miles per day. The length of this race and the winner's time may seem improbable to modern horsemen, but at that time the American economy depended on horses and they worked hard. In 1893, a cavalry officer stated their ordinary horses were expected to maintain sixty miles a day as long as necessary. The same horses could easily make 100 miles in twenty-four hours without injury. The key to this success was conditioning and increasing the feed to cover the energy expenditure.[1] Argentine gauchos also believed a horse who could not consistently travel sixty miles a day was useless.[2]

Organized endurance races began in the United States as early as the mid-1800's, all too often without any concern for the welfare of the horse. This new sport soon became notorious for its high equine death rates. The Massachusetts SPCA was started in 1869 as a direct result of the death of two horses during a forty mile, $1,000 trotting match. Endurance trials by the European military also had a high death rate. In 1892, the Berlin to Vienna race resulted in 29 dead horses, including the winner. During this time, Buffalo Bill Cody and others believed all these races needed was controls to prevent damage to the horses. By the 20th century, such controls had been universally imposed and equine condition had begun to play a role in some of the award programs. From 1919 to 1923, the Morgan Horse Club of Vermont co-sponsored a series of testing races with the Army Remount Association. In 1926, the Green Mountain Horse Association began sponsoring carefully monitored endurance rides. In one of these earlier rides, the fastest horse was eliminated because his back showed damage from an ill fitting saddle.[3]

In 1955, the first race for the Tevis Cup occurred. It is an endurance competition still held in California and designed to prove modern horses can perform as well as their ancestors. In this grueling competition, the horse has to cover 100 miles over rugged mountain trails in 24 hours. It is strictly monitored both by veterinarians and the SPCA. The first horse to arrive at the finish line receives the Cup, but a trophy is also given for the horse among the top ten in the best condition. Every horse who completes the course in time is honored with a special award.

1) Joe's Story

The name of the horse Frank rode in this long race was Joe. In Frank's real memoir, he describes how he found him.

"When I rode with the bison hunters that fall, I found another great endurance horse. Buffalo Jones had bought a string of horses and there was a small Buckskin in this lot who was wild and had never been handled. Jones said he'd bought the lot and this one was thrown in with the bargain and said, 'If you can break this one in your spare time, he's yours. I don't think that mustang will amount to anything, he's too small.'

I roped the pony, took him away from the bunch. Every evening I worked on him, but he did not get friendly. Finally, I got the saddle on him; he fought hard and threw himself. All of the men told me there was no use fooling with that pony - that he was the worst kind of outlaw and it was not worth while getting hurt for the hoss was small and good for nothing. However, this did not discourage me. Every day after I rode off the runs, I went to the small corral and spent an hour or two with that little yellow plug. Then I got him to lead fairly well - still he would fight the saddle. Every evening when I put the saddle on him, it was quite a job, but I put it on just the same.

A month of fighting and this horse got no better. I began to lose patience. I fed him; then for a week did not bother to saddle or do anything with him. The men noticed and began to poke fun at me to work me up so I thought I'd try again. One evening I rode into camp ahead of the skinners - went to the pony and he seemed friendly. I got the saddle and this time he didn't mind it on his back. I led him around the corral and he did not fight. Then I stepped up with intention of staying. He seemed surprised at me being up there and he didn't buck. When the skinners rode in I was riding that yellow colt around the camp and from then on that hoss and I were friends. I named him JOE.

Soon, I used him on buffalo runs and when he got hardened to the work he was something. He could stick to it all day then go out the next day and do it all over again."[4]

Editor's Comment: Frank may have named him after Buckskin Joe, an army horse with exceptional endurance who Buffalo Bill rode from 1869-1872.[5]

Frank describes him further in the comments below.

"When Joe became used to the crack of a gun, he was the best buffalo horse I ever expect to hear of. He could stay with a run of buffalo until they were all shot down and then race off after another run; he could lope off all day without dropping back to a walk. Joe was not fast, but he could wear other horses off their feet in a few days."[6]

"This horse [Joe] had been caught from a wild herd and like most of his kind he was tough. Although I owned him until he died, I never knew the limit of his endurance."[7]

"There's a little yellow stallion lying beneath the soil of old Fort Laramie, Wyoming who never weighed over 800 lbs - often less, ... to me he was like his color - a golden hoss. Horsemen then and today would not give $25.00 for him; he was lazy, his back was short without the least rise at the withers. He was very meaty in the hindquarters."[8]

"The best endurance horse I ever knew weighed eight hundred pounds and stood less than fourteen hands high and I was his proud owner. He never won any blue ribbons, neither did he take a silver cup, for pedigrees were unknown to my 'little yaller plug', but I want to say that little stallion earned his feed and a few thousand dollars to boot. He was one of those mutton-withered fuzztails that no one would care much about owning. ... He had the heavy, strong bone, cords [tendons], muscles, required for hardship, although I admit he did lack style and action. This pony seldom carried his head above the level of his back; his joints were short in the ankles [canon bones]; all four feet were placed well under his body. I never saw him rest a foot - he stood on all four. Often, I gave him three months of the hardest training a horse could stand, yet there was no sign of filling in of the tendons or bone trouble of any kind, neither do I recall a single day that he did not shake his head and let his heels fly when the saddle was taken off, but I do remember my many narrow escapes from being hit by those flying hoofs! On a long ride, that little horse could not be beaten."[9]

2) Before the Race

In his authentic memoir, Franks tells how he found out about the race.

"On my return [from Arizona], I was told there was a race in the making. This was to be a real race across the United States; then I heard it was to be run from Galveston, Texas to Rutland, Vermont. I saw Buffalo Jones at Fort Russell and he was eager for me to get into that race."[4]

Editor's Comment: This race has been described in three articles, published in 1937, 1940, and 1969. The author of the first one was Charles B. Roth and he included Frank's responses to interview questions.[10] The author of the second one was Frank Hopkins and it had been edited by his wife, Gertrude.[6] The author of the third one was Anthony Amarel.[11]

Frank states,

"Buffalo Jones ... paid his $150 entry fee and backed him to win. ... [He] signed on in a small store opposite the post office at Fort Russell, Wyo."[7]

"Three days later I ... started training Joe for the long Trail Ride. In three months, he was in the best of shape - fifty miles a day, three days each week without a bandage on his legs or artificial courage (such as stimulants) of any kind. I allowed him to travel as he wished, not trying to force him to any particular gait; he preferred to lope or a flat-footed walk. Trotting was out of the program with this little stallion. Most of those wild ponies can lope along without much action - that is, they [efficiently] clear the ground and put their feet down lightly. Joe had carried me on many long rides. I was sure he would reach Vermont ahead of the other mounts. Some of them were of the thoroughbred blood. I watched them exercise for a week while we waited down there in Texas. Fine looking horses they were, but too snappy and nervous to start out on a long ride of that kind."[6]

3) The Race

"On the sixth day of September, 1886, we started from the Old Point Ferry Slip, Galveston, Tex. There were fifty-six riders in all - some were cowboys, others cavalrymen and six were bridle path riders. (I was amused to see them bobbing up and down on their small flat saddles for I had never before seen the English type of saddle.)"[6]

"We started and headed north. I remember particularly a man named Gifford from Texas, a James Waldron, Charlie Austin from South Dakota, a man named Green from Idaho, and a little chap called Shorty Price from Colorado."[10]

"All of the riders left me at the very start. Joe never cared about racing away with the bunch; he would just put one foot ahead of the other all day and never seemed to tire. The first day of that ride Joe was a little sluggish, which I thought might be due to change of drinking water. I did not urge him on, but after riding twenty-three miles, I called it a day.

Under the rules of that ride you could ride ten hours or less if you wished. Each rider carried small cards that were to be signed and the exact time the rider stopped was marked on his card. This was done where the rider stopped and then checked by the judges.

It was September 13 before I came up to the other riders. Four ... were out of the race for good. The next day I passed twelve more tired horses. Joe was feeling fine. When I took his saddle off at the end of the day he would swing his head and let his heels drive at me. I always let him roll after taking of the saddle. This may not be any good to a horse, but they all like to roll. On the 17th, Joe and I had passed the last horse and rider. We were in Mississippi where there had been a heavy rain and the yellow mud stuck to Joe's feet like soft snow, but he would shake his head, jump and play at the close of every day.

Our route was marked with red paint daubed on trees, fences and stones, so it was easy to follow. On this ride I weighed 152 pounds, my saddle, blanket and slicker weighed 34 pounds; Joe weighed 800 pounds when we started the ride. I used a six-strand rawhide Hackamore without a bit. Joe did not like iron in his mouth - it seemed to worry him.

I got word from the judges when they caught up with me in the towns, that I was putting a lot of hills and valleys between me and the other riders, but I could not believe I had gained so much mileage. I had stopped to feed at mid-day in the town of Gallatin, Tenn. One of the judges stepped out in front of Joe as I was riding away and said, 'You are riding against time now for there's not another rider within many miles.'

Joe and I were in Rutland thirteen days before the second horse and rider arrived. ... The third [and last] horse came a few days later. ... I weighed Joe the following day after arriving at Rutland and he had gained eight pounds on the ride; he was seven years old at that time and I claim that is the best year of a horse's life - at least I have found it so with endurance horses.

Joe was buckskin in color. When I rode him into Louis Butler's small stable at Rutland that October evening many men of the town gathered to look him over - more on account color than anything else for many of them had never seen a horse of that color. Although Joe had covered 1,799 miles in thirty-one days, without a day's rest on the trip, many of those horsemen criticized his color. 'Joe's' average per day was 57.7 miles. I received $3,000 from Elias Jackson for that ride. Three weeks later I shipped Joe to Wyoming and bade farewell to those good people of Vermont. To me it was just one more long ride for my daily work had always been in the saddle."[6]

Charles B. Roth comments, "Mr. Hopkins kept a log of his journey, which is the most eloquent tribute ever paid to the endurance of a horse and the skill of an American horseman. It shows that doughty little Joe made the 1,799 miles in 31 days' time. Figure out his average daily mileage - 57.7 miles. Can you find another record to equal this in the history of the horse?"[10]

Evaluation (3 above)

a) In a later article, Frank states,

"In sixty years of long distance riding I never used a bit in my horse's mouth believing the bit will worry any horse a little - many of them pull on the bit and fret, some will hold their heads higher than is comfortable for them. All these little things help wear the horse out on a long trail."[9]

Editor's Comment: Like so many of the old time vaqueros, he made his own gear. He probably fitted bosal hackamores, like the one Joe wore, for everyone of his endurance horses.

b) In the later part of the nineteenth century, too many horses had died during endurance races and SPCA organizations had become concerned about the need for stopping such abuse. In Roth's article, he states the starting point of the race had been kept secret until the last minute because of the SPCA of that day.[10] This statement may or may not be true. It was not included in either the 1940 or the 1969 articles. According to endurance rider, Karen Paulo, this race was regulated. All of the horses in it were monitored along the route; those who could not continue without injury were eliminated.[3]

c) The 1940 article included two derogatory statements about other horses in the race.[6] Sadly, the 1969 article included one of them.[11] Since the condition of the horses was monitored, these horses should have been eliminated well before they reached the state described in the article. In my opinion, the derogatory statements were added to this article by Frank's wife, Gertrude, probably without his knowledge.

4) During the Race

Frank describes how he cared for Joe during the race.

"I do not think it is a good to rest too long in the middle of the day. Some riders do rest their mount two or three hours but I have learned that a long rest is not good for horse and rider will both get tired. One hour is plenty. And keeping your horse on his feet fussing over him and rubbing him after the day's work is done is not good. I always taught my horse to lay down and rest after I had rubbed his back with a damp cloth, and let him rest for two hours before feeding. I gave him a good bed where it was quiet and let him alone for the night. A good rubbing in the morning will make him feel fresh on the start of a new day."[6]

In one of his answers to letters, Frank describes some of his experiences on the way north.

"Horsemen ... kept me up all night talking and I'd listen, farmers told of a hoss their father once had who could draw the old democrat wagon with the whole family in it, 60 miles a day and these tales were handed down for generations. Men at the livery stable told of particular horses that drew a 'hack' about the streets 200 miles a day, that horse had to have that kind of work every day or else you couldn't do anything with him."[12]

"I stopped to a place where there was a half mile race track; this man had fine brood mares and two studs, speed horses, trotters and pacers. It was very hot so I asked the owner if I could stop there till sunset. He was pleased to have me. I noticed out on the track one of his men driving a bay stallion that was pretty well lathered up from the heat and the driver used the whip freely. I asked him what was wrong with the horse and was told 'that hoss has got too much pep in him if you don't drive hell out of him every day, no one could do anything with him - he's liable to jump the track fence anytime if the driver don't wallop him to keep his mind on the road ahead of him. Jesus, that dog out there has got to work every minute or else there's trouble.'

I walked out to the track with the horse breeder and watching this crazed horse. I told the owner there was something bothering the horse and I asked him to have the driver stop where he came to where we were standing. As he came around, the owner raised his hand to stop and the driver began to saw and jerk on the reins, the horse reared and plunged, finally stopped. As I stepped up to him, I noted one of the most cruel bits in his mouth. Pointing to it, I said, 'there's your trouble' but the owner said, 'that hoss will kill you if the bit wasn't in his mouth he'd rear away and kill anyone who sat behind him - he's a bad one, that stud'.

When they took him to the stable I asked if I might drive him in the afternoon. I found a straight bit in the harness closet; wound it with a strip of bandage so the iron wouldn't come in contact with his mouth. In a short while that hoss was stepping along as pleasant as you could ask a horse to be."[12]

5) The End of the Race

There are still some unanswered questions about exactly where the race ended in Rutland.

In 1886, Rutland was not just a small New England village where everybody knew their neighbors. In 1893, it had officially become a city. In 1886, a specific location could have been in Central, West, or East Rutland or in Sutherland Falls which later turned into the town of Pittsford.[13]

Frank states he finished at the small stable of Lewis Butler. According to the Vermont Vital Records, the daughter of a Louis Butler did live close to Rutland, Vermont.[14] In 1886, he could well have lived in Rutland. His small stable could have been a livery stable, a stable attached to a private house, or stalls rented in a public stable. So far, its exact location has not yet been identified.

One Frank's friends, Edward M. Dickey (Nevada Dick) comments on the race in a published article. He states in 1944 Frank visited Rutland and found Louis Butler's stable. It still contained the iron ring where he had tied Joe and the initials, FTH, he had craved on one of the beams.[15]

Editor's Note: The complete name of the man who presented the prize to Frank in Rutland was Elias Jackson 'Lucky' Baldwin. He was a wealthy man from California who ran racehorses there and in the East.

Evaluation (Chapter 3)

Did this race actually happen?

a) When horses worked for their living, they were taken for granted and newspapers typically did not include any reports of equestrian sporting events. Two of the early American endurance races did get into the news, but one was sponsored by a newspaper and the other one initiated by a newspaper correspondent. Richard K. Fox was one of the sponsors to the Texas to Vermont race. He had always reported boxing events in his magazine, the Police Gazette, but he choose not to report on this race in his magazine. In the early 1900's, he tried adding reports on Thoroughbred racing and that topic proved to be so popular, it soon spread into the newspapers. Even today, millions hear about who wins the Kentucky Derby, but how many hear about who wins the prestigious endurance race, The Tevis Cup?

There is one exception to this situation. Judging by the violent reaction of SPCA organizations to the reported deaths or injuries of horses in endurance races, this information probably did get reported in the public media. Since the Texas to Vermont race was monitored to prevent such incidents, there would have been no dramatic events to report to the general public.

Searches of the local newspapers in Galveston, Texas and Rutland, Vermont produced no mention of the race, but these results do not prove it didn't happen. According to the Rutland Herald website, their editor at that time was Percival W. Clement and he used the newspaper to promote his business and special projects. He may or may not have been interested in the publication any equestrian items. In the relevant time frame, only one race was mentioned in the Galveston papers and it was observed by a tourist in Paris, France. A general search of all archived American newspapers in that time period only produced one article and it was about paint horses. If no races were reported, then there is no reason to believe this endurance ride should have been an exception.

When automobiles came along, horses found a new role as pleasure animals. New markets for equines emerged and the publication of specialized equestrian magazines catered to these markets. Western Horseman began publishing in 1936 and the Chronicle of the Horse in 1937. With the exception of Thoroughbred racing, modern equestrian news is usually just published in such specialized magazines or in newsletters sponsored by various equestrian organizations.

In my opinion, the fact that this race was not mentioned in the newspapers does not constitute proof it never happened. Some positive evidence suggests it did occur.

b) The Pyles were one of the families involved in endurance racing in the late 1930's and they had known Frank T. Hopkins well. When Walt and Edith Pyle were interviewed, Walt stated,

"Everyone knew about the Texas to Vermont race. The old timers who were alive back then all knew of it. We all did."

Later, he expressed surprise at the idea the race should have been reported in the newspapers.[16]

c) In 1952, a well respected Professor from the University of Texas at Austin, choose to write a delightful children's story, *They Were Made of Rawhide,* about the race. Her name was Leigh Peck and the book was published in 1954 by Houghton Mifflin Company. Before writing this book, she did extensive research, including a visit to Rutland in 1952.[17] The route of the race in her book is the same one Frank describes. It is also the route currently shown on MapQuest. It goes east from Galveston to Louisiana, north to Tennessee, east to the coast, and north to Rutland. Sadly, her library and personal papers were lost when her home was destroyed in a hurricane.[18] If this material had survived, it might have contained records from her research and proof the race did happen.

d) In 1870, historians made a public appeal to find anybody who remembered the race. They did get one response from Texas. He found a reference to it in 1901, but was skeptical about the distance traveled and the reported times.[19]

Final Comment: What more would Frank and Joe be able to accomplish in the years to come?

Footnotes:

[1]Dodge, Theodore A., "The Soldier's Pluck", Riders of Many Lands, NY, Harper & Row, 1893, pp. 77-84.
[2]Cunninghame, Graham R. B. The Horses of the Conquest. University of Oklahoma, 1949.
[3]Paulo, Karen, America's Long Distance Challenge. Trafalgar Square, 1990, pages 2-3.
Harris, Fredie Steve, "America's Great Distance Horsemen", AERC Endurance News, April, 1991. Reprinted from Horseman, Aug. 1979, pp. 66-69.
[4]Hopkins, Frank T., Memoir, Letter 1, pages 9-11, Hopkins Papers, Robert Olney Easton Collection, American Heritage Center, University of Wyoming.

[5]Spring, Agnes Wright. Buffalo Bill and His Horses, 1968, p. 5.

[6]Hopkins, Frank T., "1800-mile Trail Ride - Texas to Vermont", Vermont Horse and Bridle Trail Bulletin, April, 1940, pp. 43-4, 63-4.

[7]Hopkins, Frank T., "Mustangs", Vermont Horse and Bridle Trail Bulletin, Jan. 1941, page 4.

[8]Hopkins, Frank T. As told to Charles B. Roth, Letter 4, Unpublished manuscript dated August, 1940, page 18. Hopkins Papers, Robert Olney Easton Collection, American Heritage Center, University of Wyoming.

[9]Hopkins, Frank T. "Endurance Horses As I know Them", Vermont Horse and Bridle Trail Bulletin, July, 1941, pages 81-2, 92.

[10]Roth, Charles B., "The Toughest Race", The Horse and Horseman, Jan., 1937, pp. 31, 49-50.

[11]Amaral, Anthony, "Frank Hopkins: best of endurance riders?" Western Horseman, Dec. 1969, pages 110-11, 191-194.

[12]Hopkins, Frank T., Answers, Letter 6, page 22-23. Hopkins Papers, Robert Olney Easton Collection, American Heritage Center, University of Wyoming.

[13]Dorr, Julia C. R., "Rutland, Vermont", The New England Magazine, vol. 24, issue 2, April, 1898, pp. 201-219.

[14]Vermont Vital Records, 1760-2008. Records of Lyanehs King, daughter of Louis Butler.

[15]Nevada Dick, "Stamina of the Horse Past and Present", Vermont Horse and Bridle Trail Bulletin, Jan., 1948, p. 12.

[16]"He was quite a horseman", http:www.frankhopkins.com/articles 27.html.

[17]"Undated newspaper article in the Hopkins file at the Vermont Historical Society.

[18]"In Memoriam: Leigh Peck, 1901-1969. University of Texas at Austin.

[19]"News and Notes", Vermont Historical Magazine, v. 21, no. 10, Aug. 1970.

Chapter 4: Traveling with Buffalo Bill's Wild West, 1886-1888

Background Information: Wild West Shows

As the western frontier was closing down, the era of wild west shows began. It started around 1880 and lasted about thirty-five years. These shows used cowboys and Indians to put on special exhibitions and present various dramas of frontier life. The two biggest and most successful shows were Buffalo Bill's Wild West and the Miller Brothers 101 Ranch Wild West Show, but less successful shows and many smaller ones also proliferated.

Once the tribes had been driven onto reservations, they became curiosities to their conquerors. The managers of the wild west shows allowed them to live in tepees and wear their native dress, as well as maintain their language and normal rituals. In my opinion, the main motive of these men was probably to enhance the Indians status as novelties. In the era of wild west shows, Indian tribal cultures were not yet understood or valued. When the Office of Indian Affairs allowed Indians to get jobs with these shows, they got off the reservations, traveled with their families, and earned some money. In the performances, they rode, danced, did tableaus, and joined in dramas where they always lost. Unfortunately, their appearance and activities did set a stereotype in the public mind. Indians were perceived as mounted war-bonneted warriors and the last impediment to civilization.[1] In the photograph below, Buffalo Bill is shown in 1890 with his Indian staff wearing war bonnets.

Human societies have usually regarded herding cattle as a low status job and this tradition applied to our cowboys. In the

Revolutionary War, cowboys were rustlers who sold stolen cattle to both sides. In our war with Mexico, the cowboys took cattle away from the natives to feed to the American troops. When the Americans first moved into Texas, settlers who had ranches and worked with cattle called themselves vaqueros. This job required special skills, long hours, and dealing with potentially dangerous cattle. The term, cowboy, did not come into general use until after the Civil War. Unlike the Mexican vaqueros, the American cowboys didn't spend all their time with cattle or horses. They were expected to engage in a lot of hard, manual labor. About one-third of them were black and this was a sign of their generally low status. Before Buffalo Bill became famous, cowboys were never seen as heroes. The Wild West Shows helped dramatize the American West as a place of romance and glamour.[2]

From 1860 to 1898, the melodramatic stories in dime novels romanticized cowboy life and they became the new folk heroes. A cowboy had to be white, fearless, and fair, as well as enjoy hard drinking and fighting. To defend the right or rescue imperiled white maidens, he fought and often killed dirty villains; whites, Mexicans, or Indians. His life was full of adventure and to survive, he had to be an expert shot. The public image of romanticized cowboy was inextricably linked to his trusty colt 45 revolver.

The wild west shows built on this romantic image. Groups of cowboys showed their riding and roping skills, but the real stars were the sharpshooters who demonstrated their expertise with rifles, revolvers, and shotguns. During the shows, the bands played cowboy folk music. These tunes were later adapted for use in film and television westerns.

The demise of the wild west shows can be explained by several factors. During their golden age, frontier dramas with galloping horses could not be shown on a conventional stage; but the new movies had this ability. By the time they came along, Indians had ceased to be curiosities and rodeos had become the new showcase for cowboy skills.

1) Buffalo Bill's Wild West, 1886-7, New York.

This wild west show was founded in North Platte, Nebraska on May 19 1883 by William F. Cody. In 1884, Nathan Salisbury joined him as a managing partner. This partnership turned out to be a winning one. Buffalo Bill was a great showman, but a poor business man.

Salisbury also began as showman, but what he excelled at was business management. For three years, Bill's show toured American cities and it grew bigger every year. In 1886, they leased Madison Square Garden for the winter season. They planned to present "The Drama of Civilization", alternating historical dramas with exhibitions of special skills.

Beginning with this show, they decided they had to have an elite group of cowboys who became part of the Congress of Rough Riders. They planned to have the Congress include troupes of cowboys, Mexicans, and Indians. The number of cowboys varied, but averaged about twenty-five. Frank Hopkins spent thirty-one years, from 1886-1916, as a rough rider with them. He did not spent the first three years with Bill's show, but his time with it has been incorrectly described as thirty-two or thirty-four years.

Frank comments,

"He [Salisbury] turned out the finest show of horses and horsemen the world has ever seen. Every individual rider was subjected to a real test before being hired to ride in this show. Many who thought themselves first-class horsemen were turned down."[3]

Frank Hopkins passed this test when he and Joe won the Texas to Vermont race. After they had returned home, Cody and Salisbury met with Frank and offered him a place as a rough rider. Frank was looking for the excitement he had known as a dispatch rider. He comments,

"They offered what seemed to me at that time a big price to do it, but I learned soon afterwards that their price was a mere nothing to what I actually earned for them. However, I joined their show on the twelfth day of November, 1886. It was held in the old Madison Square Garden. This Garden was an old wooden building located on the exact site where Stanford White, the famous architect, built the second Garden in about 1890.

When I rode into the ring where rehearsal was going on, some of the Indians charged at me with their ponies to count coop [coup] as they would to an enemy, this was now only in fun, although we had really been enemies on the Plains not many years before. I spoke their language fluently, so it was easy to get along with them. Among these

Indians were many warriors. Occasionally, one would tell me how near he had come to getting me at some spot where I had passed with a message in my dispatch-carrying days. It was told good-naturedly, sometimes in truth, other times jokingly.

After a few days' practice, the Bill Show started with a parade up Fifth Avenue, New York, Cody riding at the head of it, waving his sombrero to the onlookers. Coming straight from the western plains as I did, these many people crowding so around our horses worried and confused me, and I didn't like it.

When the show started - it was the afternoon performance - the Garden was packed; the aisles were filled with standees. First, all riders entered the ring on their horses, then Salisbury spoke to the audience about Cody's career and continued telling about me as a dispatch rider. My act was on first - it was to change horse five times around the ring at full speed, changing to a different style every time, the horses going as fast as they could. I made it without a miss.

The cheering of the crowd upset me so badly I was too upset to take part in the rest of the show. Salisbury tried to comfort me by saying if the crowd didn't like the act, they wouldn't cheer and that they did not cheer so much when Cody did his shooting act. But talk didn't help much - I wanted to leave at once and get back to the wide-open spaces of the West away from the crowds. I refused point blank to bear [a] dispatch in the evening performance of the show if Salisbury announced my act. He promised he would wait until I had done my riding and gone out of the ring. He kept his word and it helped, for in a few days, I was over the panic, although I never did like to hear the crowd cheer - it gave me the chills even to the last days as a show rider.

Cody had me ride with him in the Buffalo Hunt which was only chasing a dozen buffalo out of the ring with blank shots. Later on, I learned that this was done to get me used to a crowded house. For the first month, they would not let me do any trick riding. When I'd gotten for used to the crowds making fools of themselves, Salisbury asked me to do a little trick riding, warning me about keeping calm as the audience would probably whoop it up after a while. He'd say, 'Now, go out there and show them something they never saw before.' Nothing bothered me much after the first trick riding except maybe the band and I still can't stand the noise of a big band.

When hired to ride in the Show I agreed to furnish my own ponies. Some of these had been schooled for trick riding, more for my own pleasure than anything else; they came in handy now. One evening, Black Elk (a Sioux) and I gave the crowd a big surprise by racing our ponies at their best speed, the whole length of the ring, changing horses when they passed each other in the center of the ring without slacking the pace. This is the hardest thing to do on horseback and I had never seen anyone perform that feat other than Black Elk and myself ... [We] learned this trick along with many others when we were small boys and now we were in our twenty's playing our tricks on pony back the same as we did then, but amusing throngs of people every day."[3]

Editor's Comment: Frank's comments on the crowds, crowding, and cheering illuminate the negative attitude he developed towards public acclaim. The cowboys in Bill's show were not stars. As a group, they had an act entitled "Cowboy Fun". It including trick riding, roping, and riding outlaw horses. They were also expected to take part in the races and dramas. Frank's first act may have been an reenactment of the Pony Express which was a popular drama in wild west shows. His special trick with Black Elk indicates Frank had learned trick riding as a boy when he was with his Indian relatives.

2) Buffalo Bill's Wild West, 1887-8, England

On April 18, 1887, Bill's show shipped out to join the American Expedition at Earls Court, London, England. It was the year of Queen Victoria's Golden Jubilee. The show opened in May, ran into October, and was a great success. A listing of events from one of the programs used in England is at the end of the chapter. Annie Oakley was one of the star attractions in London, but she and her husband left the show in October. Buffalo Bill choose not to mention them in his book about his show in England.[4]

a) Frank at Earls Court, London

Frank comments,

"I didn't relish the idea of an ocean between me and the Western plains."[3]

He describes three incidents from his six months in London.

"The first evening performance, Black Elk and I performed many of our tricks, the last one changing horses riding toward each other from opposite ends of the ring. Then something happened - the crowd cut loose and swarmed into the ring. In a few seconds our ponies were completely surrounded by people and it was a good half hour before we got the people back in their seats. Salisbury ordered Black Elk and me out of the ring and told us not to come out in the other acts that night. Cody liked to tease me and often played friendly tricks. This time he said, 'your trick riding out there with Black Elk was so bad the crowd almost mobbed both of you and if you go out here again tonight they'll finish the job.'

Queen Victoria attended often. Once, she rode around the ring in the old Overland stage coach. One evening in August, Nate asked me to come to his office. Thinking he was about to lay down the law about something he thought I'd done (I was usually cutting pranks in those days with the other riders) I walked into his office ready to face whatever he had waiting for me.

[He greeted me] with 'Frank, I have something very special for you to do. I'm confident you'll do it right. Queen Victoria requests that you and Black Elk give a special performance on the Buckingham Palace lawn before her guests. This is quite an honor and you must not whoop it up or use any rough stuff outside of your trick riding and both of you must dress in your best parade clothes. Cody and I'll be there and if you don't act right we'll square with you later.' Then he poked me in the ribs with his thumb and said, 'I know damn well you fellows will do things right out there and we're going to be mighty proud of you both.'

The following afternoon, about two, Black Elk and I were ready to perform. Each took along three well trained horses. That side of the Palace facing the tennis grounds was packed with people who cheered as we rode onto the lawn. Men in bright uniforms rushed up to take charge of our extra ponies - some carried blankets for the ponies when we changed [horses]. No signs of Cody or Salisbury - they kept in back out of our sight fearing we might get nervous.

The lawn was soft; our ponies threw large pieces of sod high into the air and I rode over and apologized to Her Majesty, fearing that the lawn would be destroyed entirely if we continued. She just laughed and said it could be replaced and to go right ahead. So I went back to Black Elk and told him we'd go on and do it right and we did; after about two hours of trick riding, changing ponies often, that lawn looked liked a lot of hogs had been rooting in it all summer!

The crowd shouted continuously while we were performing and we gave them all we and the ponies had. Her Majesty gave us tea on the second balcony - Black Elk could not speak English nor understand it so I acted as interpreter. The Queen talked freely with us and asked a lot of questions. She was just the grandest, motherly little lady. Cody and Salisbury were not so far in the background, taking everything in but we could not see them.

That evening while getting ready for the evening performance, Cody came into the stable looking very serious; he said, 'You fellows made one awful mess out of things over there this afternoon and if anyone asks if you know anything abut trick ridin' tell them the truth - say NO.' I stared at him - finally, when he could hold out no longer he broke into a hearty laugh, 'You two can have the evening off - you surely earned it; you gave 'em all you had and I'm tickled.'"[3]

Editor's Comment: Both of these stories illustrate how well the details of such dramatic episodes stayed in Frank's memories. Without written records and a gap of thirty or more years, his memories of similar events blurred together and sometimes got confused about when and where certain events on the show's tours actually happened.

Frank describes one more incident from his time in London. He comments,

"Early in June, Nate put on a long race from Earls Court to Land's End, Cornwall, England (about 212 miles one way).The rider and horse who got there and back first was to get one thousand dollars in gold. This race was widely advertised; for a week many riders signed up to take part in it. Most of them used hunters.

I asked Salisbury's permission to enter that race. At first he thought it might be foolish to attempt to ride one of my small ponies against those fine-looking hunters. Cody said to him, 'you might get the surprise of your life, Nate, if Frank takes one of his own ponies over the road with those hunters eating his dust.' Cody was willing to bet my pony would return to Earls Court hours ahead of the bunch; Salisbury took Cody's bet, told me to train my pony and ride in the race.

I chose a pony who had been ridden seven hundred miles in as many days by a famous rider - King Stanley. I raised this little stallion - his sire and dame were got wild from the Red Desert Herd - those ponies were well named for their toughness and Uney was just as tough as his forebears - he loped away out to Land's End and back in forty-six hours of actual traveling and I rode him into the stable Cody remarked 'this talk about lopin' hosses tiring is the damdest lot of rot I've heard and how many horsemen here ever saw a true loping horse?'

Cody knew what he was talking about; that same pony sired some of the best endurance horses the world has ever known, including my Hidalgo, the stallion who beat some of the best Arabs in their own country and he was a true loping horse; all his family before him was true to that gait. Well, old Uney won the Earls Court race; he finished fourteen hours forty-five minutes ahead of the next best horse.

Cody was kind to man and horse. He liked to think of the riders as one large, happy family. He'd walk through the stable, calling every horse by name and often petted and fondled the animals. The evening of my return from that long ride, I went to the stable to care for Uney and found Cody talking to the pony. He asked me if I could teach Uney to go out into ring alone. He thought it would be nice to have Salisbury announce the winning horse of the race.

I promised to have the pony ready for that act in three days. I placed a small stand at the far end of the ring underneath the big light, put some carrots on the stand, then walked across the ring with Uney. This was repeated many times when the show was not going on. Every time the pony got the carrots I stayed a little farther back from him. After [three] days of training Uney walked across the ring alone.

Then came the evening performance when all the riders who had taken part in the race rode into the ring circled about and rode back through the curtain. The small stand was then placed at the far end of the ring with a small piece of carrot on it. Uney, wearing his best saddle and a hackamore, loped across the ring, took his bit of carrot and posed; then he pawed the tan bark and whinnied, much to the delight of Cody and the audience. When Cody spoke, Uney started for the curtain at a fast lope. Even hard-shelled Salisbury rubbed Uney's nose after that performance!"[3]

Editor's Comment: Frank's estimates of distance could be over or under stated. The roads or trails he followed may have varied considerably from modern roads. When maps of our western frontier were developed, King Stanley's ride on Uney turned out to have only covered five hundred and thirty seven miles.

If the race to Land's End extended to the rocks in the edge of the Atlantic Ocean, Frank had underestimated the distance by about seventy miles. However, the distance may have been shorter if the race actually ended in one of the cities in Cornwall, such as Penzance. The distance may have been less if the route chosen headed straight west, instead of looping to the north to touch Wales. The distance and time Frank gave averaged about nine miles per hour which is about right for a loping horse.

b) Provincial Towns in England (Birmingham, Manchester, Hull)

For the tour of the provincial cities, the program was changed to include more episodes from frontier life. After a brief stay in Birmingham, the show spent the winter in Manchester because it had a roofed amphitheater. In the spring, they stopped at Hull to give a few shows before heading home.

Frank comments,

"Riders had to keep themselves will trained and physically fit for their acts - no pleasure in the show business then for a rider, we had to put in sixteen to eighteen hours every day. I have actually dropped to sleep while in the saddle. The parades were worst of all - I'd cut out sometimes and go back to the horse-top for a snooze. Cody soon stopped that, however, by having me ride beside him at the head of the parade."

Along with two performances a day, riders had to train horses for new acts.[3] One of Frank's acts called for much horse training. He explains,

"When Cody, with his cowboys, freed the Deadwood stage coach from a band of raiding Indians, I was shot off my horse in the ring and lay there until the sham battle was over and the ring cleared of all riders. My horse then lay down beside me, pushed himself over till his saddle touched me, then, pretending I was badly wounded I grasped the saddle with one hand and my pony rolled up on his haunches bringing me to a reclining position on the saddle, when he got to his feet, took a step ahead, turned back, picked up my hat and then started to carry me out of the ring, to the thunder of applause."[5]

"There was always something to take up our time in Europe. When not in the ring, people wanted to talk with us about the West and the horses. They'd wait around until they got your ear and when they did it was hard to get away from them. Sometimes, I hid in the stall with my favorite horse guarding me to get a little rest from them and woe to anyone who tried to get by that horse and disturb me."[3]

Editor's Comment: Bill's show offered two types of tickets. The cheapest one only allowed the buyer to watch the show. The other one gave access to the encampment where the performers lived in separate campsites. The Indians had one and so did the cowboys. Spectators could both view them and talk to the performers.

3) Return to USA

When they reached New York, they unloaded at Tomkinsville Wharf and hauled all of their staff and equipment across Staten Island to the resort city of Erastina where they stayed for some time. When the show finally closed in that city, they moved on to four more American cities.

Frank comments,

"[In the] latter part of the summer, the show played at the Richmond Virginia Fair, and here Cody placed $1500 on the man who would cover one 150 miles ahead of 51 riders. The riders were invited to contest without paying any entry fee. I came in, collected the money and finished eating my supper before any of the other riders showed up."[6]

Editor's Comment: Since rough riders were paid little more than cowboys [7], Frank may have earned more for winning this race than he did for two years of hard and sometimes dangerous work.

After the show closed in Richmond, Frank commented,

"I had made up my mind I was a poor showman who always longed to go back where there were no crowds.

The Bill Show was a hugh success but all I wanted was to square up and go home. Salisbury tried to persuade me to sign a five-year contract explaining the show would soon go to the Jubilee in Rome and that I could not leave when they needed me more now. I learned a lot about Salisbury by being around him and I was not in any hurry to sign his contract, knowing full well it was drawn up for his own benefit, not mine. The day Cody and I left for the West, Salisbury asked me to promise that I'd return ready for work in two months. I said I might consider it if my wages were doubled, but I would not sign his contract; this was the first of many breaks I had with Salisbury."[3]

Editor's Comment: This comment illustrates how time can blur memories. What did happen in 1889 was the World's Fair in Paris. There was also a Jubilee in Rome in 1890, but the show only stayed there for a short time. According to the timeline published by the Buffalo Bill Center of the West, Bill's show closed on Oct. 23, 1888, reopened in Paris, France on May 18, 1889, and was at Rome from Feb. 20 to March 9, 1890.[8]

Evaluation (Chapter 4):

According to all accounts of Buffalo Bill, he was the kind of man who wanted public acclaim, enjoyed it, and thrived on it. The photo below shows him enjoying a conversation with the London ladies.

This chapter reveals Frank Hopkins was his exact opposite. He disliked cramped spaces, crowds, cheering, noisy bands, and people crowding him. Rather than talk to his admirers, he preferred to avoid or hide from them. His distaste for publicity and public acclaim may be one reason why there is so little factual information available on his life.

Despite the way he felt about show life, he had what it takes to be a show rider. His years on the frontier had given him the necessary skills and he was a natural athletic. He had also been born with a constitution of iron. He realized alcohol would interfere with the split second timing required for trick riding and staying on outlaw horses. According to his wife, that was why he drank only water. He would not touch alcohol, coffee, or tea.[9]

By the end of his two year contract, he was exhausted and fed up with Nate Salisbury and Cody's Wild West show. Did Cody and Salisbury value him enough to negotiate a new contract? Before Anne Oakley came back to the show for the 1889 season, they had to agree to give her star billing and a much higher salary. From then until 1901 when she left the show, her act came first on the program. What would Cody and Salisbury be willing to offer Frank?

Listing of Events from a Program Used in England, 1887

1. Grand Professional Review
2. Entree: Introduction of Individual Celebrities, Groups, etc.
3. Race between Cowboy, Mexican, and Indian on Ponies
4. Pony Express
5. Rifle Shooting by Johnnie Baker, the Cowboy Kid.
6. Illustrates an Attack on an Emigrate Train by the Indians and its Defense by Frontier Horsemen. Followed by Virginia Reel on Horseback by Western Girls and Cowboys
7. Miss Anne Oakley: Wing Shooting
8. Cowboy Fun: Trick Riding, Roping, Riding Bucking Broncos
9. Lillian Smith: Rifle Shooting
10. Ladies Race by American Frontier Girls
11. Attack on the Deadwood Stage Coach by Indians: Their repulse by Scouts and Cowboys, Commanded by Buffalo Bill
12. Race between Sioux Indian boys on Bareback Indian Ponies
13. Race between Mexican Throughbreds
14. Horseback Riding by American Frontier Girls
15. Phases of Indian Life: Nomadic Tribe Setting up Camps on the Prairie. Attack by Hostile Tribes followed by Scalp, War, and other Dances

16. Mustang Jack: The Cowboy Jumper
17. Buffalo Bill: Practical All-Round Shot
18. Roping and riding of Wild Texas Steers by Cowboys and Mexicans
19. Genuine Buffalo Hunt by Buffalo Bill and Indians
20. Attack on a Settler's Cabin by Hostile Indians. Repulse by cowboys under the leadership of Buffalo Bill.[10]

Acknowledgments:

Photo 1 courtesy of Wikipedia. Photo 2 courtesy of Patrick Murfin's blog.

Footnotes:

[1]Christianson, Frank. "Editor's Introduction", William F. Cody. The Wild West in England, University of Nebraska Press, 2012, pp. xvii-xix.
Fees, Paul, "Wild West Shows: Buffalo Bill's Wild West", http://centerofthe west.org/learn/western-essays/wild-west-shows.
Russell, Don. The Wild West. Amon Carter Museum of Western Art, 1970.
[2]Russell, Don. The Wild West. Amon Carter Museum of Western Art, pp. 117-8.
[3]Hopkins, Frank. "Buffalo Bill as I knew Him", Vermont Horse and Bridle Trail Bulletin, Oct. 1942, pp. 151-4.
[4]Christianson, Frank. "Editor's Introduction: Notes", William F. Cody. The Wild West in England, University of Nebraska Press, 2012, p. 191.
[5]Hopkins, Frank T. "Horses and Horsemen", Vermont Horse and Bridle Trail Bulletin, July, 1943, p. 75-6.
[6]Hopkins, Frank T. Memoir, Letter 1, p. 13-14. Hopkins Papers, Robert Olney Easton Collection, American Heritage Center, University of Wyoming.
[7]Wilson, R. L. Buffalo Bill's Wild West. Random, 1998, pp. 261-263.
[8]"Routes", 1883-1916. Buffalo Bill Center of the West, pp. 8-9.
[9]Gertrude Hopkins to Robert Easton, letter dated 1969. Hopkins Papers, Robert Olney Easton Collection, American Heritage Center, University of Wyoming. It is available on line in their digital collection.
[10]Christianson, Frank and Cody, William F. The Wild West in England, University of Nebraska Press, 2012, p. 175.

Chapter 5: Riding with Buffalo Bill's Wild West, 1889-1893

Background Information: Blizzard of 1888

In January, the Great Plains had two days of snow, then temperatures dropped to well below zero. They were followed by high winds and heavy snow. This blizzard hit so suddenly people were unprepared, including many children who were caught in one room schoolhouses. It killed two hundred and thirty-five people and thousands of cattle on the overgrazed ranges. When cattle drifted with the wind and blowing snow, many piled up and died on the barbed wire fences like the one shown in the photo below.

Unlike cattle, horses had evolved on our prairies so their instinctive behavior allowed most of them to survive. As a minimum, the CH ranch probably lost a few horses and had storm damage to repair. When news of the blizzard reached England, Frank probably worried about what had happened to his parents, his horses, and the family ranch. If the ranch was buried in snowdrifts, there would have no way for his snowbound parents to contact him. Eventually, he would have heard from them, but he may or may not have been allowed to leave the Show until it closed in October. When he discovered the financial results of this disaster, this information may have helped Frank change his mind about working for the Wild West show again.

Introduction:

When the show closed, Frank had to be anxious to see his parents and check on his own herd of horses. The goal of his breeding program was to produce the perfect endurance horse by crossing Indian ponies with American mustangs. His winnings from endurance races helped him support and increase his stock. Although Frank's father raised horses for sale, Frank consistently refused to sell any of his horses. If

69

any of his ponies did not work out for what he wanted, he did let other cowboys put them to work on the family ranch.

His job as a dispatch rider had worked out well for Frank. It let him travel constantly to new places where he could enter or organize endurance races and Bill's show offered him the same opportunity. Cody and Salisbury often put on various types of special races because they were good publicity for the show, but they ran them outside of the regular performance hours. Unlike these events, endurance races normally took one or more days. To compete in such races, Frank could not be a star who had to be there for every show; but as a rough rider, if Frank was gone for a few days, the other cowboys could easily substitute for him. What he did have to have was support from show management and the other rough riders.

Frank did sign a new contract with Bill's show. It may well have been the five year contract Salisbury initially demanded. He probably negotiated for an increase in his monthly salary, minimal publicity, and the freedom to compete in some endurance races. In the early years, these races were either be sponsored by the Show or came from special invitations. Bill's show never ran again for two whole years and rarely traveled in the winter season. In the off seasons, Frank was free to compete in whatever races he could find or organize. In his years with the Show, Frank stated he had won over two hundred races; but in his memoir, he described few of them in any detail.

1) 1889-1890

Buffalo Bill's Wild West opened again on May 18 at the Exposition Universelle [World's Fair] in Paris, France. They camped on the grounds of the Military Zone of Paris, just outside the city wall, in the suburb of Nueilley, Pres la Porte de Terne.

Frank comments,

"There Cody put on a world horsemanship contest which included riders of all nations of the world. ... It started with the long ride to Bordeaux, which I won. Then each man in his turn, contested two hours every day. ...I had little hope of winning that contest, but when it was all over I was judged the best rider."[1]

"I signed up and rode with picked cavalrymen of all nations of the world besides riding in two performances daily with the Cody Show. At the end of contest my Mustangs were judged the most active for footwork and all around supreme for endurance and courage."[2]

In one of his answers to letters, Frank describes how these contests worked.

"The World Horsemen contests were held at the World's Fair or Exposition. The riders were picked from the Cavalry of all nations of the world. Usually the contest lasted three months. The performance went on in our Show ring. ... It made no difference what one could do - the others had to be able to do what he did besides adding what they knew. If a rider failed to compete, he was immediately ruled out.

Every country represented had different tricks, [such as]

fancy riding (pyramid riding) men standing 3 or 4 high on horses and jumping hurdles,

riders picking objects up from the ground with their hands, also teeth, while the horse is in motion,

one man handling as many horses as he could while standing up on their backs and carrying him over jumps and at the same time doing tricks without losing control of his horses.

There were many tricks and while the contestant was performing the points of good horsemanship were noted: there were judges from every nation watching. This was all "advertising" for the Bill Show. There were 5 prizes the 1st $5,000 plus what might be added by admirers. Some ranged from $2,000 to $500.

I once won the big prize and the trip to Arabia was given me from different people from different countries. Every man 'did his stuff' then and if another rider could go him one better and carry this thru the contest to end - he earned what he got.

These men all worked in our Show and were paid wages while the contest was on but were not our regular riders. There were 2 cavalrymen from every riding nation in the world. They did not travel with the Show after the Exhibition. ... Frank's specialty was making a figure eight under the horse's belly and over his back while the horse loped around the arena."[3]

During the Paris Exposition, Frank met Ras Yankin (also known as Ras Rasmussen).

Frank comments,

"[He] had journeyed from his native Arabia with a number of the finest horses his country could produce. He followed me to many places as he was deeply interested in my work. He invited me to visit his country but the show was to go to Rome, Italy, and then on to Germany, besides other countries. At that time I was under contract with heavy bond so I could not leave the show."[1]

When the Fair ended, the show went south to Lyon and Marseilles, then on to Barcelona, Spain. Next, they toured Italy where Frank rode in three races, one over three hundred miles of the roughest country he had ever seen: ... but he won it with his hardy Hidalgo.[4]

From Italy, the show traveled on to Austria and Germany.

Frank comments,

"When the show was in Berlin, I was challenged to take part in a two hundred and fifty mile race near the Austrian Border (in Germany). The riders were of the German, Austrian and Italian Cavalry. I won this race with a horse that I called Snuffbox, a full brother to Hidalgo. On my return to Berlin, I was requested to ride at the head of a cavalry revue. At this time, I learned that the Congress of Rough Riders was to pay my expenses if I wished to go to Arabia, that I was to take my own horses and to contest in three rides as well as other feats of horsemanship."[5]

Evaluation (1):

Once Frank had learned to ignore the audience, he probably enjoyed most of the work he did as a rough rider, but his real love was endurance racing. Riding with Bill's show gave him the opportunity to race against new opponents all over the world. When the show was touring, these races allowed him and his horses to get away from crowds and cities for a few days. At times, Frank may have gotten confused about the places and dates where Bill's show had been, but he never lost track of any of his races and his total number of wins kept increasing.

2) Winter, 1890-91

Cody and Salisbury had initially planned to continue performing through this winter, but their plans were canceled when a public uproar began over the treatment of the Show Indians. Cody canceled their plans and took his Indians home with him. He went west, but sent his Indians to Washington with John Burke. The show wintered at Benfield in Alsace Lorraine.[6] Frank probably left his horses with the show when he returned home for a much needed rest.

He states,

"I learned there was some good horseplay going on down in Indian Territory. There was a boom as the Territory was open for white settlers so I took my Buckskin Joe and three other horses of the White-y family and started for what is now the State of Oklahoma.

The first race was two hundred miles; the prize was to be a homestead. I rode Joe, a horse mighty hard to beat, in this race. About nine miles from the finishing line, one of the riders made a desperate attempt to pass my horse on a sharp turn in the road; as the horse passed, he leaned over to make the turn and the horse's hip brushed against Joe's shoulder. Both horse and rider rolled down a 50 foot dirt embankment, neither of them was seriously hurt, but that was the end of that ride for them.

I rode in on Joe quite some time ahead, but learned I was disqualified on account of that incident. This was my very first defeat and the last and only race in which I failed to capture the prize. I lost to the second rider [Pawnee Bill Lillie] that crossed the line and I've often thought that ride was supposed to won by him before the race started. He was an agent and educator on the Pawnee Reservation and afterwards a partner of Cody's in the show. I could not [have lost] to a better man.

The other two races I won - one seventy-five miles, the other ninety miles. They claimed there were one hundred miles of road, but there were only ninety.

When I returned from Oklahoma I went to see my old friends of the Army at Pine Ridge and got there just in time for ... the battle of Wounded Knee."[7] Since Frank was just visiting friends, he would have had no reason to participate in the battle [massacre], but he may have viewed the carnage afterwards. He described the battle "as a disgrace to Army government."[8]

Frank probably spent a few weeks with his parents before returning to Germany to rejoin Bill's show. The photograph on the next page was taken on the S.S. Princess in 1891 by Fred B. Haskett and shows people sailing east for the next European season of Buffalo Bill's Wild West.

3) 1891-1892

In the spring of 1891, the Wild West show began their next tour of Europe. They started off in Germany, then toured Belgium, Scotland, and England. The show finished by spending their last six months at Earls Court in London. A listing of events from one of the programs used in England is shown at the end of this chapter.

While they were in London, Cody put on a race of one hundred miles and afterwards Frank was invited to participate in a fifty mile race against the crack riders of the English cavalry. Frank won both races.[9] Cody may also have put on another World Horsemen contest. The photograph on the next page was taken at Earls Court in 1892. It shows how some of the cowboys looked and dressed.[10] Frank would have known and worked with these men.

That season Salisbury came up with a new name for the rough riders. Since the show now had cossacks and gauchos, as well as Indians and cowboys, he decided it should be called the Congress of Rough Riders of the World.[11] In the United States, this name was first used at Chicago World's Fair in 1893.

While Bill's show was in London, Lone Wolf, one of the Lakota Indians, died. He had originally joined the show as one of a group of prisoners of war the American War Office had turned over to Cody. He and his family stayed with the show and came back to England in 1892. He caught scarlet fever, died in the West London hospital at Hammersmith, and was buried in Brompton cemetery.[10] At that time, his wife wanted to bring his body home, but feared it would be thrown into the ocean. Buried with him was White Star, a two month old child who had been killed in a riding accident. In 1996, both bodies were brought back home to the Pine Ridge Reservation.[12]

The show closed in England on Oct. 12, 1892. Instead of returning home, Frank took his horses and spent the winter season in Arabia. What happened there will be discussed in chapter eight.

4) The Chicago World's Fair, 1893.

Although the show was located outside the actual Fair grounds, it was a great success.

a) Race from Kansas City to Chicago

Frank comments,

"It took me a couple of months to come from Arabia. Cody met me at the dock. ... [He and Salisbury] were getting ready for the World's Fair at Chicago.
Cody said, 'There is a race waiting for you from Casper, Wyoming to Chicago - 1100 miles of riding. I want you to sharpen up one of your horses for that ride.'
I had some colts out of good endurance stock back home, but I didn't know what they were good for. Then, there was old Joe, fourteen years old. Would he do? I took a train to Wyoming. Joe looked good to me - the boys had used him cutting stock; he was in good shape; none of my colts were broken.
Joe stood the training very well at the start; I was careful not to overdo it: soon, I saw that the old yellow nag was just as game and tough as he always had been."[13]

While getting Joe ready, Frank started some colts and won four endurance races.[14]

"I sent word to Cody that I was ready to take on any rider or riders anywhere. Then came a stroke of bad luck - all the riders shipped their horses to Casper; we were met by a real Western sheriff whom I had known for years and he said sternly, 'If you riders try to start this ride in this here state, all of you will get locked up, and I have the law behind me.'
I got in touch with Cody and in a few days he sent word that all of us should ship our horses to Kansas City, and there we rode a little to

keep our horses in shape, and not riding in one bunch. The ride was laid out at last and we rode up the [Missouri] river as far as Sioux Falls [SD], then tacked back to Rock Island [IL], then straight into Chicago. This route was laid out so we would cover the eleven hundred mills that the riders had signed up to ride. Old Joe came in hours ahead of the rest; the game old pony rolled his eye as I stepped down out of the saddle, as much as to say, 'Boy, that last mile was tough!' Joe never looked at me like that again, for he never wore a saddle again; although he had the best of care, he did not live out the year."[13]

According to Gertrude Hopkins, the prize for winning this race was $1,000.[15]

Editor's Comments (4a):

Later in the year, nine riders entered the Great Cowboy Race from Chadron, Nebraska to Bill's show in Chicago. With one exception, they started with two horses, riding one and leading the other one. Only one horse had to cross the finish line. Two riders dropped out of the thousand mile race and some of the others did not actually ride the whole distance. In addition to the $1,000 prize offered by the race managers, Buffalo Bill added $500 to be awarded to the riders whose horses finished in the best condition.[16]

This race began as hoax, but was well publicized. At that time, endurance racing had a bad reputation because so many horses had been injured or killed in them both here and abroad. Before this race, many organizations and individuals raised a tremendous outcry about potential abuse. This reaction kept many riders from entering and almost stopped the race, but two officials from the Minneapolis Humane Society agreed to let it go on if they were allowed to inspect the horses at scheduled stops along the way.[17]

b) Back at the Show

When Frank finished his long race with Joe, he probably sent him home while he stayed with the show. If Cody put on another contest for World Horseman, Frank may well have reached the show in time to compete in it. One of Frank's friends, Nevada Dick, remembers seeing him at the Fair. He was riding with Buffalo Bill and tossing up glass balls for him to shoot down.[18]

Frank comments,

"Cody was believed to be a great shot with the rifle; the audience in the Bill show saw him shoot clay balls which he never missed. How could he miss when he used mustard-seed shot in the shells? Every shot covered a radius of about six feet. Cody was not an extra good shot - just fair."[19]

Editor's Comment: To avoid accidents to people or property, normal ammunition could not be used during show performances.[19]

Evaluation (Chapter 5):

Whatever compromise Frank, Cody, and Salisbury had worked out on Frank's contract was obviously working well for all three of them. Frank now thought of himself as a show rider, but one who could also enter endurance races. He may not have cared much about publicizing the Show, but he must have enjoyed beating all the cavalry riders who challenged him to races.

The golden years for Bill's show begin in 1887 and ended in 1893. Each year it got bigger, better, and more popular with record breaking crowds. If the listing of events below is compared to the one in Chapter 3, some changes and improvements can be identified. After the Chicago World's Fair ended in 1893, Frank would have had no way to know the golden years had come to an end.

Listing of Events from a Program Used in England, 1892

1. Grand Professional Review
2. Miss Anne Oakley
3. Horse Race Between a Cowboy, a Mexican, and an Indian on Spanish Mexican Horses
4. Pony Express
5. Attack on an Emigrant Train by Indians and Repulse by the Cowboys

6. Captain Jack Burtz's Lightning Bolt
7. Cowboy Fun
8. Across Country with riders of all nations
9. Johnny Baker, celebrated young American marksman
10. Russian Cossacks
11. Racing between American Backwoods Women
12. Troupe of Gauchos
13. Capture of the Deadwood Coach by Indians, which will be rescued by Buffalo Bill and his attendant cowboys
14. Racing between Indian Boys on Bareback Horses
15. Life Customs of the Indians
16. Col. W. F. Cody in his unique feats of sharpshooting
17. Buffalo Hunt
18. Attack on a Settler's Cabin with rescue by Buffalo Bill and Cowboys
19. Salute[8]

Acknowledgments:

Photo 1 courtesy of Capper's Farmers. Photo 2 courtesy of the Amon Carter Museum. Photo 3 courtesy of the Royal Borough of Kensington and Chelsea Library.

Footnotes:

[1]Hopkins, Frank T. Memoir, Letter 1, p. 14-15. Hopkins Papers, Robert Olney Easton Collection, American Heritage Center, University of Wyoming.
[2]Hopkins, Frank T. "Mustangs", Vermont Horse and Bridle Trail Bulletin, January, 1941, p. 4.
[3]Hopkins, Frank T., Answers, Letter 6, pp. 5-6. Hopkins Papers, Robert Olney Easton Collection, American Heritage Center, University of Wyoming.
[4]Hopkins Memoir, p. 15.
[5]Hopkins Memoir, pp. 15-16.
[6]Russell, Don. The Lives and Legends of Buffalo Bill. University of Oklahoma Press, 1960, p. 353.

[7]Hopkins Memoir, pp. 16-17.

[8]Hopkins Memoir, p. 17.

[9]Hopkins Memoir, p. 13.

[10]Walker, Dave, "Wild, Wild West: Buffalo Bill in Earls Court". The Library Time Machine, 9-27, 2012.

[11]Fees, Paul, "Wild West shows: BuffaloBill's Wild West". http://centerofthe west.org/learn/western-essays/wild-west-shows.

[12]Sprague, Donovin Arleigh. Pine Ridge Reservation, Arcadia Publishing, 1904, p. 23.

[13]Hopkins Memoir, pp. 20-22.

[14]Hopkins, Frank T. "Buffalo Bill as I Knew Him", Vermont Horse and Bridle Trail Bulletin, Oct. 1942, p. 154.

[14] Hopkins, Gertrude, "Answers, Letter 6, pp. 21-2. Hopkins Papers, Robert Olney Easton Collection, American Heritage Center, University of Wyoming.

[15]Wilson, R. L., Buffalo Bill's Wild West, Random, 1988, pp. 162-6.
 Russell, Don. The Lives and Legends of Buffalo Bill. University of Oklahoma Press, 1960, pp. 375-6.

[16]Dickey, Edward M. "I knew Frank for almost half a century", undated letter to Robert Easton (1960's?), Hopkins Papers, Robert Olney Easton Collection, American Heritage Center, University of Wyoming.

[17]Serrano, Richard A. American Endurance: Buffalo Bill, the Great Cowboy Race of 1893, and the Vanishing Wild West. Smithsonian Books, 2016.

[18]Hopkins, Frank T., "The Truth About "Buffalo Bill". Vermont Horse and Bridle Trail Bulletin, Oct. 1944, p. 121.

[19]Russell, Don. The Lives and Legends of Buffalo Bill. University of Oklahoma Press, 1960, p. 319.

Chapter 6: Riding with Buffalo Bill's Wild West, 1894-1906

1) 1894

Bill's show spent the whole season in Ambrose Park, South Brooklyn, New York. It was no longer a novelty and did not draw enough spectators to break even. This result taught management a lesson. To stay in business, they had to change.

During this season, Frank won the endurance races he describes below.

a) "I got acquainted with a veterinary from New Hampshire; he was interested in endurance races and asked me book on. This race was from Westmoreland to Hillsborough Bridge, New Hampshire. I rode in it. The horse was four years old, also of the White-y family. When I unloaded, the doctor told me I didn't have a chance.

'Why?'

'Because that horse is too small and he is spotted and a spotted horse has no endurance.'

'I said I have no other horse so I will have to use this spotted colt and I wish he was older.'

The Doc admitted on looking him over that he looked sure like a nice put together pony, but said, 'Well, boy, you'll never run that stallion against these strong horses that are entered in this race.'

Three days later I had four hundred dollars of the Doc's money in my pocket besides the prize money from the race and he was the most surprised man in all New Hampshire. He wanted to buy that horse Turk, but I had not sold a single horse of the White-y strain and it was too late to ask me now. Turk was good on mountain roads - a great horse in muddy going."[1]

b) "Doc was not easily discouraged; three months later, he sent me word there would be a good race on and he'd like me to sign on for it? I made a train that got me into Hancock, New Hampshire the next day. Everything looked alright to me so I signed on and laid down the required money. This ride was from Hancock to Hollis, New Hampshire, said to be one hundred and twenty-five miles, but I have always doubted it was that far, for Turk carried me to Hollis in nineteen hours, forty-six minutes of actual riding. There were six Morgans in this race - they were in their own country, but they failed to show their ability as mountain climbers.

At the start of this race, I was some distance behind when a large man drove up beside me in a buggy and demanded that I halt.

'Where are you going', he demanded in a gruff voice.

'I'm riding this horse to Greenfield.'

He pointed to a short red post driven in the ground at the side of the road - 'What's that?'

I answered, 'I don't know - maybe its an engineer's mark or something', but he came back with the question 'Are you sure it is not a marker for a long distance race?'

I said 'What sort of race is that?'

'He answered, 'Well, they are horse-killing races. There is one on now and if I am not mistaken, you are riding in it.'

'Well, mister, does this horse look like a race horse, or was he traveling like I was trying to win a race? This horse is to stand as a stud for one month in Greenfield.'

Then he showed me his badge -'Well, I'm sheriff on this county and I'm sorry I hailed you in suh a manner; I can see you're alright!' He rode along the road with me for a mile or two. I saw a sign which read, 'Wines and Liquor'. I asked him to have a drink. I slid to the ground and tied Turk to a large elm tree. Sheriff was acquainted with the man behind the bar.

After buying my friend some few drinks of whisky and myself some of the worst cigars I ever had to smoke, I started to send Turk along. There were the Temple mountains before me - a long ride of over eight miles of steady climbing. Turk never slacked his fast walk. At the summit I set him to a swinging lope; now I could see the other riders. Between three and four o'clock that afternoon, I passed them all and did not see any of them again until they came in at the finish, late the following evening. Not all bad for a four year old colt."[2]

c) Later that fall, Frank met Albert Knowles, who was an agent of the Arapahoe Agency. He told him of the many fine ponies his Indians had at the Agency and asked him to come and see them. Frank needed a good stallion and wanted a straight Indian pony so that winter, he visited the Agency.

He comments,

"I found the Arapahos very friendly - they were good horsemen - they asked me to ride in three different races. Now, I didn't have a horse with me, so they insisted I ride their horses. I had spotted a nice stallion which I wanted to buy. First, I must find out what this horse was good for, so I agreed to ride that one. Sure enough. He was just what I thought he'd be and I won all three of the races with him. My winnings were - nine good ponies. I bought the stallion and gave the nine ponies back to the Indians."[3]

2) 1895-1902

Nate Salisbury died in 1902, but by 1895, he no longer wanted to take an active part in managing the show. He was replaced by James A. Bailey of Barnum & Bailey and he was the one who revolutionized their travel arrangements. Now the show could be quickly loaded onto two trains with fifty or more cars and special loading ramps. The whole show could be struck down, loaded, and moved to a new town overnight. Their efficiency was much admired.

In these years, the show no longer stayed at any one place for more than a few days and played to many one night stands, but it did shut down in the winter. For example, in 1899, it covered 11,000 miles in 200 days and gave 341 performances in 132 cities.[4]

Frank comments,

"After the Chicago Fair was over, the 'Bill' show began to get ancient. Cody was in bad health from which he never recovered. We toured the States and Canada each year, the show growing smaller as each season came around."[5]

a) In the fall of 1895, there was considerable talk about a long race in Canada. Frank comments,

"Cody wanted to boost the show so he offered $1,000 to the rider who would ride one hundred miles and come in first, but told me to stay out of it people might think the race was fixed for me to win, so I let it go at that.

After the race, there was talk about me being afraid I might lose in that race as there were riders from the Mounted Police who took part in it, that made Cody sore and he challenged the winner, who was a Royal mounty. Cody even said I must ride one hundred and twenty-five miles against the Police who wouldn't ride more than one hundred. I didn't like the idea, but stopped riding in the show and began sharpening up Turk for that hard ride. He was then five years old and about nine hundred and fifty pounds with a lot of fight in him when it came to long rides. On two previous hard rides, he covered the ground without wearying. ... Now he had one more year on his age and that was a lot to an endurance horse - training only seemed to harden his flesh.

The big day came; nothing to fear - the people up there did not object to the race. There were two of us - the officer's horse a fine looking animal but high strung and I knew before we started that rider and horse were beaten. Cody said, 'Boy, you've got something on your hands now that you never had before'.

'Yes, Colonel, and I'm sitting on something that they never saw before and I'll bet you $100 that I will finish ahead of the Mounted Police.' Johnny Baker held the money and we rode to the starting line.

The large horse plunged like crazy with fright. After a few miles, I came up behind and there I rode for over twenty miles; the big horse worried and sweated; he did not like my horse tagging on behind. I thought I'd worried the big horse long enough to make him lose the race and I picked up Turk to make a bid to pass the big horse.

Not so easy though - the big fool wanted to race, so I dropped back. I tried again several times to pass. Turk was still cool and fresh. I rode along, and when the day was done, Turk was in good shape.

Next day I rode until four o'clock and the finish. I'd come to the line five hours and twenty-eight minutes ahead. I must admit though on all my years in the saddle, it was the only time that I ever tried to worry the horse of another rider and was ashamed for doing it."[6]

b) In 1896, Frank discovered the army ran endurance races under a different set of rules. They rode their horses together and stayed at a walk until one mile of the finish when they would race against each other to determine the winner.[7]

Frank explains,

"I was invited to ride in a 600 mile race at Fort Ethan Allan, Vermont, but after learning about the rules, would not book on. However, I said I'd ride against the winner of that race and would put down $1,000 if anyone wished to cover it. When the race was over, many soldiers were willing to place their money on the winner, but the officers who had conducted the race would not hear of it - arguing that it would be against the humane law.

Some of the troops got together and asked me if I still wanted to back up my offer; I would, but the race could not be run over the same ground. So it was arranged that we would start from a small town in New Hampshire - the town of Peterborough. Our route led out of the State into Massachusetts. Passing the outskirts of Nashoway this ride was to cover six hundred miles.

After I rode to Pepperall, a distance of two hundred and sixty-one miles according to men who laid out the route. I stopped at Pepperall to feed at noonday where two men stepped into the stable and ordered me not to ride any further, for the other rider's horse had 'gone to pieces' and could not compete against the pace as I was going. They said the horse I was riding against had won the six hundred mile race three different years and he was considered to be the best endurance horse in this country; he was a full-blooded Morgan.

Their horse was a wonder - when he was ridden under army rules - but when he got out on the road against a real endurance horse where the first horse to finish was the winner, their great horse could not stand up to the work. ... I rode Turk in that race; he was in his prime (7th year). ... I won over $2,000 and sure would have liked to go the 600 miles. Turk could have done it."[8]

c) A troupe of Mexican ropers, led by Vincenzo P. Orapeza, had joined the show in 1894 and stayed until 1907.[9]

In 1897, Frank comments,

"One of these Mexicans was the best rope thrower I ever saw. He told me of the many long races in New Mexico and along the border and how he had taken part in many of them, so, when it was all over that Fall, I went with him and I brought three of my endurance horses along - they'd been rode all summer as cow ponies, and they were in good shape. I rode in nine 50 miles races. Over in old Mexico, I rode two more - one 125 miles, one 100 miles."[10]

Editor's Comment: Presumably Frank won all eleven races.

d) In June of 1898 when the show was in Keene, NH, Frank finally got a chance to ride Hightower, the champion bucker of the show. He states,

"This horse had killed a number of men in his time and when he was in the Show, it was understood that no man should ride him more than once a month.

For some reason, Cody had put off permitting me to ride him; but in the city of Keene, New Hampshire where a number of Cody's friends came to visit here as I was sitting at the table eating (Guernsey Hotel) he called across to me and said, 'Frank, I think its your time to ride Hightower tonight.' I always liked a good game horse and was pleased but said 'You think he's going to hurt me Colonel?' He said to one of his friends 'It's a good performance where 2 bad actors meet - I've been keeping this feller off that horse all seasons for a time like this and this horse has never been ridden for more than two jumps by any man.'

That night, I went into the horsetop and told the head horseman to turn Hightower into the ring for me where the buckers came in. This was not a rodeo - we did not use squeeze pens for our buckers; in those days you had to be a real bronco-buster, rope your horse in the ring before the audience, leg him down by drawing his two hind feet together, saddle him yourself and step up on his middle and ride him. We didn't have 16 inch bulge forks on our saddles to hold us there.

Well, I rode Hightower that night. There was no whistle blowing for me in 3 minutes to dismount as there is in a rodeo. Hightower bucked around that the ring for some twenty minutes: the blood was flying out of my nose and ears. Finally, he came to a standstill and by then I was blind as a bat - I could make out Cody's voice calling 'Climb off him, Frank, climb off him.' But I thought the horse had only stopped to sulk and was ready at any time to whoop her up again so I kept my pants glued to the leather. Then some of the boys rode up and dropped me from the saddle.

I never saw Hightower alive again. He died right there in the ring while I was carried to the hospital. He had broken some arteries and bled to death thru the nose. I've seen many buckers in rodeos, here and in Mexico but I never saw one equal to Hightower. Some young riders tell me 'they do it different now, Pop, than they did in your day'. Mebbe, but its a sure thing they get unloaded easier too than we did then."[11]

Editor's Comment: Frank did not kill this horse, he just did his job. He was supposed to stick on this horse until he stopped bucking and he was justifiably proud of his success. In his day, horses were cheap and often left on the range until they were mature. When they were broken, some turned outlaw like Hightower. He fought until he did himself a fatal injury. He was not the only mustang who killed himself rather than accept a rider on his back.

e) In 1899, Frank was recovering from an injured leg when he heard about an interesting race. He comments,

"I heard from an old friend who lived in Idaho Falls of a race that was in the making and would I come and take part in it. I was still quite lame but said I'd go out there and look things over. I did. This was one of the old time races - the Plains Indians were first to indulge in it, then the white man joined in. It was run over trails - some of them very rough - no place for nervous horses. Some riders had the wrong kind of mounts for that rough country and soon found out their horses were no good after they had trained for a short time. Seeing how my horses stood the steady grind for training, they were eager to get horses of the same breeding. I had a good supply of them at that time, but none for sale. I made a deal with these riders - they could ride my ponies, cost would be their feed and shipping bill.

I was putting myself in a tight spot for there were 18 horses in the race who were of White-y strain - some might fool me. At the same time I wanted to see them race against each other. Winning the stake did not mean much to me for I had plenty to lose. That was the hottest race of one hundred miles I've see yet. I rode a six-year old stallion named Blaze named on account of the white mark on his face which ran down over one eye.

I won that race only by eight minutes and three seconds with that bunch of ponies hammering the trail behind me. That was the closest ride I had been in. All of those ponies covered that hundred miles in less than nineteen hours of actual traveling. Some of them could beat Blaze I found out later when I rode them myself. Three weeks later I rode one of them over the same route against two horses. My pony Colonel covered that one hundred miles in eleven hours of traveling with one night's rest between the mileage."[12]

As well as his endurance ponies, Frank had to have horses for Bill's show who had been trained for trick riding. Not all horses could do both jobs. Three of his favorite horses are shown in the photograph below. Their names were Darkie, Blaze, and Blueskin, but only Blaze and Blueskin were mustangs. This photograph was used in two articles, "The Toughest Race", by Charles B. Roth, Horse and Horseman, Jan. 1937, "America's great distance horseman", by Fredie Steve Harris, Horseman, Aug. 1979, and Anthony A. Amaral, "Frank Hopkins", Western Horseman, Dec. 1969, p. 110.

f) In 1901, tragedy struck the show. On Oct. 29, a freight train crashed into one unit of the circus train. One hundred ten horses either died or were so badly injured, they had to be put down. One of them was Frank's tough horse, Turk.[13]

g) In 1902, when the show played in Cheyenne, Wyoming, Frank's mother came to see him and her beloved Gypsy Boy. Frank tells his story below.

"Gypsy Boy had the best set of legs of any horse I raised, but for some reason he had the body of a running horse - little too long in the back to suite me. His mother died when he was born so he was hand raised and ran about the place.

Now there was a band of horse-trading gypsies known as the Coopers who camped near our place and then [went on to] Sundance, WY. They'd buy a large drove of horses each Spring, drive them east selling all.

The colt I called Gypsy Boy wandered down to the gypsy camp; for three days I searched the country looking for him, knowing he needed milk and without he'd soon die.

At sundown the third day, I saw that little rascal, he was with a small gypsy boy who was watching over the horses as they grazed near camp. I led the colt home and my mother called him Gypsy Boy and she always spoke of that colt as her horse for she raised him by hand.

The colt got too much petting and this I did not like so well. Once I got him to the Show where I rode him I got him to do what I wanted. I know he longed to feel the gentle touch of my mother's hand and the following season while the show played at Cheyenne mother came to see him. He made such a fuss when she stepped up to him I didn't have the heart to ship him away from his old home - he was then 12 years old and spent the rest of his life [with her]. I never took him away again although he was one of the best for trick riding."[14]

Below is a photograph of Frank on Gypsy Boy shaking hands with Bud Tobel, his opponent, after a hard riding contest, which he won. This stallion weighed a little over 900 pounds and was one of the White-y family. The photograph was published on page 19 of an article, "Brains Plus Endurance", by Charles B. Roth in The Horse, March-April, 1935.

3) 1903-6

In these years, the show toured Europe again, but this time they made short stays in many cities. By then, they had also added side shows to attract more customers. They spent two years touring England, Wales, and Scotland. From England, in 1905 they went to France and wintered at Marseille. In 1906, they left Marseille and covered Italy, the Austro Hungarian Empire, Germany, and Belgium.

a) Charles E. Griffin spent these years touring with Bill's show. He comments,

"At the opening performance [in Manchester, England] Colonel Cody was thrown from his horse, or rather, the horse stumbled, severely spraining one of the Colonel's ankles, consequently he was unable to ride .., but was driven around the arena in a carriage."[15]

"The first fatal accident occurred at Bristol, July 23, Isadore Gonazlez, one of the Mexican riders, was thrown from his horse and instantly killed. ... It is just as well, perhaps, that the general public do not realize the danger that forever attends the participants of the Wild West performances. Every time they enter the arena, especially in the bucking horse act, they practically take their lives in their hands."[16]

"Shortly after leaving Paris glanders broke out among the bronchos, and government veterinaries were placed with us to combat the dread disease. Forty-two horses were taken out and shot in one day.

When we closed the season at Marseilles we only had about one hundred bronchos left to give the performance, two hundred having been killed during the season.

Our magnificent draught stock ... never came in contact with the bronchos, so they did not become contaminated. When the show was finally put away in Winter quarters, Mr. Bailey and Colonel Cody, equal owners of the Wild West, held a consultation, and it was decided to kill the remaining hundred bronchos and burn all the trappings, that being the only way of stamping out the plague, and importing new bronchos and trappings from America for the next season."[17]

Editor's Comment: According to both Mr. Griffin and Agnes Spring, the results of the glanders epidemic were never publicized.[18]

When the show was in Germany, army officers studied the show's methods of quick transportation and cooking for large groups so they could apply them for military purposes.[19]

When the show closed in Belgium in 1906, "All of the bronchos, except the buckers, and a few culled from the draught stock, were sold in a bunch to a Brussels firm, who sold them at auction in Ghent."[20]

b) Frank tells us little about these years in Europe, but he did lose the horses he had brought to France in the glanders epidemic.[21] He does mention the races he won in France, Italy, and Germany. He also rode in a relay race against the Cossacks and competed in three races near the Russian border.[22]

In 1906, Frank agreed to help a Belgian who owned trotting horses. He explains,

"I told him I did know a little about trotters and he asked me to his stables and to drive one of his horses with whom there was something wrong. 'He did not go right.'
I drove the horse over a 1/2 mile track; he would break and run if I tried to get any speed out of him. When I came off the track, the owner asked me, 'Why did his horse break and run and was there any cure for that?'
I said, 'Mister, your horse is not balanced.'
He said, 'Trotting horses were something new in his part of the country. Could I help his horse?'
I could and did. We took him to the shop; I swept the ground for about a hundred feet and trotted the horse over it, then measured his tracks and found the horse traveled too slow forward; he did not get his forward feet out of the way of the hind ones. So I shod him a little heavier forward, then drove him over the 1/2 mile track. That horse could trot and he did, but there was no running. Soon the news got around and any man who owned a trotter in that part of the country called to see me."[23]

Editor's Comment: Frank's reputation was growing. This story is the first record we have of someone asking Frank for help and he responded generously.

c) When Frank was riding races on the Russian border, he met a man who traded for wool in Mongolia. When the show closed in Belgium, they met in Hamburg and used the Trans Siberian Railroad to travel through Russia. After Frank spent some time trying to catch one of Prewalski's horses, he decided they really were impossible to handle. He had brought five of his horses with him and won seventeen races with them. Since he would not sell them, he paid to have them shipped home.[24]

Evaluation (Chapter Six):

The stories in this chapter suggest Frank's new contract gave him more freedom to organize endurance races. He had found a life style suited to his personality. He enjoyed the challenge and potential dangers in trick riding and staying on bucking horses. By traveling with the Bill show, he found interested backers and new people willing to face him in endurance races. In my opinion, he never wanted public acclaim, but he did want to be accepted by other horseman who respected his skills. He soon earned the respect of his fellow rough riders and enjoyed responding to anyone who asked him advice.

Acknowledgements:

Photo 1 courtesy of the American Heritage Center, University of Wyoming. Photo 2 courtesy of the Horse, March-April, 1935.

Footnotes:

[1]Hopkins, Frank T. Memoir, Letter 1, p. 22-23. Hopkins Papers, Robert Olney Easton Collection, American Heritage Center, University of Wyoming.
[2]Hopkins Memoir, pp. 23-24.
[3]Hopkins Memoir, pp. 25-26.

[4]Fees, Paul, "Wild West Shows: Buffalo Bill's Wild West", http://centerofthe west.org/learn/western-essays/wild-west-shows.

[5]Hopkins, Frank T., "Buffalo Bill as I Knew Him", Vermont Horse and Bridle Trail Bulletin, Oct. 1942, p. 154.

[6]Hopkins Memoir, pp. 26-7.

[7]Hopkins Memoir, p. 32.

[8]Hopkins Memoir, pp. 28-30.

[9]Dean, Frank and Rodriguez, Dr. Nacho. Charro Roping. Wild West Arts Club, 2003, p. 9 - Confirmed by records on Buffalo Bill's Wild West, kept at the McCracken Research Library, Buffalo Bill Center of the West.

[10] Hopkins Memoir, p. 30.

[11]Hopkins, Frank T. Answers, Letter 6. pp. 2-3. Hopkins Papers, Robert Olney Easton Collection, American Heritage Center, University of Wyoming.

[12]Hopkins Memoir, pp. 31-32.

[13]Hopkins Memoir, p. 30.

[14]Hopkins Memoir, pp. 50-51.

[15]Griffin, Charles Eldridge. Four Years in Europe with Buffalo Bill. Stage Publishing Co., 1908, p. 27.

[16]Griffin, p. 30.

[17]Griffin, pp. 67-68.

[18]Griffin, p. 68.

Spring, Agnes Wright, "Buffalo Bill and His Horses. 1967, p. 20.

[19]Russell, Don. The Lives and Legends of Buffalo Bill. University of Oklahoma Press, 1960, pp. 371-2.

[20]Griffin, p. 83.

[21] Hopkins Memoir, p. 15.

[22]Hopkins Memoir, pp. 33-35.

[23]Hopkins Memoir, pp. 33-34.

[24]Hopkins Memoir, pp. 34, 39-42.

Chapter 7: Staying with Buffalo Bill's Wild West, 1907-1917

1) 1907

When Bailey died on March 22, 1906, Buffalo Bill no longer had a partner and for two years, he managed the show alone. Before the 1907 season, he got rid of the side shows and circus elements, as well as revising the show program He started the 1907 season at Madison Square Garden and followed it with a series of one night stands. His new program is shown below.

Listing of Events from Program Used in 1907

1. Grand Review
2. Race of Races: Race between a Cowboy, Cossack, Mexican, Arab, and Indian
3. U.S. Artillery Drill
5. Pony Express
6. Attack on Emigrant Train
7. Feats of Agility by Arabs and Japanese
8. An Attack on the Deadwood Stagecoach by Indians
9. Expert Shooting by Col. W. F. Cody
10. The Battle of Summit Springs. June 11, 1869, Colorado
11. Lightning Drills and Wall Climbing by Devlin Zouaves
12. Mexicans Illustrate Use of Lasso
13. Veterans from the 6th U.S. Cavalry in military exercises and exhibitions
14. Johnny Baker Marksman
15. The Great Train Hold-Up and Bandit Hunters of the Union Pacific
16. Indian Boys' Race
17. Cowboy's Fun
18. Feats of Horsemanship by Cossacks from the Caucasus of Russia
19. A Holiday at the T. E. Ranch in Wyoming: Mail is delivered, Indians attack[1]

2) 1908-1912

In 1908, Buffalo Bill began negotiating with Pawnee Bill (Major Gordon Lillie). Their two shows eventually merged under the name of

Buffalo Bill's Wild West combined with Pawnee Bill's Great Far East. It was also known as the Two Bills Show.

a) Frank comments on the merger,

"Major Gordon Lillie's small show joined up with us. That was the beginning of the end for the 'Bill' Show. Lillie was a little too much of a business man; our old riders lost their old spirit and many of them quit; the show was on a downslide."[2]

"Then Major Gordon Lillie joined the show with his elephants - this was a funny thing in a wild west show! The show started down grade from the time Lillie joined partnership with Cody,"[3]

"He [Cody] was a life long friend of mine, yet I must say he was a very poor business man, spending his spare time drinking with his so-called 'friends'. As he grew older, the old Barley-corn burnt him out, though he looked the picture of health, when riding in the ring, he was only the outside shell of the man I knew in my boyhood. ... But for all of this he never lost his pose as a showman. He was always kind to his riders and horses and often spoke of them as one big family. Maj. Gordon Lillie joined up with Cody and from the first day Lillie started in to run things to suit himself, for his own benefit; nine years later Cody was without a dollar, the Bill show was something of the past."[4]

b) In the winter seasons, Frank was free to concentrate on racing, visiting his family, and training his horses. After the end of the 1908 season, Frank agreed to take charge of a shipment of horses going to Singapore. When the horses had been delivered, he went to India, bought a scrub horse for $25.00, won four races on him, and sold him for $600.00[5]

c) Frank's father had been breeding old type Morgans for years and had always sold many of them to eastern dealers as prospective carriage horses. The advent of the automobile had destroyed the market for driving horses and the CH Ranch was overstocked with unsold horses. Since his father was now in his nineties, Frank took over the responsibility for selling his horses. One of Frank's friends, Bud Tobel, found a solution for him. Like Frank, Bud was half Sioux.

Frank explains,

"Ed Tobel came to see me. I had always called him 'Bud'. We had given certain performances together in England and contested, he was as good a horseman as ever looked down over a horse's ears, but he had one bad habit - drink. He would go on a month long spree; stop, not drink even with best friends, then break out again.

When he came to see me, he was broke. He'd been training polo ponies for George Minnick down in Texas, went on a spree, [and] lost his job. Bud could train a polo pony with the most expert riders but the drink ruined him. He was at home with my people - knew we could not let him drink here.

He spoke of my horses and told me the polo teams were using larger horses and mine were the right type for the game. He had been into the Argentine with shipments of polo ponies. He said if those horses of mine were trained to play the game he could sell all of them in the Argentine. By the first of May, Bud had many of those colts as handy as a pocket in a shirt.

Bud told Dan Monet, the dealer from the Argentine that I was a long distance rider and I soon was invited over there. There were about 20 rides none over 60 miles - most of them with cattle raisers. That winter I shipped 12 of my little nags and had Bud go along. You'll be surprised when I say I rode 68 rides from the 14th day of Oct. to the 4th of March. All of the stallions came home with me.

I sold the horses old enough to train - knew the trade would not last for long (autos were coming in). If I bred any more mares I'd have a lot of back yard pets on my hands. I figured right - the rush for polo ponies slacked off after 3rd year. Many mares that had been shipped for polo playing had been used as brood mares after they played the game for a season. From time to time I see pictures of polo ponies - most of them a wide white blaze running down their faces and that mark is surely the stamp of Whitey, [the stallion] who was at the head of my [father's] herd for twenty years.

I always rode my own horses in the Show; the few that were left were soon used up. Tobel rode with us in the summer of 1911."[6]

Editor's Comment: Bud Tobel was killed by one of the vicious buckers in Bill's Show.

3) 1913

Different disasters happened to Buffalo Bill and to Frank in 1913.

In 1908, the Two Bill's show had been a great success, but it went downhill rapidly. In 1913, the two shows began to break apart. Buffalo Bill made a bad mistake when he borrowed money from Harry H. Tammen and didn't repay it. Tammen forced Bill's show into bankruptcy on July 20, 1913. Along with all the other show property, the receivers grabbed the ticket wagon with all of the show's business records. The property was finally sold at a deferred auction on Sept. 15, 1915.

Frank comments,

"Winter of 1913, Stable in Bridgeport, Conn.: 48 horses in all, 36 of them colts weaned when I sold their mothers to go to South America - colts now four years old - a fine lot, other 12 last of the White-y family. I was training the colts to play polo. Some of 'em broke to harness.

I put on a sleigh-riding party. ... but on return trip as I drove eight-horse team down to where my stable was and saw a large fire. I knew where was and sent that team into a dead run with the people screaming with fright.

I jumped from the sleigh ran to the burning stable. The firemen grabbed me, I left my coat in their hands and ran into the burning stable; there were horses in there I had to save. Burning timber was falling all around and smoke and heat almost blinding but when I called to the horses they answered me. I called first to Chenango and he answered; then I heard Blue.

As I cried out most of them whinnied out their answer - that was the only way I had of finding them. One by one, they came after me over the falling timbers. 'Come on, boys, come here.' I could not see them but I knew they were trailing on after me as best they could as fast as I could cut their ropes. How we got out of that stable with the falling timbers I don't know but when I reached the street, all of the Indian ponies were huddled about me. I noticed Silver was in bad shape - he coughed and held his nose to the ground. Doctor Shelby came to me, told me to put the horses on his lawn.

As I started for his lawn, I noticed my left arm was helpless where the shoulder was broken - there were bruises and burns on my body which by then was nearly naked. Silver walked around me; I laid the good hand on his head to calm him for I knew that little silver tailed horse was dying on his feet, finally he did lay down and he went out like a light. I looked at the house - it was burned to the ground [and] the big stable had fallen. In it was a collection of many things including hundreds of photographs and pictures of me in contests; they did not matter much compared to my horses. When I saw Silver lying at my feet, it was too much. I was badly hurt and had to be carried away from his body stretched out on the snow covered lawn.

I lost 18 horses in that fire, two of White-y family had to be destroyed; I was in the hospital until the following June."[7]

Editor's Comment: In 1911, Frank used Chenango, Blue, and Silver in races in Tennessee. Blue was a game little horse and slate grey in color. His full name was Blueskin.[8] In the photograph below, he is the third horse and the only one who is completely shown.

Chenango outlived all the rest of the White-y family and died in 1928.[9] Silver was by the stallion Frank bought from the Arapaho and out of his albino mare, Josey II. He was seal brown with a silver mane and tail.[10]

4) 1914-15

Harry Tammen made Buffalo Bill add his Wild West show to his Sells-Floto Circus.

Frank comments,

"The next year the show was on the road. But the Colonel never became the same man again. he was sick and broken in spirit. I have no idea how Cody lost the large fortune he made with the show, but now it was all gone. In two years, his hair grew snow white and the old plainsman had to be helped into the saddle - he was only the shell of the Buffalo Bill I'd known since childhood."[3]

Editor's Comment: Frank probably did everything he could to help and cover for Buffalo Bill, including sometimes acting as ringmaster. Frank's wife, Gertrude, commented Frank was the only person who could get Buffalo Bill out of a saloon without a fight.[11]

Before the fire in 1913, Frank had received an interesting letter from Japan. He explains,

"Japanese Army officer wrote me he'd like some nice saddle horses for breeding up stock (Sang Wo). I met him once across sea and contested against him. He said he'd come to America to get a few Bison and at the same time would buy some horses to improve saddle stock in his own country."[12]

"The army officer came in the fall [of 1914] bought all the horses I had not of the White'y family - he also bought 6 bison. He said if I would take 2 of my ponies he'd see I got a few long rides and that I'd get beat in his country (looking sad). When it came time to ship the stock, I went with him, but I took 4 ponies. I won 38 rides -none less than 60 miles, the longest about 110. The Japs are good sports and friendly, they wanted to pay my expenses home."[13]

Editor's Comment: When the horse market died, many ranchers converted to cattle. As the his father's horses were sold, Frank probably began buying cattle with the proceeds. This may explain why he waited until 1915 to apply for a livestock brand.

5) 1916-17

Buffalo Bill broke away from Tammen at the end of the 1915 season. In 1916, he combined his Wild West show with the 101 Ranch Shows. He died on Jan. 10, 1917. Johnny Baker wanted to keep the show going and Jess Willard bought into it. It lasted one more season.[14]

Frank comments,

"[When they] took the show on the road the following spring [1917]: they agree to pay me $1,000 per month, but no contract. On the 1st of June the government took me from the show to work to do some confidential work for our country which was at war with Germany."[15]

Evaluation (Chapter 7):

Since Frank had grown up at an army fort and had many Indian relatives, he had to have been all too familiar with what the abuse of liquor could to humans. Although he didn't drink himself, he accepted it in his friends and helped them when he could. Some of Bud Tobel's sprees may have been triggered by the way people treated half breeds.

Frank's career as a show rider certainly paid off when he found a way to sell his father's horses. He speaks of Buffalo Bill and a friend and an employer, but was he also a family friend? Frank and his Father could both have known him; but given the way people felt at that time about Indians and half breeds, I doubt if he would wanted to become a family friend. The photograph below is a painting of Buffalo Bill done by Rosa Bonhuer in 1889.

As Buffalo Bill and his show gradually went down hill, Frank had begun to wonder how much longer he could continue as a show rider. He believed his performance and enjoyment was being affected by his age and the results of his many injuries[16], but he choose to stay with Buffalo Bill to the bitter end. According to David Dary, such loyalty to employers, like Buffalo Bill, and friends, like Bud Tobel, was a critical part of cowboy culture.[17]

With the end of Bill's show and the family ranch now raising cattle; when the war ended, what kind of career could Frank find with horses? How could he continue to challenge himself to learn, do, and succeed?

Evaluation of Buffalo Bill's Wild West (Chapters 4-7):

Bill's show ran from 1883-1916. At this time, the federal government was financed by custom duties. Individuals and business enterprises did not pay any income tax. There was no safety net for individuals, such as social security, unemployment, or worker's compensation. Since there was no government mandated withholding, what employees received in their gross pay was every penny they earned. Their employer did not have to keep any form of quarterly or annual records for them or the government.

Unfortunately, the business records of the show were lost in the 1913 bankruptcy, but several volumes survived in the files of a legal firm. They did show the names and amounts paid to each employee. Payments could be made weekly or monthly, but groups, such as the Indians, could be paid in lump sums at defined intervals.[18] What was received and when would have depended on their contract with the show.

The show essentially had three levels of employees. The top level was the management staff and the stars who had individual billing on the show program. The next level was performers who had group billing on the show program. They belonged to the Congress of Rough Riders. Each group had some form of leader who organized their performances and monitored their behavior. For example, the cowboys had a foreman while the Indians looked to their tribal elders. The last level was the employees who kept the show running, such as the ticket sellers.

As the show moved from place to place, keeping track of all these different types of employees had to have been a difficult task. As new employees were hired and people wandered off, the total population may have varied from day to day and place to place. The Indians were allowed to come and go just like the other employees. Some of them accidentally got left behind, others wandered off, and some just stayed in Europe.[19]

Over the years, the Buffalo Bill Center of the West has built a database of people associated with William F. Cody. While they do have records, they can come from a variety of sources, including newspaper articles and shipping records. The Center estimates their records are only 70% complete.[20] Frank Hopkins mentions several injuries and states Bud Tobel was killed during a performances. The Center admits deaths and injuries in the arena did happen, but all they normally have is records of the ones who were reported in the newspapers.[21] The Center's records of Buffalo Bill's Wild West do not show either Frank Hopkins or Bud Tobel as employees. Given the incomplete state of their records; in my opinion, this lack does not constitute proof they did not work for the show.

According to Frank's wife, Gertrude, he inherited his straight black hair from his mother and he left it uncut when he was performing for Bill's show.[10] Since he was a half breed, he could perform as a cowboy or an Indian. When he was a cowboy, he probably braided his hair and tucked it up under his ten gallon hat. We do not know what names the show actually used to identify him in their business records or in the arena. Did they identify him as a white, Indian, or half-breed? Presumably he had an Indian name, but we do not yet know what it was. In my opinion, his comments about Buffalo Bill and stories about his time with the show his show indicated he did spend thirty-one years with it. Proof of his claim was probably destroyed in the Bridgeport fire.

Frank does claim he worked for Buffalo Bill in the two years he spent with the Sells-Floto Circus and his statement is supported by the man who donated his parade bridle to the Wyoming State Museum. More information on this bridle is in Appendix A. The donator states Frank used this bridle with Bill's show from 1900-1915[22], but another set of records contradicts this statement. The records at Circus World just show a Frank Hopkins who worked for Ringling Brothers in 1914-1915 as a baggage stock handler, but they do not have any additional information to prove which Frank Hopkins held this job. Unfortunately, the census records show thousands of men named Frank Hopkins. Even a middle initial would help narrow this list. In my opinion, this man was just another man named Frank Hopkins, but not the real one. Ringling Brothers did purchase the Sells-Floto Circus in 1929, but their Museum in Sarasota, Florida does not have any records of Frank T. Hopkins.

Evaluation (Chapters 4-7): Document Validity

All too often, the real Frank T. Hopkins has been misrepresented as the sole author of material that had been extensively edited and included misleading information. His writing style is terse, concise, focused, and precise, but frequently lacks adequate punctuation. His friend, Nevada Dick, describes his speaking style as similar to his writing style.

He states,

"When speaking he was one who did not waste words, or did he favor any one interrupting, until he had finished. He at times was called upon to address, a body of horsemen, and he was a man who could hold the attention of his audience, as he gave some of his experiences. In his speech, he spoke in a clear ringing voice, which held the audience spellbound, but was not given to a lot of flamboyant gestures, etc., but made himself clear, and to the point."[24]

Frank had lived through many dramatic experiences and had turned most of them into stories he could share with others. Although these stories were based on his memories, they were probably told soon enough and often enough to stay relatively accurate. Such stories can be found in both his published and unpublished material. When such stories were identified; they were extracted from the mass of available material and quoted in this book. The only change to them has been to add punctuation where needed to improve their readability. Place names, dates, and distances were checked for every story. When multiple or conflicting stories were found, the ones with the most verifiable detail were used. If the narrative had not been written in Frank's style or if the details could not be verified, it was not used.

.e versions of his memoir appear to exist. An unpublished
ᴧs found in the archives of the American Heritage Center at
ersity of Wyoming. Judging by the poor quality of the
ᴧing and the added notes, this one was dictated directly by
ᴧo his wife and unedited. It is the one quoted in this book. At
best, this manuscript was semi-chronological. It appears to represent an
outpouring of memories as they came into Frank's mind. Sometimes
Frank included a clue to tell us when the event he is describing
happened, but often he gave us no helpful information. Fortunately, the
Buffalo Bill Center of the West does have a detailed list by date of
everywhere Bill's Show went. They sent me a copy of this list and it
was invaluable in determining when and where various events had
happened. If one of Frank's stories conflicted with the information on
this list, it was not used.

Acknowledgements:

The first photo is courtesy of the American Heritage Center,
University of Wyoming. The second one is courtesy of Wikipedia.

Footnotes:

[1]Griffin, Charles Eldridge. Four Years in Europe with Buffalo Bill.
Stage Publishing Co., 1908, pp. 91-94.
[2]Hopkins, Frank T. "Buffalo Bill as I Knew Him", Vermont Horse and
Bridle Trail Bulletin, Oct. 1942, p. 154.
[3]Hopkins, Frank T. "Memoir, Letter 1, p. 42. Hopkins Papers, Robert
Olney Easton Collection, American Heritage Center, University of
Wyoming.
[4]Hopkins, Frank T. "The Truth About Buffalo Bill", Vermont Horse
and Bridle Trail Bulletin, Oct. 1944, p. 121.
[5]Hopkins memoir, pp. 42-43.
[6]Hopkins memoir, pp. 44-46.
[7]Hopkins memoir, pp. 51-53.
[8]Hopkins memoir, pp 47-50.
[9]Harris, Albert W. The Blood of the Arab. The Arabian Horse Club of
America, 1941, p. 49.

[10]Hopkins memoir, pp. 27-8, 35.

[11]Gertrude Hopkins to Robert Easton, letter dated 1969, p. 1. Hopkins Papers, Robert Easton Olney Collection, American Heritage Center, University of Wyoming. This letter is available on line in their digital collection.

[12]Hopkins memoir, pp. 51-52.

[13]Hopkins memoir, p. 54.

[14]Russell, Don. The Life and Legends of Buffalo Bill. University of Oklahoma, 1960, pp. 473-4.

[15]Hopkins, Frank T. Memoir Addendum, p. 5. Hopkins Papers, Robert Olney Easton Collection, American Heritage Center, University of Wyoming.

[16]Hopkins, Frank T. Memoir Addendum, p. 4. Hopkins Papers, Robert Olney Easton Collection, American Heritage Center, University of Wyoming.

[17]Dary, David. Cowboy Culture. NY, Alfred A. Knopf, 1981, p. 278.

[18]Wilson, R. L. Buffalo Bill's Wild West. Random, 1998, pp. 261-263.

[19]Russell, Don. The Lives and Legends of Buffalo Bill. University of Oklahoma Press, 1960, p. 351.

[20]Preis, Karen. E-mail to author, dated 9-2-14.

[21]Preis, Karen. E-mail to author, dated 4-1-15.

[22]Schultes, Domingique. E-mail to author, dated 1-13-16.

Mrs. Katherine Halverson to Mr. Robert Easton, letter dated 6-19-1970. Hopkins Papers, Robert Olney Easton Collection, American Heritage Center. University of Wyoming.

[23]Shrake, Peter. E-mail to author, dated 10-17-14.

[24]Dickey, E. M. to Robert Easton, undated letter, p. 1. Hopkins Papers, Robert Olney Easton Collection, American Heritage Center, University of Wyoming.

57, a parade bridle was given to the Wyoming State Museum in nne, Wyoming. A photograph of it is shown on the next page. The donor stated, "Parade bridle made and used by Mr. Frank T. Hopkins, c. 1900-1915. Mr. Hopkins was once a member of the troop [troupe] and also a ringmaster for the Buffalo Bill Wild West Show."[1] The Museum had cataloged it as G-1967.64.1. Anyone who wishes to see it must place a request three weeks before the date when they want to see it.

Evaluation has established this parade bridle should be described as a vaquero bridle. The quality of the leather and the workmanship is excellent. It is decorated in mother of pearl and silver in an intricate design. Unlike most American cowboys, vaqueros made their own equipment and some of them became works of art, as is the parade bridle created by Frank Hopkins.

In vaquero horsemanship, horses were trained in three phases. In the first one, the horse is ridden a bosal hackamore. Frank always rode his endurance horses in such a hackamore. In the second phase, the horse is ridden with double reins, one attached to the bosal and one to a bit. In the third one, he can be ridden in just a bit.[2] The bit with Frank's bridle is a half breed curb. Like a spade bit, it is a signal bit, but less severe. This kind of bit could only be safely and humanely used by a rider with a solid seat, steady hands, and a light touch. With this bit, a horseman needed a highly trained horse and the ability to use considerable finesses as he communicated with him.

There are no markings on the bit to indicate where it had been made. The bit shanks are in the form of a lady's legs. A slight bend in the knee gives the shanks a curve and the rein ring is attached to the lady's shoe. The unusual bit with this elegant bridle had mother of pearl inlaid on the shanks and slobber bar. Copper had been used in the cannon on either side of the bit port.

Frank left no record to tell us when and where he learned about vaquero horsemanship. He certainly would have seen it when he was a dispatch rider in Arizona and he may have discovered there how well a bosal suited Joe. Buffalo Bill usually had Mexican cowboys (vaqueros) in his show and Frank may have learned more from them. Since his mother's Christian name was Vallez, there may also have been a family connection.

Footnotes:

[1]Mrs. Katherine Halverson to Mr. Robert Easton, letter dated June 19, 1970. Hopkins Papers, American Heritage Center, University of Wyoming.
Dominique Schultes to author, e-mail dated 1-13-16.
[2]Ladendorf, Janice. Spanish Horsemen and Horses in the New World. CreateSpace, 2015, Chapter 7.

Photo courtesy of Wyoming State Museum, Dept. of State Parks and Cultural Resources

Chapter 8: Race in Arabia (3,000 miles)

1) Hidalgo

The horse who won this race was a product of Frank's breeding program he named Hidalgo. He was a member of the White-y family. White-y was the little mare he bought from the Army when the Sioux were forced back onto the reservation. He bred her to Jigger, the spotted stallion he bought from the Apache White Mountain Band. This cross produced five mares, one of whom was a dark chestnut with a small white spot on her neck. She was the dam of Hidalgo and Frank called her Josie.[1]

Editor's Comment: In his letter to Mr. Harris, dated 2-18-49, he describes Hidalgo's dam as spotted cream and white.

Hidalgo's sire was a horse called Uney, who had once been ridden seven hundred miles in seven days by King Stanley. Frank comments,

"I raised this little stallion - his sire and dam were got wild from the Red Desert Herd - those ponies were well named for their toughness and Uney was just as tough as his forebears. ... that same pony sired some of the best endurance horses the world has ever known, including my Hidalgo.[2]

When Frank saw Hidalgo as a handsome two year old, he yearned for the day when he could start riding the spotted colt.[3] Unfortunately, no photographs of Hidalgo have survived, but what we do have is a wooden carving of him done by Frank. Some think the color of his spots was a light gold or dun. Others think they were a darker color. Hidalgo is being ridden by an Indian. This fact suggests Frank may have felt like an Indian when he did some of his endurance rides. A photograph of this carving is shown below.

There is a story behind the seven hundred miles ride. When Crow scouts shot Frank at Grantrice Pillars, news spread among the cavalry that he could not live. King Stanley was at Ft. Custer when he heard and started out on Frank's horse, Uney. To reach his dying friend, he rode one hundred miles for seven straight days.[4]

Editor's Comments:

There is no longer any record of a place called Grantrice Pillars, but it may only have been known to the Army dispatch riders, like Frank and King Stanley. Frank was probably shot there and carried to Fort Bridger.

Later research established the seven hundred miles was an overestimate. According to Colonel Parker, Grantrice Pillars was on the edge of the great basin and the actual measured distance of the ride was 537 miles.[5] This is close to the distance between Ft. Custer, MT, and Ft. Bridger, WY.

2) Dates

Background Information:

Buffalo Bill's Wild West was an outdoor show and they carried their arena and stands for the spectators with them. When it played in the United States, normally it stopped and rested during the winter season. This policy gave Frank time to spend with his family, friends, and horses, as well as enter a few endurance races.

Taking the show to Europe was an expensive proposition. When the show was there, it typically spent the winter playing in an indoor amphitheater or traveling in the south. For example, in Italy it could play outside during the winter months. Their normal stay in Europe would normally begin in the spring and continue for two or three years. When the show returned to the States, it would normally be in the fall so the performers and stock could rest during the winter.

In the States, the best seasons for endurance races were spring and fall. In Arabia, summer was the worst time and winter the best time. In the winter, temperatures averaged around 80 degrees and camels can go three weeks without water; in the summer, they need water every three days.

When the information in Frank's memoir was compared to the route listing of the show's travels, the only possible time when this race could have occurred was the winter of 1892-1893.

a) In 1889, Bill's show crossed the ocean and played at the Paris Exposition from 5-18-89 to 11-14-89. Afterwards, the initial plan for the show was to move from place to place for the next two years, finish with six months in London, and close in October of 1892.

While Frank was in Paris, he met Ras Rasmussen (also known as Ras Yankin), a fine Arabian gentleman who controlled the camel freight in Aden, Arabia. At that time, Frank believed he was committed to the Show until the fall of 1892. He states,

"[Rasmussen] had journeyed from his native Arabia with a number of the finest horses his country could produce. He followed me to many places as he was deeply interested in my work. He invited me to visit his country but the show was to go to Rome, Italy, and then on to Germany, besides other countries. At that time I was under contract with heavy bond so I could not leave the show."[6]

Editor's Comment: This statement explains why the race could not have happened in the winter of 1889-90.

b) After the Show left Paris, Ras Yankin followed it to Marseilles, Rome, and Germany. Frank mentions winning a tough race in Italy with Hidalgo and another one in Germany with Snuffbox, one of Hidalgo's brothers.

In July of 1890, when the Show was in Berlin, Frank states,

"At this time, I learned that the Congress of Rough Riders was to pay my expenses if I wished to go to Arabia, that I was to take my own horses and to contest in three rides as well as other feats of horsemanship."[7]

Editor's Comment: Even if Frank had been allowed to leave the show at that time, Ras Yankin would not yet have had time to organize the contests. Also, races in Arabia were not normally run in the brutally hot Arabian summer.

When a scandal suddenly exploded over the treatment of Indians in Wild West Shows, Buffalo Bill decided he had to take his Indians home to defend himself. Without Buffalo Bill or any Indians, the show had to close for the winter season. Their last stop was in Strasburg, Germany where the show closed on Oct. 26, 1890.

At this time, the plans for the contests in Arabia were probably still being made. Frank left his horses behind in the show's winter quarters and went back to the States where he rode in three races and visited his friends at Pine Ridge just before the Massacre at Wounded Knee. He was back with his horses before the show opened again in Strasburg on April 19, 1891.

Editor's Comment: With the distances and travel times between the States and Arabia, as well as the travel time from south Arabia to northeast Germany, the race could not been run in the winter of 1890-91. Three months plus three weeks would not have been enough time for Frank to return to Europe, pick up his horses, get them to Aden, condition Hidalgo, spend 68 days racing with him, return to Aden with Rasmussen, and still get back to Strasburg before the show opened on April 19.

In 1891, the show toured through Germany and played at two cities in Belgium before it moved on to England where it opened on June 20, 1891. It closed there in London on Oct. 12, 1892. Ships often traveled from London to India. If Frank caught one of them with his horses, he would have reached Arabia with just enough time to condition his horses, win the long race, return to Aden with Rasmussen, leave his horses there, and reach home in time for the World's Fair in Chicago.

When Frank reached New York, Cody and Salisbury met him at the dock. They were getting ready for the World's Fair at Chicago and wanted him to condition one of his horses for a special long race.[8]

Editor's Comments:

When Gertrude wrote Frank's letter to Albert Harris in 1940, it stated Bill's Show closed after the Paris Exposition in 1889 and Frank went to Arabia in 1890[9], but this was misinformation. Frank was tied to the show until it closed in England in the fall of 1892.

This letter also stated the race had been run annually for 1,000 years.[9] In my opinion, this race may have existed, but it could have varied considerably in both location and length. If the 3,000 mile race was new, Ras Rasmussen was probably the perfect person to organize it, but setting it up could have taken him many months.

In his memoir, Frank stated racing in Arabia began as soon as horses were brought there in 2,000 B.C.[10] Racing was popular in the Middle East. In the third century AD, "King Bahram [Persia] owned 40,000 horses, constantly racing them to sift out the best mares and stallions for breeding."[11] The time span for the annual race suggests it dates back to the beginning of the Muslim empire.

Annual races are not unknown in Saudi Arabia. When Ibn Saud rose to power, his men rode camels. When he was firmly in control, he started an annual endurance race for camels.[12]

3) Arabia in 1892

Today Arabia means Saudi Arabia to most people, but there are five geographic regions within the general area of Arabia. These regions are described below.

a) The lands along the Mediterranean Sea. They include the modern countries of Jordan, Israel, Lebanon, and Syria. In 1892, all these lands were part of the Ottoman Province of Syria, as were parts of the modern countries of Turkey and Iraq.

b) The Hejaz contains the middle part of the coastal lands that lie along the eastern shore of the Red Sea. It includes the holy cities of Mecca and Medina. In 1892, it was controlled by the Ottoman Empire and is now part of Saudi Arabia.

c) The Nejd is the central plateau of Arabia. It lies between the Hejaz on the west and the Al-Dahna desert on the east. In 1892, the feuding tribes there were under the nominal control of the Ottoman Empire. It is now part of Saudi Arabia.

d) Al-Rab Al-Khali Desert (The Empty Quarter)

For many centuries, nomadic tribes roamed the Nejd and the Al-Rab Al-Khali Desert. They usually pastured their stock in the Nejd in the summer and in the Desert in the winter. Nomads tend to pay little attention to political boundaries. Most of this desert is now part of Saudi Arabia.

e) Southern Arabia contains the modern countries of Yemen, Oman, and the United Arab Emirates. In 1892, North Yemen was under the control of the Ottoman Empire, but most of South Yemen had become an British Protectorate. The British took control of Aden in 1839. When the Suez Canal opened in 1869; the British had to maintain its firm grip on Southern Arabia to protect their shipping as it moved up the Red Sea. In 1892, Oman included the United Arab Emirates. It kept its independence, but had a long standing treaty relationship with the British. The Ibadi form of the Muslim religion is practiced only in Oman and is relatively accepting of strangers.

Editor's Comment: Since the Ottoman Empire never ruled South Yemen or Oman, it never controlled all of Arabia. In 1892, they did control most of North Yemen. At various times, they did have alliances with the tribes who lived in the Central Arabia. The map on the next page shows the shrunken Ottoman Empire in 1914.

In classical times, South Arabia was well known. Some of its major products were and still are frankincense and myrrh, aromatic resins produced by special species of trees. There was a climate change just before the collapse of the Roman Empire which dried up both North Africa and South Arabia. In the Dark Ages, Europeans lost what they had known about Arabia south of the Mediterranean coastal region.

Not until 1875 did Central and South Arabia open up to European explorers and travelers. At that time, the British and Ottoman Empires maintained a friendly relationship. In the nineteenth century, passports were not needed to travel anywhere in Europe or in the Ottoman Empire. The one exception was Russia where passports were required. This rule explains why Buffalo Bill's Wild West never traveled there. Since Indians had no birth certificates and were not yet citizens, they could not obtain passports. Travelers in the Ottoman Empire and South

Arabia reported no administrative problems. The most they had to do was pay a special fee as they moved into the territory of a new tribe.[13]

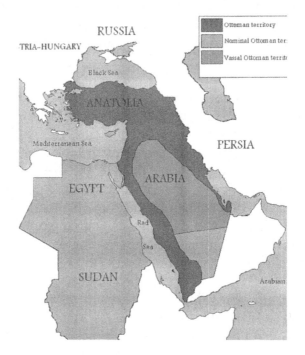

Conclusion (3): In 1892, there was no political reason why the race could not have happened just as Frank described it. It had to cross tribal boundaries, but not national ones. Given the unrest in the Middle East today, such a long race would no longer be feasible; but shorter endurance races have occurred within national boundaries. For example, Saudi Arabia has been holding an annual endurance race since 2005.

4) The Race

a) The Horses of Arabia

The breeding of Arab horses begin early in South Arabia. In biblical times, King Solomon presented a delegation from Oman with a horse who became their foundation stallion, Zad-Ar-akib. Breeders studied pedigrees and maintained bloodlines by breeding only the best class animals. The result was healthy, reliable horses who could be sold for good prices to India and Mauritius.[14] Yemen has a similar history,

114

but their foundation stallion was a gift from King Soloman to the Queen of Sheba. In 120 AD, a deposed king of Yemen supposedly went to Syria with 80,000 Arabian horses.[11]

Contrary to popular belief, the Arab horse did not originate in Central Arabia. In classical times, the Arabs rode camels. In the Hejaz or Nejd, small scale horse breeding did not begin until just before the birth of Mohammed. Their homeland did not have enough water or grazing to support more than a few horses and they were not always of the best quality.[15] When Ibn Saud rose to power in the 1930's, his men did not ride horses, they rode camels.[12]

b) In his memoir, Frank does give us a detailed description of the race. He states,

"The long ride started from Aden: a hundred of the finest desert horses and many from the limestone sections entered the race, the most perfect group of horses I ever expect to see - those from the desert were gray or white, those from the high land chestnut, some sorrel and a few black. The route led along the Gulf of Aden where the air was not too dry for our mounts; then the trail went along the seashore to Syria. We then turned from the sea and rode up the border between Syria and Arabia; part of the way was limestone and the rest flaming fine desert sand. Water was scarce, the air dry and hot. The Arabian horses could get along without water pretty well, but my Mustang began to gain ground once he got into the desert although he got water only once a day. At times there was no water for almost two days, still my 'Hidalgo' went on and at no time did he appear weakening although he grew gaunt and lost flesh. There were days of sand storms and then it was impossible to go on. Horse and rider rested between the camels that carried our feed. When a rider got out in the lead, two camels were sent ahead with him and these camels were changed three times on the ride. Many horses dropped out; when we entered the desert only five finished."[16]

Frank identifies Arabs from two locations. One is the gray or white horses from Syria who had been bred and trained to go without food or water for long distances. An American cavalry office said riding one of their horses felt like sitting on the edge of a knife.[17] The horses from the highlands would have been from North Yemen. Since South Yemen and Oman both had some fine Arabs, they could also have entered a few in the race. Since it never went near the Nejd and the tribes there had so few good horses, they probably did not enter any horses in the race.

5) The Route

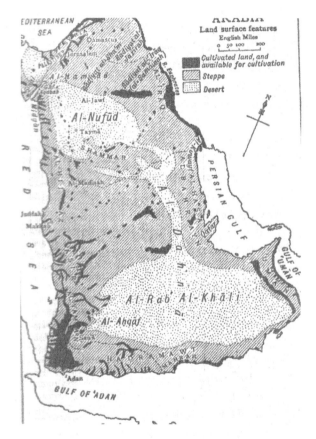

As the map above shows, there are three real deserts on the Arabian Pennisula. They are the Al-Nufud, the Al-Dahna, and the Al-rab Al-Khali. The rest of the Pennisula is dry steppe land, including the Syrian desert. If water can be found, most of this land could grow crops. The black areas show cultivated or cultivatable land.

The route described by Frank Hopkins did not go near any of the three deserts or the Nejd and it did not attempt to cross the Al-Rab Al -Khali. It began in Aden and followed the coast line through South Yemen and Oman until it reached the Hajar Mountains. As long as it

116

followed the coast, logistic support could easily have been provided by dhows. These ships used lateen sails, traveled in the Red Sea and the Indian Ocean, and were especially designed to carry large stores of water and food, as well as heavy merchandise.

South Yemen is broken up by a series of fertile canyons where both food and water could easily have been obtained. In these canyons, one good year can produce enough food for five years. The first photograph below shows the old city of Aden while the next one shows a view of one of the canyons in South Yemem.

The western most province of Oman is Dohfar. This fortunate area normally recieves twenty-five inches of rain per year and still produces aromatic resins. The phograph below is of this fertile province.

From there, the race continued through Oman across the gravely plain shown in the first picture on the next page. Again, logistic support could be provided by dhows. After the race reached the Hajar mountains, it left the coast line and turned north to cross the Dahira plain. This plain parallels the Gulf of Oman and lies between the Al-Rab Al-Khali and the Hajar Mountains. For many centuries, the Faflaj channels have brought water down from the mountains to irrigate this fertile area. An Aflaj channel is shown in the second photograph on the next page. East of the mountains lies the fertile heartland of Oman.

When the race reached the end of the Dahira plain, it turned northwest to follow the dry, barren coast of the Persian Gulf. At the time of the race, this desolate area was populated by few people. The photograph below shows a fragile raft being built out of the mid-ribs of date palms.[18] Again, dhows could have been used to provide logistic support. Today this coast is full of cities, oil piping, and oil drilling sites.

When the race reached the head of the Gulf, it continued on between the Ottoman Province of Syria and the Valley of the Euphrates River until it reached the shores of the Mediterranean Sea possibly near a large city like Aleppo or Damacus. To reach the coast, the race would have had to travel on the edge of the Syrian desert. This was probably the most difficult part of the race. Instead of limestone hard pan, sometimes the horses had to travel over fine desert sand. Logistic support could only be provided by camels so water was scarce. The photograph below shows a view of this desert.

The route of the race was well planned. In such races, some horses drop out early days while others drop out later. At the beginning when there were the most horses, the race began a relatively fertile area where it was relatively easy to provide logistic support. At the end when there were the fewest horses, it ended in the most difficult area for logistic support.

When the race was over, Frank commented,

"I'll say that those people they were fair in every way - no trickery amongst the judges or the riders."[19]

Frank and Hidalgo took 68 days to reach the finish line and they passed the finish stone thirty-three hours ahead of the second horse.[9] After his return to Aden, Frank won two races with Hidalgo's brothers, one on limestone for 150 miles and one on sand for 500 miles.

Although Frank did leave all three of his mustangs in Yeman with Ras Rasmussen, he brought an Arabian stallion home with him. He considered him the prettiest horse he had even seen and so intelligent he learned tricks easily, but found him too high strung for endurance work.[8]

Conclusion (5): There was no geographic reason why this race could not have followed this route in 1892. After the discovery of oil in the barren lands on the western side of the Persian Gulf, such a race would no longer have been feasible.

6) Food, Condition, and Water

In his letter to Harris, Frank states,

"The only feed available were plants called vatches [vetches] and to my surprise these weeds were very nourishing food for our horses if they were dry - some of the riders fed the vatches green. The only grain was barley."[9]

Barley is an excellent substitute for oats and widely fed in Europe. It is normally fed with water. There are several species of vetches. They are not weeds, but make excellent hay. Both barley and vetches are commonly fed in the Middle East and California.

Frank does comment on the fact Hidalgo lost condition.[9 and 16] There were probably two factors involved. The Cavalry Manual of Horse Management states,

"When horses are expected to march 35 miles a day, they will typically show considerable loss in flesh after a week or ten days of marching.[20]

Depending how fit Hidalgo was at the beginning of the race, he probably would have had this type of weight loss. In the last stretch through the Syrian desert, water was scanty and he may have had some dehydration. Hidalgo never had to go more than a day and 1/2 without water and mustangs were expected to be able to go two days without water.

Conclusion (Chapter 8):

In 1892, this race would have been both politically and geographical feasibible. At that time, if Europe knew little about Central and South Arabia, then Americans probably knew less. Buffalo Bill got away with presenting Berbers from Morocco as Bedouins from Arabia. How could Frank have known so much precise and accurate detail about Arabia, if he had not ridden around the coast and through the Syrian desert?

Could an American Mustang actually beat purebred Arabs on their own ground? Colonel T.A. Dodge was a former cavalry who knew mustangs well and had spent a lot of time with the Syrian Bedouins. He states,

"I would stake my money on a hundred broncos of the Western plains, ridden in their own way by cowboys, against a hundred Arabians of the Syrian desert, ridden by Bedouins - for a pull of one to five hundred miles under conditions fair to each."[21]

Acknowledgements:

Photo 1 courtesy of Albert W. Harris. Photos 2-5, 8 courtesy of Wikepedia. Photo 6 courtesy of World heritage Sites, Photo 7 courtesy David Fairchild.

Map 1 is courtesy of Mapsof.net. Map 2 is courtesy of Emery Walker Ltd.

Footnotes:

[1]Hopkins, Frank T. Memoir, Letter 1, p. 39. Hopkins Papers, Robert Olney Easton Collection, American Heritage Center, University of Wyoming.
[2]Hopkins, Frank. "Buffalo Bill as I knew Him", Vermont Horse and Bridle Trail Bulletin, Oct. 1942, pp. 151-4.
[3]Hopkins, Frank T. Memoir, Letter 1, p. 12. Hopkins Papers, Robert Olney Easton Collection, American Heritage Center, University of Wyoming.
[4]Hopkins, Frank T. Answers, Letter 6, p. 16-7. Hopkins Papers, Robert Olney Easton Collection, American Heritage Center, University of Wyoming.
Hopkins, Frank. "Buffalo Bill as I knew Him", Vermont Horse and Bridle Trail Bulletin, Oct. 1942, pp. 151-4.
[5]Parker, Colonel. "Riders and their records", Vermont Horse and Bridle Trail Bulletin, July, 1942, pp. 105-7.
[6]Hopkins Memoir, p. 14-15.

[7]Hopkins Memoir, pp. 15-16.

[8]Hopkins Memoir, pp. 20-22.

[9]Harris, Albert W. The Blood of the Arab. Chicago, Arabian Horse Club of America, 1941, pp. 50-52.

[10]Hopkins Memoir, p. 18.

[11]Fox, Charles P. A Pictorial History of Performing Horses. NY, Bramhall House, 1960, pp. 14-15.

[12]House of Saud, DVD, Martin E. Smith, 2005.

[13]Dodge, T.A. Riders of Many Lands. NY, Harcourt, 1894.

Bent, J. T., "Hadramut", Living Age 103:81-94, Oct., 1994.

J. Theodore Bent, "The Land of Frankincense and Myrrh", Living Age, v. 207, issue 2679 Nov. 9, 1885, pp. 342-356.

[14]"Horses of Oman"

http://www.omanet.om/english/culture/horse.asp?cat=cult.

[15]Hendricks, Bonnie. International Encyclopedia of Horse Breeds. University of Oklahoma, 1995, pp. 40-41.

[16]Hopkins, Frank T. "Mustangs", Vermont Horse and Bridle Trail Bulletin, Jan. 1941, pp.

[17]Dodge, T. A. Riders of Many Lands. NY, Harcourt, 1895, pp. 365-66.

[18]Fairchild, David Fairchild, "Travels in Arabia and Along the Persian Gulf", National Geographic Magazine, April 1904, pp. 139-151.

[19]Hopkins, Frank T., Memoir, Letter 1, p. 18. Hopkins Papers, Robert Olney Eaton Collection, American Heritage Center, University of Wyoming.

[20]Devereauz, Frederick L., editor. The Cavalry Manual of Horse Management, A.S. Barnes & Noble, 1979, pp. 144-5.

[21]Dodge, T. A. Riders of Many Lands. NY, Harcourt, 1894, p. 340.

Chapter 9: Last Years

1) 1917-1923

a) Frank spent World War I doing confidential work for the government. Before he left in 1917, he comments,

"I had not raised any colts for a few years - now my horses had been reduced in number for there were only 5 of the White-y strain left - they were getting along in years. There was no one interested in long rides as the roads were hard and even then there were cars to annoy a horse on the road. I noticed that I was not the man in the saddle I had been for I was getting hurt more often; it was a sure thing that many injuries were telling on me now: as I looked back over my long trail I remembered I had lived quite a few years and it was not easy for me to compete against the younger riders who joined the Show. I was not the same as I had been a few years before though many told me I was as good as ever, some said better - I knew better than any one else that the work in the saddle was getting to be real hard work for me now where before the same work was pleasure for me - even the playing of the Band made me shudder it got on my nerves and now I can't stand the blare of a Band."[1]

b) When the government finally released him, he states,

"When I returned home things began to happen. I got a telegram from California- -Buffalo Jones was very ill and wished to see me. I got there just in time - he passed on a few hours later [Oct, 1, 1919].

I faced then what was the worst thing that could happen - my father, who would have been ninety-eight years old if he had live three days longer, passed on [Dec., 1919]. He was a true plainsman and loved scout duty. He was often called in on bad cases in the army like taking off an arm or a leg which in those days was not such an easy experience in those days for the patient as now. But he preferred to scout. He served as a scout over fifty years. .... He talked very little. Maybe it was his living alone with his horse so much on the plains.

After his death, my mother was broken in spirit. She was only seventeen years older than I, a large woman who stood six feet two inches tall, who before his death was so happy. Although I was her only child, she did not notice me [when] bereft of him. She was always loving, kind, and thoughtful to me. Five months after father passed on she followed [May, 1920].

I've been shot 7 times, bones broken, smashed up at lot and always came through but this blow brought me to earth, until I realized there was still much to be thankful for."[2]

Editor's Comment: Frank does state his father came from Illinois. He probably left to go to California in 1849.[3]

c) Later that year, Frank went east and he comments,

"I met a Belgian at the Old Glory Hambletonian sale in the armory, New York City. He'd come to the sale to buy colts for the horsemen of his country and wanted me to return with him and assured me there would be a great demand for me on their race tracks.

I'd been in his country when they first took interest in trotting horses and I was sure there were some friends there I knew. I bought several two year olds at that sale for my friend as he turned the buying over to me. When the colts were loaded, I sailed with them. As soon as they were on shore, I got the job of breaking and training them. I also drove in races.

Not long before I was in great demand and most of the horse owners remembered me from my first visit to their country for I had taught them several things about balancing and showing off their horses. Now these men saw that I was able to get speed out of many of their horses with my method of training. Of course, this is not horsemanship in the saddle; still, it is skilled horsemanship.

Some of these owners got to be very good drivers, most of them laid aside their methods after they saw me drive their horses and lower their marks. One horse I recall that could not turn a mile better than 3 minutes, after I had handled him for a month could pace a full mile in 2 5-1/4 [2.525 minutes]. Many of these horses could trot in the 2/10 class [one mile in 2.1 minutes] where before a horse that could trot in 2/10 was called fast in that country.

Most of those horses were bought in America and were of the best Hambletonian blood. The next year, trotting races was the greatest sport in all Belgium. We turned out a number of good drivers. The second season they built more tracks and there were races all over the country. I drove in many of them - some days I drove in 10 classes. I was making money, but the heavy strain was wearing me out. The trotting association wanted me to sign a 10 year contract - I simply told them I was going home when the season was ended, and referred to the good drivers that became experts in a short while.

I left that country a tired worn out man having put in two years of the most tedious long hours every day spending most time on horses, drivers, owners and without recreation. I left behind warm friends and happy thought of how hard these good people had worked to give the trotting horse place in their land. I hadn't done much myself, but there is a class of horse who will long remain in Belgium. I have been sent for since and visited that country twice in recent years and I must say that those people have some of the finest trotting and pacing horses - even our horses and drivers would have to do their best to compare [to them]."[4]

Editor's Comment: Like most of the old timers, Frank probably thought automobiles would eventually replace horses. Since he believed endurance racing had come to an end, he turned to harness racing as an alternative. He began working as a trainer and teaching his training methods to others.

Historical Note: In the nineteenth century, harness racing began in various European countries, including Belgium. In 2010, Belgium still had three tracks which sponsored one thousand races.

d) When Frank returned home, he took some time off to spend with the ponies he had left. He comments,

"Caring for those little horses was more pleasure for me than it was work, for I had so longed to be with them. The five ponies all old now - none of them less than 18 years; still I treasured them and as I worked cleaning and shoeing them the memories of other days appeared often before me."[5]

e) When Frank's old friend, Dr. Petersen, stopped at the ranch he asked Frank to break some fine Hambletonian colts for him. He also wanted Frank to train one of them to trot fast around a one mile track without a driver. Frank succeeded and the colt was a great success when he was shown at county fairs. Unfortunately, he was poisoned before his second season by a jealous rival.[5]

2) 1924-1926

a) When Frank was fifty-five years old, he foolishly tried rodeo riding. He states,

"I rode for Tex Austin at Fort Worth, Texas, where I covered all the real buckers in the outfit and never hit the ground. After touring with the rodeo for three months I learned a thing or two - no matter how well I did, I was gypped out of the money - so I bid them goodbye and good luck to the broncos who were sure to break a few more bones before the end of the season. I knew there would not be any of mine broken unless I got paid for pains I might suffer."[5]

b) In the spring of 1925, Frank was engaged to drive and train trotters for a local association headed by Dr. Peterson. One day, he overhead Dr. Petersen talking about some of my long rides to an outspoken horseman from New York who was standing nearby. He refused to believe any horse could cover sixty surveyed miles in ten hours.

"Frank stepped away from the horse he was shoeing and said 'Gentlemen, allow me to settle this for you. I will ride that 60 miles on any mile race track and place one thousand dollars that I will cover 60 miles in less than 7 hours.'

I added the horse I would choose for the ride was over twenty-two years old. Then I asked them to allow me one month before the ride. The following day the agreement was written up and I was to get $1400 if I covered the 60 miles in less than 7 hours. If I took ten hours on the ride, I would receive only $500. Before sunset, each had laid down his money and we were well pleased.

I began to train Perko [Purko], a silver grey stallion who was at that time 23 years old. When he was in good flesh that hoss weighed 900 pounds; after one week of light training, I was sure that little Mustang could still do his stuff. I had ridden him in long rides in his younger days and knew him to be as tough as they come.

The word passed from one horseman to another. Many of my old friends called to learn the facts of the ride. I assured them the ride would be made in less than 7 hours and that the old Gutenberg track was the place chosen for the race to take place.

The morning I was supposed to ride, I got to the track at 6 o'clock and jogged Purko around until the ride was to start. AT 8 o'clock I rode out to the old starting post and got the word to GO. ... I headed Purko out into the center of the track bed and set him into a swinging lope - not a fast gait. I looked at my watch to gauge the horse's speed. After he had turned the mile a few times, he knew what I wanted him to do for he settled down to a steady gait. I watch him very careful until 12 o'clock, then spoke to him, urging him along to a faster gait; when the horse settled down to his new pace there he stayed until the ride was ended at 25 minutes of 2 o'clock in the afternoon.

That ride settled a big argument for all times and also fattened the purse of a number of my friends as well as my own."[5]

c) The brand record for the family ranch ended on 12-31-1925 presumably because Frank had sold the ranch.[6]

d) In 1926, Frank rode his last race. It was a relay race of 120 miles, twenty miles to the horse. He comments,

"A group of cavalrymen who were arranging for the race, some of them older men who knew me on the plains years before, spoke to the younger riders about me, told them of some of my rides. I said nothing. But I could see that my reputation didn't make much of an impression on these self-confident young men.

Then a few of these youngsters crowded around me and began asking me questions, which I answered. At length one of the boys remarked that he supposed I was like all of these old-timers - I could tell about what I used to do, but I couldn't show'em. Well, that got me. I asked if I could sign for the race. I could. I did. I paid my entry fee, signed my name on the book. The race was from Willimantic to Manchester, Connecticut.

I did the 120 miles in 7 hours, 48 minutes, 9 seconds, and I finished first. I raced to show those wise lads how it was done. It was half an hour before one the chaps hove into sight. I was in bed for a week afterward from being hip-locked and with a bad back, but it was worth it. I showed'em."[7]

Editor's Comment: As compared to the 1925 race, Frank rode twice the distance cross country and on six different horses. Since he now had only five aging mustangs, he had to ride a trotter in the first lap of the race. These differences may explain why he was laid up for a week after he won the race.

e) In 1926, a reporter from Philadelphia's Evening Public Ledger interviewed a man named Frank Hopkins. At that time, he was the foreman of a subway construction job. This interview was published on March 28, 1926 under the title, "Call of the Wild".[8] This interview contains much information that does not agree with what Frank T. Hopkins said about his life. It also gives him credit for the accomplishments of other western heroes.

The undated copy in the Hopkins Papers at the University of Wyoming was missing a section[9] which includes a photograph of the interviewee. The man in this photograph was not the one who appears in photographs of the real Frank T. Hopkins. Since this article has been used as evidence to prove the real Frank Hopkins was a fraud, it will be analyzed in the appendix to this chapter.

The interviewee may once have been an out-of-work cowboy who knew about the real Frank T. Hopkins and envied him his reputation and job with Bill's show. Since they had the same name, he could have started by pretending to be the real man to entertain himself and his friends, but his story probably grew as he claimed more and more of the accomplishments of other real heroes. In my opinion, when he allowed this interview to be printed, he stepped over the line into fraud.

3) 1927-1940

a) In 1928, Chenango died. He was the last of the White-y family.[10] Frank had always had horses ever since his grandfather had given him his first pony to ride. For the first time in many years, now he had none. When Frank had sold the ranch, he had already lost his home, but when he married Gertrude Nehler in 1929, he found a new one.

b) Frank needed the stimulus of stepping into danger so he got interested in establishing a new career as a deep sea diver.

According to his wife, Gertrude, he was inspired by the General Slocum disaster in 1904.[11] The excursion steamer, General Slocum, caught fire on June 15, sank, and over one thousand people died. The remains of the steamer were salvaged and converted into a barge which sank in 1911.

Gertrude states he worked at the sea wall construction project in Galveston, Texas. This city had almost been destroyed by a hurricane in 1900.[12] Getting the first segment of the sea wall up took from 1902-1904. She states he also worked in the Copper River Railroad project in Alaska.[13] Building the railroad bridge across the Anchorage Harbor began in 1915 and ended in 1917.

In these three letters, there are two memories involved. Gertrude had to describe what she remembered from what little Frank had told her about his life before they married. Frank had to remember events which had occurred well before their marriage. This information could not be verified, but there is some evidence to support it. On their marriage certificate, Frank states his occupation was diver. The American Heritage Center also has three photographs of Frank working as a diver, probably on the Copper River Railroad project. One of them is shown below.

Frank might have begun doing some diving in the off seasons of Bill's show. Gertrude states he worked at fortifying New York Harbor during World War I.[11] This could be the confidential work he did for the government. As the public interest in harness racing waned, he could have decided to try turning diving into a full time job.

c) On Oct. 11, 1929 Frank T. Hopkins married Gertrude A. Nehler in Queens County, New York.[14]

Their marriage certificate states
Frank Hopkins lived at 4505 23rd St., Long Island City.*
His age was mistakenly entered as 44 when it was 64.
He was white, single, and this was his first marriage.
His occupation was diver.
He was born in Laramie, WY [Territory].
His father's first name was Charles.
His mother's name was Vallez Nauqua.

*He had same address in the 1935 and 1940 censuses.

Gertrude Nehler lived at 18 Ely Ave., Long Island City
Her age was 38.
She was white, single, and this was her first marriage.
She was born in the USA.
Her father's first name was August.
Her Mother's name was Lisette A. Motzer.

Gertrude and her family were easily traced in the census records.
Her birth certificate shows she was born on May 14, 1890 in L. Bergen, NJ.
The 1905 NY state census shows her family had moved to Manhattan. At that time, her father's brother lived with them.
The 1925 NY state census shows her family had moved to Long Island City in Queens, New York. Instead of her uncle, her paternal grandfather now lived with them.
The death certificate of her father, August Nehler, shows he died on Nov. 20, 1925 at the age of 61 in Queens, N.Y.
The US census of 1930 lists Gertrude's mother, Lizisette [Lisetta, Lizette, Lisette] Nehler. She was age 65, born in 1865 in NY, white, female, and widowed. She was the head of the household and her parents had been born in Germany. Her household included her daughter, Gertrude, and three boarders.

Editor's Comment: Both Frank and Gertrude's mother were born in 1865.

After the death of her husband, Gertrude's mother had to turn their home into a boarding house. When Frank and Gertrude were married, he lived at this boarding house and may have met Gertrude there. At the time of her marriage, Gertrude could have been working outside of her home. When the 1930 census was taken in April, Frank may well have been out of town working on a construction project.

d) In her letters to Robert Easton, Gertrude describes her husband as the strong, silent type. When she knew him, she thought he was about six feet tall and weighed 175 pounds. He was fair minded and had a keen sense of humor. He was slow to anger, but when aroused, he could be dangerous. He had muscles of steel and a gentle touch, especially with injured animals.[15]

e) In his years of endurance racing and riding with Bill's show, Frank had made friends who stayed in touch with him. Since he now had a new home with Gertrude, they could enjoy having dinner with them. Gertrude knew little about the West and less about horses. From listening to their conversation, Gertrude picked up most of what she knew about the West.

Sometimes Frank and Gertrude did more for his friends. When Broncho Charley Miller was in his nineties, he often spent weekends with them. At that time, he lived near the old Madison Square Garden. He wore his hair in two braids and tucked them up under his ten gallon hat. Frank had tanned the leather and made his grey leather coat while Gertrude had made his gauntlets.[16]

f) 1940 Census (information released April 2, 2012)

For the first time, the real Frank T. Hopkins stayed in one place long enough to be recorded in the bicentennial US census. Whenever records had been gathered in April, he was on the move when he was a dispatch rider, traveled with Buffalo Bill's Wild West, or worked on various construction projects.

In this census, Frank is identified as the Head of the Household living at 4505 23rd St., Long Island City, Queens County, New York. It included his wife, Gertrude, her mother, and three boarders. He had lived in the same house in 1935.

His mother-in-law owned her own home, valued at $5,500 and her only income came from her lodgers. Since Frank paid her rent, she treated him as one of them. In 1939, he made $1,340 working part time as an insulating mechanic. Her other boarders worked full time and made $1400, $850, or $526 in that same year.

The census information states Frank was born in Wyoming, about 1886, and his age was 74. He identified himself as an Indian. While his education had not gone beyond 4th grade, his wife and mother-in-law had completed 8th grade.[17]

Evaluation: Chapter 9

In his last years with Bill's show, Frank had begun to feel the results of his many injuries and realized what had once been pleasure had become hard work. When he returned home from the War, he was devastated when his parents died within five months of each other. When he found a temporary career in harness racing, he was forced to defend his reputation in his two final endurance races. Later, he found a new career in deep sea diving and a new home when he married Gertrude Nehler.

When a fraudulent Hopkins was interviewed by a newspaper reporter, he took credit for many of the exploits of Buffalo Jones. He stated he had a Canadian wife and ten children. His photograph reveals he is not the real Frank T. Hopkins. For the first time, the real Frank Hopkins was listed in the 1940 US census. These records validate his age, birthplace, and race.

Acknowledgements:

Photo courtesy of American Heritage Center, University of Wyoming.

Footnotes:

[1]Hopkins, Frank T. Memoir Addendum, p. 4. Hopkins Papers, Robert Olney Easton Collection, American Heritage Center, University of Wyoming.

[2]Hopkins, Frank T. Letter 1, Memoir, pp. 54-55. Hopkins Papers, Robert Olney Easton Collection, American Heritage Center, University of Wyoming.

[3]Bourke, John G. On the Border with Crook. Skyhorse Publishing, 2014, pp. 154, 210.

[4]Hopkins, Frank T. Memoir Addendum, p. 5-6. Hopkins Papers, Robert Olney Easton Collection, American Heritage Center, University of Wyoming.

[5]Hopkins, Frank T., "Training Trotters"
 http://www.frankhopkins.com/articles24.html.

[6]Wyoming Livestock Board, Wyoming Brand History (Frank Hopkins 7OL Brand).

[7]Roth, Charles B. "The Toughest Race", The Horse and Horseman, January, 1937, p. 50.

[8]"Call of the Wild", Evening Public Ledger (Philadelphia), March 28, 1926.

[9]"Call of the Wild Subway Lures Hero of Novel Here".
http:www.frankhopkins.com/articles 23.html.

[10]Harris, Albert W. The Blood of the Arab. Chicago, The Arabian Horse Club of America, 1941, p. 49.

[11]Hopkins, Gertrude letter to Robert Easton, Oct. 1968, p. 3. Hopkins Papers, Robert Olney Easton Collection, American Heritage Center, University of Wyoming.

[12]Hopkins, Gertrude Letter to Robert Easton, April 25, 1970. p. 2. Hopkins Papers, Robert Olney Easton Collection, American Heritage Center, University of Wyoming. This letter is available on line in their digital collection.

[13]Hopkins, Gertrude Letter to Robert Easton, 12-24-68, p. 3. Hopkins Papers, Robert Olney Easton Collection, American Heritage Center, University of Wyoming. This letter is available on line in their digital collection.

[14]State of New York, The City of New York, Dept. of Health, Certificate and Record of Marriage, #3220.

[15]Hopkins, Gertrude, Response to Letter from Robert Easton, March 10, 1968, p. 1, Hopkins Papers, Robert Olney Easton Collection,

American Heritage Center, University of Wyoming. This letter is available on line in their digital collection.

Hopkins, Gertrude, Letter to Robert Easton, Nov. 30, 1968, p. 2. Hopkins Papers, Robert Olney Easton Collection, American Heritage Center, University of Wyoming. This letter is available on line in their digital collection.

[16]"Broncho Charley Miller", note on the back of the article by Gertrude Hopkins. Hopkins Papers, Robert Olney Easton Collection, American Heritage Center, University of Wyoming.

[17]US Census Bureau. Records of the 1940 Census for Long Island City, New York.

Chapter 9: Appendix A

An Implausible Newspaper Article

"Call of the Wild: Subway Lures Hero of Novels Here, Buffalo Bill Rider Who Saw Woolly Days on the Frontier Bosses Broad Street Gang." Evening Public Ledger (Philadelphia), March 28, 1926.

Analysis of Misinformation and Errors

1) Interviewee states he was the son of "Lonesome Charles Hopkins", a famous scout of pioneer days.

Analysis:

a) Frank's father was not a famous scout. He was a packer and a civilian employee. There is no record stating his nickname was, "Lonesome".

b) Interviewee may have confused him with Lonesome Charlie Reynolds, a famous scout who was killed at the Battle of the Little Bighorn.

2) Interviewee states he was the only successful rider of Dynamite.

Analysis:

a) Dynamite was a bucker who performed in the early days of Buffalo Bill's Wild West. Broncho Charley Miller was the man who conquered him.

b) In 1898, the real Frank Hopkins rode Hightower to a standstill.

3) Interviewee states "I don't talk more than two words for days;"

Analysis: If this is true, how did he supervise a construction crew?

4) Interviewee states he spoke six or seven dialects.

Analysis: Indian tribes spoke different languages. If he called them dialects, he may not have been as familiar with Indians as he claimed to have been.

5) Except for two errors, the story of Frank's first dispatch ride is correct. The interviewee states he was 12 when he set out on his first dispatch ride and he was sent because none of the men could be spared.

Analysis:

a) The real Frank Hopkins states he started his first dispatch ride on his thirteenth birthday.

b) The army preferred to use military staff to carry dispatches, but there were no maps of the frontier and they did not know the country. Frank was probably sent with this message because he was familiar with the appropriate trails.[1]

6) Interviewee states "he has figured as hero of several novels of Zane Grey, and incidents of his life have furnished material for a moving picture of William S. Hart." He also acted as a guide to Zane Grey and Richard Wallace when they wished to scale the north rim wall of the Grand Canyon.

Analysis:

a) In his memoir, the real Frank Hopkins states his only contact with Zane Grey was through Buffalo Jones. In 1906, Buffalo Jones and Zane Grey used one of his horses in a mountain lion hunt.[2] He also knew Buffalo Jones was the hero of Grey's novel, *The Last of the Plainsmen.*

b) The real Frank Hopkins could not have guided them on their climb in the summer of 1907 because he was still traveling with Bill's Show.

c) The real Frank Hopkins mentions William S. Hart only once in his memoir. In 1913, he had his stable in Bridgeport, Connecticut. When he put on a sleigh riding party, he invited both Bill Hart and his sister, Sarah.[3] This was the same day a fire destroyed his home and stable.

7) Interviewee states "I was kind of prominent on Frontier Day in Wyoming that year and riding all over the lot. Colonel Cody somehow took a notion to me and invited me to join his outfit. ... I used to manage his animals in winter quarters, and in the shows I did fancy roping and riding."

Analysis:

a) The Frontier Days in Cheyenne did not start until 1897 and the real Frank Hopkins joined Bill's show in 1886. The Frontier Days are still held in July and Buffalo Bill would have to had stayed with his show to make his contracted performances. He could not even leave it in 1898 when he wanted to serve in the Spanish American War.

b) When Bill's show was in the US, his ranch in Nebraska was used as their winter quarters and his cowboys would have tended the stock. The real Frank Hopkins enjoyed his winters off and never mentions staying with the show stock.

c) The real Frank Hopkins did trick riding, but not trick roping. From 1894 to 1907, a highly skilled troupe of ropers from Mexico did the fancy roping for Bill's show and he probably would not have needed to hire an American cowboy for that job.

8) Reporter states his interviewee had married young, a Canadian girl with whom he had fallen in love while a boy. He had eight husky sons and two daughters and a home in Bergen County across the Hudson from New York.

Analysis: When the real Frank Hopkins married in 1929, he was sixty-four years old and single. His wife, Gertrude, was also single and thirty-eight years old. Their home was Long Island City, NY. The 1940 census shows they had no children.

9) Interviewee states he kept the ranch in Wyoming for his children.

Analysis: The brand records show the ranch was sold in 1925.

10) Interviewee describes how he took part in a disastrous gambling game in the town of Jackson's Hole, Wyoming.

Analysis:

a) Jackson's Hole is not a town. Jackson sits in the valley of Jackson's Hole. The town was incorporated in 1894.

b) The real Frank Hopkins bet on himself and his horses, but there is no record indicating he otherwise engaged in gambling. In his spare time, he made equipment and carvings.

c) This story may have been about the real Frank Hopkins or interviewee may have used his own experience to construct it.

11) Interviewee stated he left Buffalo Bill's Wild West in 1906 and engaged in construction work.

Analysis:

a) After 1906 Bill's show did not exist as a separate entity. It first merged with Pawnee Bill's Great Far East, then with the Sells-Floto Circus, and finally with the 101 Ranch show.

b) The real Frank Hopkins stayed with Buffalo Bill until he died in 1917.

12) The reporter describes the man he interviewed. He had a wonderful breadth of shoulder and a lean brown face with heavy square jaw.

Analysis: As the photographs on the next page show, the real Frank Hopkins did not have these characteristics.

The photograph below shows the Frank Hopkins who gave the interview in the 1926 newspaper article. The heading states "Zane Grey Hero Here."

The three photographs on the next page are of the real Frank Hopkins. He is shown as a young man, as an older man, and at age 65.

The real Frank T. Hopkins had an oval face and did not have a heavy square jaw. His shoulders are sloping and narrow, not magnificent. Also, his ears are a different shape and set differently on his head. He could pass for white, but he had his high cheekbones, deep set eyes, and nose from his Indian heritage. The man in article photograph shows no sign of Indian blood.

Acknowledgements:

Photo 1 courtesy of the archives of Philadelphia's Evening Public Ledger and Minnesota's Dakota County Library Interlibrary Loan Service.
Photo 2 courtesy of the American Heritage Center, University of Wyoming.
Photo 3 courtesy of the Horse, March-April, 1935, p. 18.
Photo 4 courtesy of Green Mountain Horse Association.

Footnotes:

[1]Parker, Col. R., "Riders and Their Records", Vermont Horse and Bridle Trail Bulletin, July, 1942, pp. 105-107.
[2]Hopkins, Frank T. Memoir Addendum, p. 1. Hopkins Papers, Robert Olney Easton Collection, American Heritage Center, University of Wyoming.
[3]Hopkins, Frank T. "Memoir, Letter 1, p. 52. Hopkins Papers, Robert Olney Easton Collection, American Heritage Center, University of Wyoming.

Chapter 10: Growing Reputation

Background Information: Endurance Racing in the Early 20th Century

Frank was right in assuming the time for long rides had passed, but racing did continue for shorter distances. Strict rules were enforced to reassure those who were concerned about equine welfare and they no longer offered the kind of prize money Frank had so often earned.

Prior to World War II, the US cavalry wanted to gather information about the best breed of horse for their requirements. With the Morgan Horse Club of Vermont, they sponsored the first modern endurance race on Sept. 13, 1913. The race covered 154 miles and the horses had to carry a minimum weight of 160 pounds. The winner was a mare named Halcyon who was 7/8 Arabian. She won a silver trophy and $100. A similar race was organized in Oct. of 1918. This time the distance was 162 miles and the horses had to carry a minimum of 200 pounds of weight. The joint winners were two Arabians with the same time.

The same two organizations sponsored the US Mounted Service Cup competitions. From 1919 to 1923, they held a race every year. The horses had to carry a minimum weight of 200 pounds and cover sixty miles a day on five consecutive days. Any horse who looked like he might be injured was immediately ordered out of the race. If a horse was not moving freely on the sixth day, he was automatically disqualified. There were three judges. Horses could earn twenty-five points for speed, twenty-five for low feed consumption, and fifty for condition. In these races, the emphasis was no longer on who was first, but on who was the best.

The first race was won by Ramal, an Arabian mare. The horse who actually made the best time was disqualified on the sixth day. The horse who came in second was Kingfisher, the son of Halcyon. The next year, the required weight was increased to 245 pounds and the winner was a grade thoroughbred mare named Mille Denis. The third race was won by an Arabian named Crabbet, the fourth by Vendetta, another thoroughbred mare, and the last race by Gouya, an Anglo-Arabian.

Breeders made a great effort to select and condition their best horses for these tests. Of the one hundred and two total contestants, twenty-four had 50% or more of Arabian blood, twenty-seven had 50%

or more of Morgan blood, and thirty-six had 50% or more of Thoroughbred blood. There were also nine Anglo-Arabs, four Kentucky saddle horses, and two Standardbreds. One of the half Arabs was a mustang cross. Three of the horses were considered to be outstanding. They were the Arab, Crabbet, the Arab, Rustem Bey, and the Thoroughbred, Pathfinder.[1]

The Green Mountain Horse Association was founded in 1926, to develop trails and encourage trail riding in Vermont. They held a sixty mile two day ride in 1927. Beginning in 1937, they held a hundred mile ride on Labor Day weekend. It continued throughout World War II and is still held every year.

1) Roth Articles

Given his extensive experience in endurance racing, the real Frank T. Hopkins had much to offer the people who were interested in promoting the new type of races. At that time, few eastern horsemen were familiar with his name and exploits. When Charles B. Roth interviewed Frank and wrote three articles about him, that situation begin to change.

"Brains Plus Endurance" was published in the March-April, 1935 issue of The Horse, the Official Journal of the US Army Remount Service. In this article, Frank explains for Mr. Roth what he believes are the qualities of the ideal endurance horse, including Joe and Hidalgo.[2]

"Great Riders" was published in the March-April, 1936 issue of The Horse. In this article, Frank describes some of the great riders he had known, including King Stanley, Yellowstone Kelly, and Black Elk. Mr. Roth believes Mr. Hopkins belongs at the head of the list of great riders. He quotes Frank as saying,

"The test of a good horsemen is that he can do what he sets out to do with his horse and at the same time manage the horse so skillfully and considerately that the horse does not suffer a single ill effect in the feat."[3]

"The Toughest Race" was published in the January, 1937 issue of The Horse and Horseman. The focus in this article is on the Texas to Vermont race, but some of Frank's other races are also described. When asked about the qualifications of an endurance horseman, Frank responded,

"The only answer to that question is that it takes just plain horsemanship in all that the word implies. I had to study my horses to find the right one. Then I had to use common sense in riding him. That is horsemanship, nothing else."[4]

All three articles are on the Hopkins website[5], but without any of the original photographs. Included are the three shown below. The first one is from "Brains Plus Endurance" and the other two from the "The Toughest Race".

Editor's Comments:

Since all three articles were based on interviews with Frank, the material in them is authentic. The opinions he expresses are similar to what he has said in other articles and unpublished material.

Even though two men share the same name, they cannot be the same person. The Charles B. Roth who wrote these articles was a publicist who headed a Denver firm. He is not the man who wrote so many best selling books on salesmanship.

2) Vermont Articles

As Roth's articles appeared in print, Frank was discovered by the eastern equestrian community. His knowledge and skills impressed many expert horsemen. He was asked to write a series of articles for the Vermont Horse and Bridle Trail Bulletin, published by Green Mountain Horse Association. A list of these articles is given in the first appendix to this chapter. Some of the information in these articles indicates Frank was still riding and training horses when he lived on Long Island.

The first article, "1800 Mile Trail Ride - Texas to Vermont", begins with an introduction by Harvey Wingate. He comments,

"His [Frank's] patience and native ability have enabled him to train horses other people could do nothing with and even today he can train them very well. He loves horses and good horsemanship and has had many a fight with men who used cruelty, in the place of training, to make a horse do the proper things."[6]

At the end of the article, "Understanding Horses", the editor comments,

"If our readers think this kind of horsemanship is just 'talk', call around some day and watch old man Hopkins in the training pen!"[7]

At the end of the article, "Trail Horses", the editor comments,

"Visitors at the Trail Ride have told me they would be well repaid for the time they had spent there, if they had seen and done nothing excepting talk to Frank Hopkins. There is no one in the country who had the experiences with horses that Frank has. We all hope that in spite of his eighty-two years, he will come for many Trail Rides to give us his expertise and help."[8]

At the beginning of the article, "Horsemen and Horsemanship", the editor explains this article is a reprint of one written by Charles B. Roth in The Horse. He comments,

143

"Frank Hopkins has told us a great number of things about horsemanship in the past and we are happy to reprint this splendid article."

The first and second comments imply Frank is still training horses. The third and fourth comments suggest Frank's articles reinforced what he had already said verbally.

In 1942, Frank was asked to be one of the judges of the Sixth Annual One Hundred Mile Trail Ride put on by the Green Mountain Horse Association. For their Bulletin, he describes this experience in an article, "A Judge's Impression of the Ride". Since Frank included much valuable advice about endurance riding, it will be reprinted in Part III. Frank's friend, Nevada Dick was there and his description of what Frank had to do and did is reprinted in Appendix B. The photograph below shows Frank at the ride talking to the Association President, Dr. Earle Johnson, as he shows his horses to Frank.[9]

Editor's Comment: In these articles, Frank's speaking style is reflected in the information on horses, horsemanship, and endurance riding. He was focused, intense, accurate, forthright, and includes just enough detail to make his point.

3) Albert W. Harris discovers Frank Hopkins

Albert W. Harris of Chicago loved mustangs and began breeding his own in 1903. The Harris family rode and drove their mustangs everywhere, including downtown Chicago. Mr. Roth believed the quality of his horses came from their Barb and Arab ancestors. While the Barbs and Arabs have some characteristics in common, such as endurance; they are not the same breed of horse, but many people still confuse them. Modern research has established there is no Arab blood in any of the Spanish breeds nor in the true Barb.[10]

Mr. Harris was deeply interested in endurance racing and soon began acquiring Arabs. He eventually became the President of the Arabian Horse Club of America. In 1940, Charles Roth sent Albert W. Harris a copy of his article, "Great Riders"[3], he reviewed it, and sent many questions back to Mr. Roth. He asked Frank to respond to them and Frank sent him the two long letters shown in Appendix C. In these letters, Frank describes his ponies and two longest races. Mr. Harris published Roth's article and Frank's two letters in his book, The Blood of the Arab.[11] In the photograph below, Mr. Harris and his wife are riding two of their mustang stallions.

LITTLE BEAR AND PONCA
Mustang or Spanish Barb Stallions

a) Mr. Harris was highly respected and his book well known. One of the first authors to use the information about Frank Hopkins in this book was Frank Dobie. He put information about the Texas-Vermont race in his classic book, The Mustangs.[12]

b) Jack Schaefer also found an account of this race in The Blood of the Arab. The sentence quoted below convinced him the race had actually happened.

"My friend Buffalo Jones induced me to enter and backed me to win."

Mr. Schaefer knew how Buffalo Jones felt about mustangs and believes if such a race had been in the making, Buffalo Jones would certainly have had a hand in it.[13] In 1963, Mr. Schaefer mentions the Texas to Vermont race twice in the introductory history to his book, The Great Endurance Horse Race: 600 Miles on a Single Mount, 1908, From Evanston, Wyoming, to Denver.[14]

c) John Richard Young discovered the letters and in 1954, he used the information in his book, The Schooling of the Western Horses. He describes the fate of the mustangs and states,

"The fate of the Mustang presents one of the most disillusioning commentaries on the wisdom of American horsemen that it is possible to find in our history. ... The crime might be excusable if we had succeeded in breeding a better horse than the true Mustang, but we have not even come near it. ...Almost all of them [the old-timers] can tell of examples of Mustang endurance and stamina which, by modern standards, seem extraordinary, but which the old-timers accepted as commonplace. ...Really outstanding Mustangs set almost incredible records for traveling amazing distances."

He draws on the letters when he lists multiple examples of extraordinary rides, which naturally included Frank's two longest races.[15]

4) Frank's Reputation Spreads

After Frank's death in 1951, his reputation continued to spread among horsemen as more authors used the material in the Roth articles, the Vermont articles, and the Harris letters.

a) Anthony Amarel published two articles about Frank. In 1962, he described the race in Arabia. It includes a drawing of Frank and a map of the race. The map is shown below. The political geography is not correct, but it shows a route similar to the one described in Chapter 8.[16]

His second article was published in 1969 by Western Horseman. It describes Frank's beliefs about mustangs and his two longest races. It uses the photograph shown below.[17]

Both articles can be found on the Hopkins website, but without the illustrations.[18]

b) In 1979, Fredie Steve Harris published an article about Frank's career in endurance racing. It begins with the early history of abusive endurance racing and describes Frank's humane approach, as well as some of his longest rides and his belief in mustang qualities. It includes a drawing, as well as the photograph above and the one shown below.[19]

The caption states, "Hopkins maintained his horsemanship long after he quit distance racing." This photograph was taken in 1948 or 1949. The horse is Blue Bird, a Canadian mustang owned by the Pyle family. They may have given him this photograph.

This article can be found on the Hopkins website, but without the illustrations.[20]

Evaluation: Chapter 10 (1-4):

The real Frank T. Hopkins had been a dispatch rider for the Army, a specialty rider for Buffalo Bill's Wild West, and a great endurance rider. In the 1930's and 1940's, there had to have been many people still living who remembered Frank's achievements yet there is no record of anybody questioning any of the published information about his career.

5) The Pyle Family

Tom Pyle worked on both the Stillman and Rockefeller estates. In his time, the Rockefeller estate owned about twenty-five thousand acres and was still expanding. It surrounded the town of Pocantico Hills, New York. Two roads ran through the estate, one of which reached the town. Within the Rockefeller estate, one area was protected by fences and security gates, but miles of trails ran through the rest of the estate. Anyone who behaved could walk or ride on them. One of Tom's jobs was to deal with the ones who didn't behave.

The Stillman family bought land on the northeastern part of the estate and eventually sold it back to the Rockefellers. When Tom caught five poachers on their land in one day, he was asked to become one of the volunteers who protected game for the state of New York. When Tom moved on to a job with the Rockefellers, he was eventually given charge of the outside patrols, as well as conservation and gamekeeping.[20]

Tom knew Frank Hopkins well and valued him as a horseman and naturalist. Frank's knowledge of medicinal plants especially impressed him. In the 1940's, Frank often drove up to visit the family and ride on the trails of the estate. The photograph below shows Tom talking to Frank Hopkins.

Tom's son, Walt Pyle, grew up on the estate. He is a decorated veteran of World War II. He comments,

"Frank was the real thing. Everyone involved with horses knew who he was and what he could do."[21]

As a young distance rider, Edith Colgate competed in the Green Mountain annual 100 miler endurance ride. She competed five times and finished twice. Frank's name was renowned among her crowd and she took pride in knowing him. She comments,

"He was quite a horseman."[21]

During World War II, after she left the service, she took a job on the Rockefeller estate where she eventually met Walt Pyle, Tom's oldest son. When they married in 1947, together they operated a stable on the D. Stillman estate. It was still connected to all the trails on the Rockefeller estate.

Tom Doyle explains,

"To give my own sons a breather and a chance to get on their emotional feet, after their years overseas, before going on to steady jobs, I decided to lease the old Stillman barn, which was not in use, and turn it into a boarding stable and kennel.

First, I talked the project over with Mr. Junior [John D. Rockefeller, Jr.] and got his permission, then I made the deal with Alex Stillman. Ann Stillman Davisson shipped horses down from her Canadian ranch for me to show and sell. We only kept the stable a couple of years, until Mr. Junior decided to purchase that section of property. He asked me if I'd like the place fixed up to continue as a stable, but I had already accomplished my purpose. My boys had a chance to get over their war nerves, and the older one, Walt, had married one of the girls who worked for me, training dogs at the estate and teaching riding at the stable."[22]

In 1952, Walt and Edith relocated to North Pomfret, VT where they bred registered Jersey cattle and Thoroughbred horses. They also won the 100 miler with one of the horses sent by Mrs. Davidson from her ranch in Alberta, Canada. Most of them had been sired by a Thoroughbred stallion, but all of them were at least half Indian pony. Their mustang blood came from the Athabascan Territory.

If they asked Frank's advice, he certainly would have helped them. When he shared his knowledge and advice with other long distance horsemen, he so inspired them that they changed their saddle fit and strategies - to winning results. Frank is shown riding Blue Bird in the photograph below. She was one of the Athabascan mustangs.

Walter Pyle comments on Frank's first ride on her,

"He mounted a horse like - he was way up in years - but he mounted a horse smoother than all the young riders around. ... We never put anyone on Blue Bird. Too much horse. ... I was amazed. He took off on her and it was like the two had been riding together all their lives. What he could do with that horse. He rode all around the courtyard and then out on the trails."[21]

In the late 1940's, Ned Wehrman picked Frank up every Sunday to bring him up to ride at Pocantico Farms. If he didn't feel up to riding, Tom Pyle would drive him around on the trails. The photograph below shows Gertrude Hopkins, Frank holding Blue Bird, and Ned Wehrman.

Walt Pyle comments,

"And Ned, Ned Wehrman - he was a horseman - he used to bring Frank up on Sundays, get him out of Long Island. His wife, she was much younger than he was, she was keeping him there for his health she said. But Ned knew that Frank didn't want to be there. He wanted to be around horses. We all knew who Frank Hopkins was, but it was Ned who kind of looked after him and made sure he got him into the country, up to our stables".[21]

Edith Pyle adds,

"Ned didn't care for her much. The wife. She was a good many years younger than Frank. But he adored Frank. The sun rose and set on Frank to Ned. ... He said that she [Gertrude] wanted to write a book about Frank and make lots of money."[21]

The Pyles never found Frank to be a braggart or boastful. They also believed he came from the West. Edith described how he taught them to use poplar bark to worm their horses. This is an Indian remedy. Walt comments,

"He was from out west - no doubt about it. ... The way he talked, the way he carried himself, the particular way he was around horses, everything. You had to know him."[21]

6) The Conroys were a family of professional horsemen who knew Frank well. They admired his knowledge of horsemanship and his willingness to share it with others. After Peggy Conroy's grandfather came from Ireland in the 1860's, he raised and trained horses in the New York City market. He knew and respected Frank's experience and ability. Her parents were distance riders in the 1940's and met Frank at one of the 100 mile rides. Her father, Tom Conroy, spent many hours with Frank discussing horsemanship, distance technique, and horse history.

Her parents bred horses and their favorite was King Patch, a grandson of Dan Patch who looked very much like him. He was a talented jumper and competed in several of 100 endurance rides. They also owned a granddaughter of Dan Patch, who produced many fine dressage horses, jumpers, and endurance horses. Late in the 1900's, they switched to breeding Thoroughbred racehorses. Peggy Conroy is still working with horses and currently getting eight horses ready for the track.[23]

7) Gertrude's mother died on Sept, 22, 1949.[24] Gertrude inherited the house and may have continued to keep lodgers.

Frank died on Nov. 5, 1951 in their Long Island home. He was buried in the Lutheran All Faiths Cemetery in Middle Village, Queens County, NY.[25] After Frank's death; Gertrude sold the house and moved south. In clearing up, she inadvertently destroyed material and had to depend on her memory for what had been said in the lost material.[26]

In 1961, Gertrude applied for social security at one of the NY offices.[27] When Gertrude contacted Jack Schaefer in 1962[28], she was living on 41-61 23rd St. in Long Island City, NY. She died on August 23, 1971 of a stroke.[29]

Evaluation: Chapter 10

The Green Mountain Horse Association gave Frank the recognition he deserved and made extensive use of his expertise in selecting, training, and riding endurance horses. For years, Frank willingly helped people with difficult horses, equine medical problems, and advice on endurance riding. In my opinion, if he had not been an expert horseman, he would have been quickly found out and rejected by this group. His reputation was never questioned until the production of the controversial movie, Hidalgo.

Acknowledgements:

Photo 1 Courtesy of The Horse, March-April, 1935. Photos 2-3, 6-7, 10 Courtesy of American Heritage Center, University of Wyoming. Photo 4 Courtesy of Green Mountain Horse Association. Photo 5 Courtesy Albert Harris. Photos 8-10 Courtesy of Pyle family.

Map courtesy of Horse Lover's Magazine, June-July, 1962.

Footnotes:

[1]Paulo, Karen. America's Long Distance Challenge, Trafalgar Square, 1990, pp. 3-5.
Lewis, Curtis L. The Great American Horse Race of 1976. Mennonite Press, 1993, pp. 13-14.
Harris, Albert W. The Blood of the Arab, Chicago, The Arabian Horse Club of America, 1941, pp. 123-140.
[2]Roth, Charles B., "Brains Plus Endurance", The Horse, March-April, 1935, pp. 18-20.
[3]Roth, Charles B., "Great Riders", The Horse, March-April, 1936, pp. 16-17.
[4]Roth, Charles B., "The Toughest Race", The Horse and Horseman", Jan. 1937, pp. 31, 49-50.
[5]Articles 2, 13, 14, and 25 on www.FrankHopkins.com.
[6]Wingate, Harvey. "Introduction: 1800-Mile Trail Ride-Texas to Vermont" Vermont Horse and Bridle Trail Bulletin, April, 1940, p. 43.
[7]Editor, "Trail Horses", The Vermont Horse and Bridle Trail Bulletin, Oct. 1946, p. 153.
[8]Editor, "Understanding Horses", The Vermont Horse and Bridle Trail Bulletin, July, 1946, p. 102.
[9]Hopkins, Frank T. "A Judge's Impression of the Ride", Oct. 1941, pp. 135-6, 142. Reprinted as article 15 on www.FrankHopkins.com. Without photos.
[10]Ladendorf, Janice M. Spanish Horsemen and Horses in the New World, 2015,
Chapter 11.
[11]Harris, Albert W. The Blood of the Arab, Chicago, The Arabian Horse Club of America, 1941, pp. 44-52.
[12]Dobie, J. Frank. The Mustangs. University of Texas Press, 1952, pp. 286-7.
[13]Schaefer, Jack. Forward to Lord of the Beasts: the Saga of Buffalo Jones by Robert Easton, University of Arizona Press, 1961, p. x.
[14]Schaefer, Jack. The Great Endurance Horse Race, Stagecoach Press, 1961, p. 7.

[15]Young, John Richard. The Schooling of the Western Horse. University of Oklahoma Press, 1954, pp. 50-52.

[16]Amaral, Anthony A., "Hidalgo and Frank Hopkins", The Horse Lover's Magazine, June-July, 1962, pp. 28-29, 64. Reprinted in SMR Newsletter, Winter, 2001. Also reprinted as article 8 on www.FrankHopkins.com.Without illustrations.

[17]Amaral, Anthony A., "Frank Hopkins ... best of endurance riders?" The Western Horseman, Dec. 1969, pp. 110-111, 191-4. Reprinted as article 4 on www.Frank Hopkins.com. Without photos.

[18]Articles 4, 5, and 8 on www.FrankHopkins.com.

[19]Harris, Fredie Steve, "America's great distance horseman", Horseman, 1979, pp. 66-9. Reprinted as article 5 on www.FrankHopkins.com. Without illustrations.

[20]Tom Pyle as told to Beth Day. Pocantico: Fifty Years on the Rockefeller Domain. NY, Duell, Sloan, and Pearce, 1964.

[21]Articles 27 and 28 on www.FrankHopkins.com.

[22]Tom Pyle as told to Beth Day. Pocantico: Fifty Years on the Rockefeller Domain. NY, Duell, Sloan, and Pearce, 1964, pp. 221-222.

[23]Leerhsen, Charles, "A Century-Old Breeding Lesson", NY Times, 5-14-08. Comment by Peggy Conway.

Article 28 on www.FrankHopkins.com.

Conway, Peggy to author, e-mail dated 3-8-16.

[24]US Find a Grave Index, 1600's-Current, Memorial #89205828.

[25]US Find a Grave Index, 1600's-Current, Memorial #10331690.

[26]US. Social Security Administration. Numident Record for Gertrude Hopkins, social security number 065-16-4276.

[27]Gertrude Hopkins to Jack Schaefer, letter, June 4, 1962. Hopkins Papers, Robert Olney Easton Collection, American Heritage Center, University of Wyoming. It is also in their digital collection.

[28]Mrs. B. G. Monroe to Robert Easton, letter dated Aug. 26, 1971. Hopkins Papers, Robert Olney Easton Collection, American Heritage Center, University of Wyoming.

Chapter 10: Appendix A

Articles published in the Vermont Horse and Bridle Trail Bulletin

"1800-Mile Trail Ride - Texas to Vermont", April 1940, pp. 43-44, 63-64

*"Gentling", Oct. 1940, pp. 127-30, 137-138

*"Mustangs", Jan. 1941, pp. 2-4, 24

*"Endurance Horses as I know them", July 194, pp. 81-82, 93

*"A Judge's Impression of the Ride", Oct. 1941, pp. 135-6, 142

"Hunting Buffalo", Jan., 1942, pp. 2-4, 20

"Riders and their Records" By Col. R. Parker, July 1942, pp. 105-107

"Buffalo Bill as I knew him", Oct. 1942, pp. 151-4

*"Horses and Horsemen", July 1943, pp. 73-6

*"The Mustang", Oct. 1944, pp. 5-6

"Carrying Notes for Uncle Samuel" By Gertrude Hopkins, April 1944, pp. 49-50

"The Truth about 'Buffalo Bill'", Oct. 1944, p. 121

*"Horsemen and Horsemanship", Jan. 1945, pp. 17-18, 24

"Only a War Horse", Jan. 1946, pp. 5-7

*"Understanding Horses", July 1946, pp. 95-6, 102

*"Trail Horses", Oct. 1946, pp. 153-4

Editor's Notes:

1) Unless otherwise noted, author credit for the articles is given to Frank Hopkins.

2) Articles marked with an asterisk will be reprinted in Part III.

3) Complete photocopies of all the articles were obtained from the Vermont Historical Society. Copies included photographs and editorial comments.

Chapter 10: Appendix B: Judging an Endurance Ride (Undated letter from Nevada Dick (Dickey, E. M.) to Robert Easton, pp. 2-3. Hopkins Papers, Robert Olney Easton Collection, American Heritage Center, University of Wyoming.)

"I recall clearly the tremendous task which was his, in the year 1942. He was asked to accept the position of Judge at the Vermont Trail Ride, which was held, at Woodstock VT. This meant his being on hand from early morning, when those riders, with their mounts must be checked, weighed, and started on schedule. The first group must leave at the break of day, so that the others entered could get off, early enough to have eight hours of daylight, in which to travel the required distance, and reach the stable.

There the mounts were closely examined, from head to foot, and this meant that the judge, personally went over each animal, to check for any faults. As Judge, he [Frank] examined every horse, and in some cases horses were of a mean disposition, or at least the kind which did not take kindly to having a man pick up their hind feet. I was standing close by one such horse, as the Kid [Frank], stepped close to examine the horse, when one of the officials shouted 'Look out for his feet. He kicks.' Without the least hesitation he stepped into the make-shift stall, and the moment the horse started to raise it's hoof, this horseman quickly changed it's mind, as it found it's foot seized, and drawn into a position, which suited the examination of the foot. (I did hear that at an earlier ride that the judge simply passed up this same animal, without risking a kick in doing the task). It was after dark, that night before his task was completed, and we were free to get supper.

As soon as he had finished his meal, Hopkins left the table, and when we again caught up with him, he was still locating some those who had found a place and were getting all set for calling it a day. The Kid however informed them that there was still the reports to be make out, and a tally made as to any faults, or other data recorded which should be completed, so that all records could be kept up date. There was some who grumbled about it, yet none the less complied, and it was some time before he came back to join the gathering.

While most of the committee sought their beds, the Kid sat upon the porch talking until it was quite late before he started to his room, yet he was the first man to appear at the stable next A.M. and ready to take up the task of preparing the first riders for their days journey."

Chapter 10: Appendix C

Letters sent by Frank T. Hopkins to Albert W. Harris

February 18, 1940

"The little stallion Joe that I rode from Galveston, Texas, to Rutland, Vermont, in 1886, was dark buckskin in color with black tips, mane and tail, weight about 800 pounds. He was caught as a wild Indian pony in the Shoshone Valley, Wyoming, and I happened to get him in this way: Buffalo Jones bought him with a number of unbroken ponies; Joe was very wild - the horse breakers soon gave up all hopes of breaking him. As I was at the time riding as a dropper for Jones that winter on the buffalo runs, the pony was given to me as a hopeless outlaw, but in two months' time of careful handling I rode him on the runs. When he got used to the crack of the gun and other things that went with the chase, Joe was the best buffalo horse I ever rode and he never seemed to tire.

The White-y family, as I call them, started with a small white mare–even her eyes were white. This little 700-pound mare belonged to one of the Sioux Indians, Red Calf by name. The Indians had been put on Pine Ridge Reservation; their droves of ponies were taken away, leaving only two ponies to each tepee. This Indian, Red Calf, asked me to buy the little White-y as he thought a lot of her, and Red Calf also told me that the mare could lope along all day without tiring. Red Calf and I had played together as small boys (his father was a government scout at Fort Laramie, Wyoming, where I was born). The following morning after I had talked to Red Calf I bought White-y from General George Crook (I was dispatch rider for him) for three silver dollars. This mare raised five colts [fillies] for me—four of them were dark cream in color with white manes and tails and the fifth colt was spotted cream and white. That spotted mare was the dam of Hidalgo, the stallion that weighed 950 pounds. It is my personal opinion that Hidalgo was the greatest endurance horse that ever carried a rider.

I might mention that I did not cross these ponies with other blood, but got the best stallion that could be found of the Indian pony blood."

I bought White-y the year 1877 and continued raising colts from that strain. The last horse of that strain, a stallion named Chenango, died at the age of twenty-two (1926) the year before my friend King

Stanley passed on. Most of these ponies weighed about 950 pounds, although the starting stock weighed between seven and eight hundred pounds.

I believe the Indian ponies are without doubt horses that were brought here by the Spanish - the Mustangs were the same horse until other horses got mixed with them, horses that got away from the Army and wagon trains during the troubles with the wild bands. The Indians kept their ponies herded and in that way kept the blood clear. Inbreeding was the cause of their ponies being so small."

March 9, 1940

"This was how my going to Arabia came about: During the World's Fair in Paris, France, I was contesting against cavalry men of all nations of the World - men who had been picked by their own government and sent there. Naturally I met many good horsemen, among them one Ras Rasmussen, who controlled the entire camel freight in Aden, Arabia. He seem to take quite and interest in me, told me of the endurance rides that took place in his country every year and asked me to visit there. He spoke particularly of one ride that was run every year for more than a thousand years and no one but Arabs rode in that race. He was a great horseman of that country and he brought some of his horses to the Fair: They were the best I had ever seen, but they were small. After the contest was over, at the end of the Fair, 1889, our Show got ready for the voyage back home, and one morning Nathan Salisbury sent for me and with him was Ras R. I got the greatest surprise of my life when they told me I was to go to Arabia! The funds for that trip were furnished by the Congress of Rough Riders of the World.

I shipped three of my ponies - one called Hidalgo and two of his half brothers; all of them cream and white spotted stallions. Hidalgo was eight years old then and I trained him for the long ride. He was as fine a looker as could be found. I had ridden him on some hard rides and knew what he could do if called upon. The long ride started from Aden (this was in 1890); we rode along the Gulf to Syria, then inland along the borders of the two countries. Much of this ride was over limestone country, the only feed available were plants called vatches [vetches] and to my surprise these vatches were very nourishing food for our horses if they were dry—some of the riders fed the vatches green. The only grain was barley. Over 100 horses started in that ride; many were ruled out the first week. My Hidalgo began passing other horses on the fourteenth day of the ride and gradually moved up toward the front every day. Hidalgo reached the finish stone thirty-three hours of actual travel ahead of the second horse. I was sixty-eight days in all on that ride of over 3,000 miles; there were a few days that we rested. Some of the way was over loose sand and the air was very dry and hot and water scarce. My horse lost quite a lot of flesh, still he finished strong and in good spirit.

I left him in that land where he belonged. I heard of him often, though, until he died - at the age of twenty-eight. Ras R. raised many fine colts from Hidalgo and Arab mares. Most of the colts were pure white; strange how that color will throw back at times."

Harris, Albert W. The Blood of the Arab. Chicago, The Arabian Horse Club of America, 1941, pp. 48-52.

Editorial Comments:

White-y's colts. Colt can be used to include fillies.

In his first letter, Frank describes Hidalgo's dam as spotted cream and white. In his memoir, he describes the dam of Hidalgo as a dark chestnut mare with one spot on her shoulder (see Chapter 7). In the second letter, Hidalgo is described as a spotted cream and white stallion. Since no photographs of him have survived, there is no way to know how light or dark his spots could have been.

The race in Arabia race was run in 1892, not 1890 (see analysis in Chapter 8).

Since King Stanley died in 1929, Chenango died in 1928 (see Chapter 9).

Chapter 11: Final Conclusion

When the movie, Hidalgo, was released in 2004, a storm of controversy had already broken out. Since it was historical fiction, criticizing both the historical background and the fictional events is legitimate. Unfortunately, the controversy spilled over into attacks on the credibility of the real Frank T. Hopkins. They took three basic forms. The first one focused on the conflicting styles and fictional elements in the available manuscripts, the second one questioned his biographical information, and the third one attacked his status as a horseman.

1) Hopkins Papers

Although an author normally does all of the original writing, some editing is usually done by various experts prior to publication. The Hopkins Papers include a mass of published and unpublished material. The degree to which any of it has been edited varies considerably with each individual article or manuscript. If it has been edited, the quality of the editing also varies.

Unfortunately, all of Frank's unpublished manuscripts are in his wife's handwriting presumably because he dictated them to her. To keep up with him, she had to write fast and sometimes go back to add clarifying notes. His original thoughts are relatively easy to recognize since they tended to lack sentence structure and punctuation, as well as occasionally using colloquial language. An example is using hoss for horse. The unpublished material selected for in this book generally follows this style.

a) Frank's education was minimal. According to the 1940 census, he barely reached fourth grade. While he learned to read, he may never have been taught the rules governing formal compositions. Since his wife, Gertrude, had completed eighth grade, she would have learned these rules, probably as they were defined in the McGuffey Readers. To be published at that time, Frank's material needed this type of editing. A good example of this process is in the long unpublished document, "Keep Your Horse Happy". The first part has been edited, but not the rest of the document.[1]

Edited Sample:

"In more than sixty years of intensive horsemanship which includes winning more long rides than any other horseman, I have discovered that the most important factor in horsemanship is the horse's mental attitude."[1]

Unedited Sample:

"I rode my first endurance race back in 1877 - a ride of 350 miles on rough trails which had been marked so every rider had to cover the ground; I rode a dun colored Indian pony who weighed less than 800 pounds."[1]

b) The articles sent to the Vermont Horse and Bridle Trail Bulletin were all submitted in Gertrude's handwriting. They were probably dictated by Frank and corrected by his wife. Traces of two distinctive styles can be found in these articles. Gertrude was romantic while Frank was forthright. Gertrude rambled while Frank was focused and never used unnecessary detail. This contrast can be seen in the excerpt below of the first two paragraphs of the article, "1800-Mile Trail Ride-Texas to Vermont."

"To one who loves the great outdoors, there is nothing quite so interesting as a Trail Ride. It makes little difference whether you ride the sage-covered plains and foothills of the far West or the rugged hillsides of the Eastern States. There is something fascinating about such a ride - the falling leaves moving about your horse's feet, the squeaking of the saddle leather beneath you. The busy horse seems to enjoy covering the trail fully as much as his rider. There is new scenery for every mile you cover, but in the distance will be a beautiful hill covered with green spruce or sugar maples, with their autumn leaves of red and yellow, you will be anxious to get to. And when you do get to this spot, there will be another that looks more beautiful beyond. As the day draws near its end, maybe you will see a glorious sunset dropping behind the far away hills. So you have come to the close of the pleasantest day of your experience.

Caring for your mount is part of the day's pleasure. As a dispatch rider for the Army during the Indian troubles on the Western Plains for nine years, I have known the thrill of many long rides. Some of them covered 200 to 300 miles. My mounts were fed on wild buffalo grass. They got the best care I could give them, although the best could not be much. There was one class of horse I liked best and would ride no other but this, even though there were many fine looking mounts offered me - I refused all but the Indian pony, a hardy little animal, no trail too long or too rough - a horse that could get along without grain and go without water for two or three days at time. Still the Indian pony has a weakness - the sound of the human voice will worry him off his feet. I never spoke to my ponies while up there in the saddle."[2]

Analysis: The first paragraph is in Gertrude's romantic, wandering style: the second shifts into the mundane and specific.

    b) Another example of Gertrude's style is in the article, "Mustangs". The excerpt below precedes the story of the blizzard told in Chapter 2.

"When I started, the sun was shining, the sky was clear and there was about three inches of light snow that had fallen during the night. As I rode along, mule deer scampered among the scrub cedars. Farther along, I saw the fresh hoofprints made by a band of wild ponies who had probably fled before a prowling cougar. Coming from the high ridge about me, I heard the bugle call of an elk. As I rode along I noticed the dark moving forms of the bison as they browsed in the valley below. A spotted eagle screamed as he soared in graceful circles above me. It seemed a fine winter's day and even the hills belonged to the man who rode them. When I stopped to graze, the long, streaming shadow of my pony was no longer visible for the sun was directly overhead (it was mid-day). I loosened the saddle girths and my pony shoved the snow aside with his nose searching for buffalo peas, while I nibbled away at the dried beef I'd taken from my saddle bag. I could easily see Harney Peak in the Black Hills, and off to the west, the Laramie Mountains, the day was so clear. That afternoon, I rode into higher country and at sundown I made camp against the ledge of a yellow crag."[3]

Analysis: If this article was fiction, this detail would help set the scene for the reader. As non-fiction, it is unnecessary detail. Such additions are relatively innocuous, but most of Gertrude's changes fell into other categories.

c) The published articles also contain evidence of Gertrude's attempts to build her husband's reputation by making critical comments about his opponents.

In the article, "1800-Mile Trail Ride-Texas to Vermont", two derogatory statements were made about Frank's opponents. They did not appear in any of Frank's other descriptions of the race. They are shown below.

Statement 1: "Four of those riding English saddles were in bad shape and their mounts were a sorry sight to look at - over at the knees and spread behind, their muscles trembled and twitched; those were out of the ride for good."[2]

Analysis: After the start, Frank only saw the other horses as he passed them. These four horses may have been eliminated before he passed them. If he had ridden past them, he would not had enough time to observe the details of their condition.

Statement 2: "That horse [the one who came in second] was broken down in spirit and body. The third horse came in a few days later, a broken-down wreck."[2]

Analysis: Since the race was closely monitored, these horses should have been eliminated before they reached this condition.

In my opinion, both these statements were added by Gertrude, probably without Frank's knowledge. Once he had dictated what he wanted to say, we do not know how often or how seriously he reviewed what Gertrude had written down and submitted for publication.

d) In her attempts to build Frank's reputation, Gertrude also added material inflating his relationship with famous men. Frank obviously knew Buffalo Bill well, both by reputation and as an employee; but since Frank was half Indian, I doubt if Buffalo Bill ever became a family friend. This claim is only made in the article, "Buffalo Bill as I

Knew Him", where Buffalo Bill is described as six feet, seven inches tall.[4] In my opinion, this error could only have been made by someone who didn't know him well, such as Frank's wife. If she had only seen him on horseback during one of his shows, she could easily have overestimated his actual height.

At various points in the Hopkins Papers, Theodore Roosevelt is mentioned. Several stories had probably been invented by Gertrude.[5] When he first came west; he supposedly stayed on the CH ranch and bounced all over the saddle when he was learning to ride in a western saddle. Since he was already a skilled horseman, this story is ridiculous. In one of her letters, she also claims Frank's father invited him to stay at their ranch on his college vacations and he worked for him for four years before he bought his own ranch. These claims violate known facts about Roosevelt's career. In my opinion, her stories invalidates all the rest of the information in the Hopkins Papers about Frank's various contacts with Mr. Roosevelt.

e) There is one article published under Gertrude's name, "Carrying 'Notes' for 'Uncle Samuel'". It plainly shows how she fictionalized information to present her husband in a more favorable light.

This article begins when Frank and some of his friends had been to see the latest shipment just in from the Remount sales. After dinner that night, the talk turned to dispatch riding. What Gertrude said in her article is based on the gossip she overheard that night and did not have the background to understand. The information in her article contained various errors.

Example 1:

As she said, dispatch riders always had to deal with the terrain and the weather, but she was wrong when she implied their trips always brought them into contact with the scouts of Indian war parties. When travel during the day became too dangerous; she also states instead they raced on at night. In any type of rugged or uneven terrain, she apparently didn't realize how easily a horse could fall and injure or kill himself. The only time night travel might be feasible was when there happened to be a full moon.[6]

Example 2: She comments,

"The alert rider [like Frank] might hear the sharp cry of a coyote - not quite perfect - for it was purposely imitated that way by the Indian scout. If the dispatch rider knew his Indians right, he would answer with the short, choppy yelp of the female coyote; then the Indians, thinking the answer came from one of their own traveling scouts, would not move from where they lay bedded down."[6]

Analysis: The scouts for war parties did use animal cries as signals, but they could not always have infested the country traveled by the dispatch riders. When they did use these signals, they imitated them perfectly and few whites had the same ability. Gertrude is probably implying her husband was one of the few who understood and used them.

Example 3: She comments,

"The worst enemies of the dispatch riders were outlaws who traded guns and ammunition to the Indian warriors; these 'traders' were lawless whites who made a living defying our Government and killing anyone who might come across their pack trains or their trail. Many a young and inexperienced dispatch rider gave his precious life by innocently crossing the trail of such outfits. Usually, seeing white men, he would ride up to have a word with them (so he thought), but he never lived to tell it; they knew a dead rider could not report having even seen them."[6]

Analysis: There may have been an occasional case of such killings, but not to the extent implied by her statement. First, dispatch riders were always in hurry and would not normally have stopped to chat. Second, if they knew the country well enough to be dispatch riders, they would presumably know enough to avoid such outfits. Third, once such a killing had been reported, other riders would soon be warned to beware of these outlaws.

Example 4:

To do their jobs, dispatch riders did not need to be able to speak any of the Indian languages. Frank was unusual in his ability to speak them, but he was never allowed to serve as an official translator. He was known to be a half breed and he would not have been trusted to fairly present the white point of view. Occasionally he might have been asked to do some informal translation for officers who knew him, but such occasions probably were rare.

Analysis: Gertrude tells a story of how some Sioux demanded Frank translate for them because they did not trust trader's sons. Since she says their demand triggered a serious investigation, her story is probably another one of her fictional attempts to enhance Frank's reputation.

f) Gertrude was the one person who could easily have added fictional elements to Frank's manuscripts. She demonstrated her ability to write fiction in her unpublished article about Hidalgo.[7] Judged as fiction, it is not a bad story and uses information from some of Frank's stories about his many horses. The author's ignorance of horsemanship is not unusual for those who write such fiction.

Judged as non-fiction, her story is a collection of misinformation.

Analysis: Her fictional horse was sired by a wild stallion caught in the Shoshone Valley and out of an albino mare caught by Frank. Possibly his sire was meant to be Joe and his dam Josie II. Frank states Josie I was not an albino, but she was the dam of his Hidalgo.

The color of her fictional horse is described as seal brown, like Frank's beloved Silver, but this horse had small white spots all over his body. Such a snowflake pattern is rare and changes with the horse's age. A carving of the real Hidalgo is shown below and the face markings match, but not the body color. Unlike her fictional horse, the horse in the carving of the real Hidalgo did not have white glass eyes.

In her story, one day Frank rode out and roped the fictional colt before leading him back to the ranch and tying him in the corral, but cowboys never roped a colt because they could damage his immature body. Unlike a typical wild mare, his dam did not try to protect her colt by attacking the human who threatened him. Instead, she just followed and entered the corral that night. When this miraculous event supposedly occurred, Frank was actually dispatch riding in Arizona.

When Frank started riding for Buffalo Bill, Hidalgo was only two years old; but in her story, Frank broke him and took him to New York to use in his first season with Bill's show. Cowboys like Frank never rode two year olds and he did not show Hidalgo at Madison Square Garden in the winter of 1886-7, but he did take him to Europe in the 1889-91 tour.

Gertrude describes two tricks Frank supposedly taught her fictional horse, but no experienced horseman would teach a horse to lie down on top of him or rear and put his hoofs on his shoulders. She probably did not realize how dangerous these tricks were.

Her fictional horse had style. A trick horse may need it, but Frank never selected or used a stylish mover as an endurance horse. Such a horse could never have won a 3,000 mile race. Frank never described the real Hidalgo's disposition, but Gertrude's fictional horse was as responsive as Frank's beloved horse, Pardner.

The real Hidalgo stayed in Arabia with his two brothers. The fictional Hidalgo did go to Arabia, but Frank brought him back to the United States where he traveled with Bill's show for many years. Such travel was hard on a horse and Frank retired his horses after a few stressful years, but Gertrude's fictional horse kept right on learning new tricks and appearing in the show ring.

Editor's Comment (e and f): In my opinion, the analysis of these two articles has identified Gertrude as the one who did all or most of the negative editing of her husband's manuscripts.

Evaluation (1):

Many writing partnerships have been successful, but Frank and Gertrude did not have one of them. Frank enjoyed telling stories, but he also described himself as a square shooter. Such a man is always, honest, honorable, and keeps his word. In one of his articles about Buffalo Bill, Frank expresses his concern about some of his legends which he knew could not have been true.[8] Somehow he kept his writings about horses, horsemanship, and endurance riding free from destructive editing, but he failed with information on his career and personal life.

His wife obviously knew little or nothing about western geography, history, or culture. She was an opinionated woman who believed Frank had been a member of a non-existent Indian Royal Family. The combination of her ignorance and active imagination is probably responsible for the appearance of so many fictional elements in Frank's biographical information.

In reviewing their published and unpublished biographical information, the first step is always to identify and ignore or remove any of Gertrude's destructive editing. The second step is to use public records to validate its accuracy. Once this has been done, what is left is usually relatively free from error. When multiple or conflicting stories exist, the one with the most verifiable detail is probably the most accurate one.

2) The Heroic Myth

Background Information: The Romantic Frontier

Life on the western frontier was first romanticized with the publication of melodramatic dime novels. Buffalo Bill had the record with over eighty novels published about his real and imaginary exploits. The wild west shows continued this process, as did the emerging movie industry. Fictional memoirs and ones that mixed fact and fiction also flooded the market. According to Jack Schaefer, the newspapers of that day added fuel to the romantic flames by favoring colorful and gooey stories over factual reporting.[9]

Gertrude Nehler was born in 1890 and probably read dime novels, as well as attending wild west shows and movies. If she did, this experience may have been one reason she wanted to marry a cowboy and fictionalize his stories. Unfortunately, by the time Robert Easton contacted her, serious research on western history had already begun and he wanted more and better information than she could give him.

a) Frank's real career

He states he had been a dispatch rider for the Army during the Indian troubles, a specialty rider for Buffalo Bill's Wild West, and a successful endurance rider. Carrying dispatches did not turn him into a western hero or an Indian fighter. His job was to deliver his messages. He only fought Indians when they managed to trap him so that he could not run away from them. He took the dangers involved in this job for granted and did not think of himself as any type of hero. Romantic western heroes killed Indians, they did not run away from them.

Charles B. Roth was a publicist and had his own firm in Denver. He helped Frank promote himself as a horseman and endurance rider. His articles never went beyond what Frank had said about his real career. As his articles, the Harris letters, and Frank's articles were used by future authors; they began dropping the dispatch and specialty riding to describe him simply as one of the greatest of the early long distance riders.

b) The Critics

Those who have called Frank T. Hopkins an Old West fraud base this opinion on several factors. Some noticed the inconsistent styles in the Hopkins manuscripts, but attributed both of them to one psychotic individual who knew almost nothing about the Western frontier. In my opinion, there were two people and the ignorant one was Frank's wife, Gertrude. Her changes and additions did much to damage the creditability of Frank's manuscripts.

Unfortunately for Frank's critics, his name is a common and uncommon one. Frank Hopkins is a common name and his critics have accumulated information about various men with this name, but without checking the type of criteria needed to verify if any of them really were Frank T. Hopkins. One of them is Frank's unusual middle name, Tezolph. The other is his Indian blood.

These critics also claimed Frank had said his father was a survivor of Custer's Last Stand. Frank states his father had survived the wagon-box fight in 1867, but he does not say he had been at Custer's Last Stand in any of his published articles or in any of the manuscripts found at the American Heritage Center.

In addition, the critics claim Frank had said his mother was an Indian princess, but there is no record of any such statement in his published or unpublished work. In his day, this term reflected a negative racist stereotype and he would not have used it about his beloved mother. An Indian princess was usually defined as the daughter of a chief. Gertrude did write a note against a picture of Sitting Bull in one of the manuscripts found at the American heritage Center. It states Frank's mother was just his cousin.[10] This story may or may not be true.

Frank's critics have also expressed some legitimate concerns about the number of careers Frank was supposed to have had. Unfortunately, there is considerable confusion of between what Frank actually said and the exploits of other western heroes. Each one of these claims is analyzed below.

Career 1: The Pony Express

The Pony Express ran from 1860-61, four years before Frank was born. Express riders carried commercial mail while the dispatch riders carried military mail. The critics may have confused these tasks.

Buffalo Bill claimed he rode for the Pony Express and it was an event in his early Wild West shows. Frank did say he had ridden in that event.

Career 2: Indian Fighter

Buffalo Bill was a scout who rode with the troops when they set out to fight and kill Indians. He legitimately described himself as an Indian fighter. Dispatch riders like Frank simply carried messages through Indian country.

Career 3: Buffalo Hunter

When Buffalo Bill held a contract to supply meat to the Kansas Pacific Railroad, he became famous as a buffalo hunter and expert shot. Since he needed meat, he killed buffalo from horseback.

When Frank was not needed by the Army, he did hunt buffalo intermittently, but so did almost anybody who lived on the frontier before all the herds were massacred.

Career 4: Star of Buffalo Bill's show

Frank never claimed he had star billing in this show. If he had, his name would certainly have shown up on the program. He was one of the Congress of Rough Riders and part of the cowboy troupe, but not a star. He did trick riding and rode outlaw horses in the Cowboy Fun event, as well as participating as a rider in many of the other events. Leaders of troupes were sometimes listed on the program, but not individual members.

Career 5: Rough Rider

The troops who fought with Theodore Roosevelt in the Spanish American war were called Rough Riders, but Buffalo Bill used this name first. When he put on an event called The Battle of San Juan Hill, Frank may have played a minor role in it.

Buffalo Bill was tied up with contracts and could not get away to participate in the Spanish American war. In my opinion, Frank would also have been in the same situation. Since he is not listed as a Rough Rider, his wife probably created the story about his serving as a scout for Theodore Roosevelt in Cuba.

Career 6:
African Explorer.
Big Game Hunter and Guide.
Zane Grey's Friend and Hero of One of his Novels.

These claims were not made by the real Frank Hopkins. They were made by the false one who was interviewed by a newspaper reporter in 1926. They applied to Buffalo Jones who was an African explorer, a big game hunter, and guide. He was also the man who was Zane Grey's friend and the hero of one of his novels.

Career 7: Secret Service Agent

This claim is an example of negative editing. Frank stated he did do confidential work for the government during World War I. When someone changed confidential secret, this statement could easily be misinterpreted. What he may have actually done was work as a diver on the fortifications of New York's harbor.

Career 8: Pinkerton Detective

This claim comes from one of Gertrude's letters. She once saw Frank exchanging signals with a trooper who stopped them on the way to visit Joe Pyle on the Rockefeller estate. She simply assumed this incident meant he had been a detective. Since they would have been visiting Tom or Walt Pyle, this story may or may not have been true.[11]

Career 9: Bounty Hunter

Although Frank's authentic memoir does not state he ever did any bounty hunting, this claim is made in the introduction to Frank's first published article by Harvey P. Wingate. Mr. Wingate had just had dinner with Frank and his wife. He had obviously been overwhelmed and confused by too much information. He states Frank had been born in Laramie, Wyoming instead of Fort Laramie. He did not realize all of Frank's endurance rides had been races. He incorrectly linked the race in Arabia to our Thanksgiving Day holiday.

He also states Frank had shot several outlaws for the government. This could well have happened when he was a dispatch rider. Unfortunately, he identifies one of these outlaws as the famous bad Harry Tracey, but he committed suicide before he was caught for the second time. On the dates when he was chased, Frank would have been traveling with Bill's show.[12]

This analysis of potential careers reveals what Frank told Charles B. Roth about his real career was probably completely accurate. None of his early articles about Frank made any attempt to establish him as any kind of romantic western hero. He publicized him as a horseman just as Frank wanted.

With the exception of one long article[1], Frank's unpublished manuscripts have not been dated. Most of Gertrude's negative editing could well have occurred after Frank's death or without Frank's knowledge. Since the Easton files could not be accessed until after his death in 1999, they could not have been used to perpetuate any type of hoax or fraud.

In his last years, Frank did spend time willingly helping many people, but he followed the frontier rules. If help was needed, it was freely given, even to your worst enemy.[13] Since he did not expect or receive any payment for sharing his expertise; he could not have been involved in any form of fraud.

3) A Legendary Horseman

Western horsemanship has evolved from three sources - the Indians, vaqueros, and cowboys. Frank knew Indian horsemanship well and had tamed his first mustang with advice from his mentor, Chief Sadheart. He also knew vaquero horsemanship and training methods. He rode like a vaquero, used a bosal hackamore for his endurance horses, and created a parade bridle with a vaquero bit and decorative design. Only a skilled horseman with an excellent seat and extraordinarily light hands could have had the finesse to safely use the half-breed curb attached to this parade bridle. Finally, like all the cowboys in Bill's show, he had the skills necessary to rope and ride outlaw horses.

His critics have generally ignored his published and unpublished material about horses, horsemanship, and endurance riding. This material reflects his tradition, his extensive experience, and his level of knowledge. It also documents his surprisingly modern belief in the value of building a partnership with your horse. Instead, they have focused on rejecting the few existing photographs of Frank and his horses.

Frank used all his knowledge, experience, and skills to win 402 endurance races. His critics have all too often misquoted and exaggerated this total. Frank rode his first race in 1887 and his last race in 1926. In fifty years, he would have averaged eight races per year.

His win record does seem to be highly improbable until it is compared to his life story.

In frontier days, the typical recreations at the frontier forts were drinking, gambling, and horse racing. Racing and gambling were also popular with Indians. In his days as a dispatch rider, Frank claims to have won 189 races with either the army boys, the Indians, or both. What he won was some money, but mainly merchandise and ponies. Given the way he moved around, this claim is feasible.

When his memoir was reviewed, it mentioned an additional 209 races. Another 4 were found in one of his published articles. Some are described in detail, but for most of them, all he gives us is location and length. He defined an endurance race as one fifty miles long or longer and he did ride in many relatively short races. Given the way he traveled around in his thirty-one years with Bill's Show, another 213 races is a believable number. If he had stayed in one location, people would soon have refused to compete with him.

The number of races may be correct, but how did he manage to win every race he entered? There were probably numerous factors involved. In my opinion, he was a perfectionist who strove constantly to find ways to improve his performance. Like so many cowboys, experience taught him what gave the best results, but usually he could not explain why it worked.

a) One factor was his athletic abilities. His friend, Nevada Dick, often called him by one of his nicknames, the Laramie Kid. He describes his stamina and strength in the quotation below.

"There was nothing out standing, in the build of the Laramie Kid, to the casual observer, but to those who KNEW him, he was far stronger physically, than any man I have ever met. Like the endurance horses he raised and trained, he too knew the value of taking care of himself, and put in his time in doing things which kept him in such shape that he could stand, long hours of work, yet always appeared fresh, and able to keep going after men of half his age were on the verge of exhaustion.

In height, he stood a trifle under six foot, and in weight around 190 lbs. Where most men are built with a normal chest, and smaller waist, he was built with a round body, so to speak, and heavily muscled, and solid as a tree trunk yet not muscle bound, just plain solid through, and the strongest man I ever knew. At one time he had to move a large stone. He picked up one end of the rock, while TWO MEN took the other end, but were unable to keep their grip and were forced to drop the load. Hopkins then told the pair, 'get out of my way'. He then picked up the stone alone and carried it to the spot desired."[14]

His description explains how Frank could handle the demanding schedule imposed on the riders in Bill's show, as well as compete in endurance races. His exceptional stamina also had to contribute to his success in endurance races. In addition to what Nevada Dick said, sticking to bucking horses and riding trick horses require required excellent balance and exceptionally quick reaction times.

Editor's Comment: When Frank was racing, his weight was 152 pounds. His wife, Gertrude, thought he was slightly over 6 ft. tall and weighed about 175 pounds in his later years.

b) Frank had an excellent seat which was similar to the one used by the vaqueros[15] and in classical dressage.[16] Both the vaquero and classical seats are ergonomically correct because they have been designed to maximize efficiency and comfort for both rider and horse. Frank's comments on sitting in the saddle are presented in Part III.

c) Another factor is a saddle that puts the rider in the correct position. Frank started out using a McClellan saddle. Frank comments,

"The McClellan Saddle has been use by the army since I can remember and I've heard it praised highly all my life, by Cavalrymen who had to do real riding. ... I've ridden enough miles in the old McClellan Saddle to girdle the globe and miles to spare - it was made for real riding men who knew how to appreciate a good seat in rough country and long trails."[17]

A McClellan saddle is shown in the photograph on the next page. All of these saddles had stirrup hoods, but the fenders were an option. They could be attached to the stirrup leathers to protect the rider's legs.

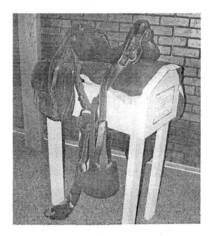

The western saddle was developed by the Mexican vaqueros. The first cowboy saddle was a Mother Hubbard and it was a vaquero saddle covered with leather.[15] When Frank was with Bill's show, this is the type of saddle he used. A Mother Hubbard saddle is shown in the photograph below.

c) Frank soon learned to use mustangs with exceptional endurance for his rides and his breeding program was designed to produce outstanding ones. Since his horses grew up on the high plains; in lower altitudes, they would have had more energy and endurance than horses who were raised in a lower altitude. Frank may have well understood what an advantage this gave them, but all of his opponents might not have been aware of it. His opinions on the right type of horses for endurance riding will be presented in Part III.

d) Experience had taught him to utilize the procedures described below.

To keep his horses comfortable, he always rode them in hackamores and never forced their heads into any type of artificial position.

After each day's ride, he used a special care routine.

He always started slowly. We now know this gave his horse time to find his second wind and his metabolism time to adjust to the stress of competitive endurance riding.

He let his horse tell him how much distance he could handle on each individual day. We now know that varying workouts from hard to easy to medium is the way to maximize the horse's efficiency will minimizing the stress on his body.

More information on these procedures will be presented in Part III.

Conclusion (Chapter 11):

Today Frank would be called a natural horseman and a horse whisperer. In my opinion, his reputation as a person and a horseman had to be validated before his writings on horses, horsemanship, and endurance riding could be taken seriously. Most of what he said is just as true today as it was one hundred years ago.

Acknowledgements:

Photo 1 courtesy of Albert W. Harris.

Footnotes:

[1]"Keep Your Horse Happy", Letter 4, Hopkins Papers, Robert Olney Easton Collection, American Heritage Center, University of Wyoming. Reprinted in Part III.
[2]Hopkins, Frank, "1800-Mile Trail Ride-Texas to Vermont", Vermont Horse and Bridle Trail Bulletin, April, 1940, pp. 43-44, 63-64.

[3]Hopkins, Frank T., "Mustangs", Vermont Horse and Bridle Trail Bulletin, Jan., 1941, pp. 2-3.

[4]Hopkins, Frank. "Buffalo Bill as I Knew Him", Vermont Horse and Bridle Trail Bulletin, Oct. 1942, pp. 151-154.

[5]Hopkins, Frank T., Memoir, Letter 1, Addendum, p. 3. Hopkins Papers, Robert Olney Easton Collection, American Heritage Center, University of Wyoming.

Gertrude Hopkins to Robert Easton, letter dated Oct., 1968, p. 2. Hopkins Papers, Robert Olney Easton Collection, American Heritage Center, University of Wyoming.

[6]Hopkins, Gertrude A., "Carrying 'Notes' for 'Uncle Samuel'", Vermont Horse and Bridle Trail Bulletin, April, 1944, pp. 49-50.

[7]Article 19, "Hidalgo", in www.frankhopkins.com.

[8]Hopkins, Frank, "The Truth About 'Buffalo Bill'", Vermont Horse and Bridle Trail Bulletin, Oct. 1944, p. 121.

[9]Schaefer, Jack. The Great Endurance Horse Race. Stagecoach Press, 1963, p. 8.

[10]"Summary of a Half Century's Events, Deed, Exploits, and Achievements in Buffalo Bill's Active Life", p. 3. Hopkins Papers, Robert Olney Easton Collection, American Heritage Center, University of Wyoming.

[11]Gertrude Hopkins to Robert Easton, letter dated 4-25-79. Hopkins Papers, Robert Olney Easton Collection, American Heritage Center, University of Wyoming.

[12]Wingate, Harvey P., Introduction."1800-mile Trail Ride - Texas to Vermont", Vermont Horse and Bridle Trail Bulletin, April, 1940, pp. 43.

[13]Dary, David. Cowboy Culture. NY, Alfred A. Knopf, 1981, p. 278.

[14]Dickey, E. M. to Robert Easton, undated letter, p. 2-3. Hopkins Papers, Robert Olney Easton Collection, American Heritage Center, University of Wyoming.

[15]Ladendorf, Janice M. Spanish Horsemen and Horses in the New World. CreateSpace, 2015, Chapter 5.

[16]Loch, Sylvia. The Classical Seat: A Guide for Everyday Riders. Unwin Hyman, 1988.

[17]Hopkins, Frank T. Answers, letter 6, pp. 12-13, Hopkins Papers, Robert Olney Easton collection, American Heritage Center, University of Wyoming.

Part III: Articles and Comments by Frank T. Hopkins
Introduction: Mustangs (Old Spanish)

During his fifty years of competing in endurance races, Frank Hopkins used what he described as American mustangs or Indian ponies. He also called them old Spanish. As a mustang advocate, he has always been popular with all those who fought to preserve these unique horses. The photograph above is of a modern Spanish Mustang named **Little Hawk.** He was owned by Ashley Newkirk from Apache Trails Ranch in Arizona. In my opinion, he might resemble Frank's powerful horse, Turk, who is described in Chapter 6.

The Spanish conquistadors brought horses with them when they came to the New World and took them along where ever they settled in North and South America. When the Pueblo Revolt drove them out of Santa Fe in 1680, they left behind hundreds of fine horses. Historians believe these horses were the foundation stock for the mustangs Americans eventually found roaming our Great Plains. Since initially they were the only horses out there, they were the horses the Indians rode, as did the early fur traders, explorers, and cowboys; but Americans preferred bigger horses like the ones they had known in the east and soon began importing them.

In Frank's day, descendants of the Spanish horses still existed, but were rapidly disappearing. A few dedicated men recognized their value and began a long struggle to preserve their unique bloodlines. The Spanish Mustang Registry was started in 1957 and other organizations followed. Today they are grouped together as Spanish Colonial Horses.

Since Frank refused to sell his horses, their bloodlines have been lost, but all these registries draw from the same root stock of Spanish horses. Wild horses still exist in the West, but few of them now carry any Spanish bloodlines. When these horses are captured, they can be adopted; but they will have an ID number branded on their necks.

Since there are so few photographs of Frank's horses and not many people are familiar with the Spanish Colonial breeds, some more photographs of horses from the Spanish Mustang Registry are shown below. The horse in the first picture is **Yellow Fox.** He was named for the Cheyenne Indian who bred him. He was one of the foundation stallions of the Spanish Mustang Registry and was owned by the Cayuse Ranch in Wyoming. In this picture, Mrs. Emmett Brislawn is riding him. The second horse is his son, **Chief Yellow Fox**, and he was owned by Kim Kingsley of Horsehead Ranch in Breien, ND. The third horse is **American Yellow Fox**, who is currently owned by Nancy Rasmussen of Free Spirit Spanish Mustangs in Wisconsin. He is the horse on the cover. All three are buckskins like Frank's Joe.

The first horse in the second group is **San Domingo**, who is another one of the foundation stallions of the Spanish Mustang Registry. He was owned by the Cayuse Ranch in Wyoming and being ridden by Mrs. Emmett Brislawn. Although he is a medicine hat paint; without his winter coat, he could resemble Frank's Hidalgo. The second horse is **Chief San Domingo** who was owned by Kim Kingsley of

Horsehead Ranch in Briein, ND. The third horse is **Blue Diamond Domingo**, who was owned by Mrs. Robin Sackett from Free Spirit Spanish Mustangs in Wisconsin.

The horse shown below belongs to the author. He comes from both of the bloodlines described above. His sire was **Chief San Domingo** and his dam was sired by **Chief Yellow Fox.** His name is **Skandranon Rashkae.**

Acknowledgements:

Photos 2 and 5, courtesy of Josie Brislawn. Photos 1, 2, and 6, courtesy of Kim Kingsley, Photos 4 and 7, courtesy of Nancy Rasmussen.

Part III - Articles and Comments by Frank T. Hopkins
Section A: Unpublished Material

Editor's Note: Minor punctuation and spelling errors have been corrected. Bold face in texts has been used to emphasize key points.

1)"Keep Your Horse Happy: How to ride hundreds of miles over unknown country without tiring your horse". As told to Charles B. Roth by F. T. Hopkins.

"Keep Your Horse Happy", Robert Easton Collection, Letter #4, Robert Oley Easton Collection, American Heritage Center, University of Wyoming.

Editor's Comment: This manuscript was dated August. 1940 and prepared for publication in the "Polo" Magazine. By this date, the magazine no longer existed and the editing was never completed.

If there's any accomplishment an outdoor man ought to have it's horsemanship. By that I don't mean the kind of horsemanship that passes on the bridle path, the polo field, or the show ring or hunting course; these are play - **the real horsemanship I refer to is the kind that enables a man to start with a single horse, ride several hundred miles or several thousand miles over unknown country and bring the same horse back in as good condition as the day he left.**

I suppose it's really a lost art in this country, horsemanship, because there is no call to master it as there was when I was a boy over sixty years ago. Still, I don't know. This horse is coming back in certain districts; notably out West, horse vacations are becoming more popular. On the whole, I still think that every man to call himself fully accomplished ought to know horsemanship.

The principles are really not difficult to learn - there are so few they are so simple. Putting them into practice really takes more time but even the practice of horsemanship can be mastered by any man who has the patience to learn the wonderful organization of the horse - what it is capable of doing, how to make it do its utmost, and what a fascinating subject this is!

In more than sixty years of intensive horsemanship which includes winning more long rides than any other horseman, I have discovered that the most important factor in horsemanship is the horse's mental attitude. That sounds like equine metaphysics. You may think that I'm about to start telling you of a horse I once had that could think as well as a Senator but I'm not. **All I mean by this statement is that a good horseman is one who keeps his horse happy at all times. A happy horse will work; an unhappy one will not.** That always gave me more concern than any other thing on my long rides, keeping my horse happy. I knew its importance. If my horse was happy, free from irritation or worry he would deliver the very last ounce of energy he has. But if he were fretted, worried, filled with care or fright, he would be under par. Then I would lose.

I like to see my mount throw his ears forward, look at the road and take in everything that is going on, not paying the slightest attention to me on his back - that's a happy horse for you. **But how do you get a horse to be happy and how do you keep him that way? It starts with adjusting yourself to the horse, not trying to make the horse adjust himself to you.**

Take the matter of gaits, a very important matter. Many horsemen believe that the rider should decide what gaits the horse should use. I've always believed that this is putting the wrong end to - I let the horse decide which gait suits him best, then I conform. It seems more sensible to reform the rider than to try to reform the horse. Learn the gait that comes natural to your horse; then ride him that gait.

To give you a personal example: In my long distance rides I always rode loping horses, not every horse I tried, when I was selecting my mounts, was a loper. Some were trotters, some pacers, some were runners. The ordinary way would have been to take a natural trotter and train him to lope out for me. I disposed of the trotter and tried until I got a horse that loped by nature.

I know that many horsemen - those who train bridle-path horses especially, engage in a process know as "gaiting". But I'm not talking of bridle-path horses. I'm talking of the horses that a man rides - really rides. **So I say my first rule of horsemanship is to become acquainted with your horse.**

Then, the selection of the right kind of horse has a good deal to do with having a happy horse. I always chose level-headed horses at least, that's what I call them. Some horsemen call them just plain lazy. It didn't make me angry. I suppose they were lazy. They would work all right, but I had to make them work. **Still, in every long distance race I ever entered I always crossed the line ahead of the rest. The reason is that my level-headed horses worked without worry. They didn't fret or stew about anything they couldn't help. At night they would sleep as well in a strange stall as they would at home. The energy which high-strung fellows used up in needless worry, my lazy boys used to win races for me.**

The way a man sits his horse has much to do with how the horse feels about life, too. Ride a horse properly and he will carry you with a minimum of discomfort to himself - also to you. Ride him improperly and neither of you will have much fun. I had to learn the proper and easiest way to ride my horses because riding with me wasn't sport - it was life. At the age of 13 I was carrying dispatches for the U.S. Army in Wyoming and Montana, riding 60, 70, 80 miles a day. When a man has to do that he soon seeks the easiest way to ride.

That way is the old time plains style of riding, not often seen these days. Old time plainsmen always rode with a real long stirrup so that their legs were almost straight. They sat down close to the leather of their saddles and stayed right there. No jouncing around, no bouncing up and down, no letting air or scenery between knee and their saddles. They really rode, those old boys did. This style of riding was much easier on the horse than today's. Riders now ride all over the horse from neck to crop, throwing him off balance by shifting that heavy weight here and there, and tiring him out. When you ride, let down to the leather. Stay there. It's hard, I know. Few men I see nowadays can do it. But when you find one who can, horseback riding is a graceful, beautiful accomplishment.

To ride properly you have to acquire a sense of balance. Actually, all there is to riding is just that - balance - your own and your horse's, only practice will give it to you. If you sit down tight in the leather, keep poised and balanced so that no matter which way the horse goes it doesn't disturb your balance, you are really riding.

If a man rides a horse correctly and keeps the horse happy in his work, he can get unbelievable service out this hardy animal. Horses vary just as humans do, however. Some are 50 mile-a-day riding animals, others will bat out 80 or 90 miles and be ready to do the same job the next day. The farthest I ever rode in a day was 124 miles; did it in twelve hours; I had to. I've heard of men riding 150, 200 miles a day, but I always thought too much of a horse to ride him till he dropped.

Proper grooming is another phase of horsemanship that is important if a man wants to get the most out of his horse. My methods differ from those of many horsemen. I don't believe in over-coddling or over-grooming. Most horsemen believe in both or seem to. I really believe fussing with a horse, bandaging his legs and tendons and hour-long brushing does more harm than good.

This is how I handle my horses; first I brush them to keep their hides clean, but I never rub or fuss with them when they should have rest. If my horse has had a hard day I clean his hide, wash out his mouth and sponge off his back where it is wet and tender from saddle; then I give him a good bye and let him rest. Next morning, he's ready to duplicate the job he did before.

In feeding a horse there is no need to go to outlandish extremes. Common sense is the best. Oats and timothy hay will keep a horse fit. In my long distance races I used to feed half a dozen eggs plus a little raw chapped steak with the oats. These gave a little extra endurance the next day. But this specialty feeding is not necessary for ordinary riding. You can't fool a horse by feeding him improperly. **A horse doesn't lie. At least, I never knew one that did. Feed him the right way and his condition will tell the truth.**

You can loiter around a horse ring or stable any day and hear much argument about this breed or that being better, about horses of a certain height being ideal, about this or that weight being preferred. But I'll tell you what more than 60 years on horseback have taught me about it. **A horse is no smaller than his ability and no worse; it depends entirely upon the horse, not upon his ancestors, size, weight, color or conformation.**

I've been in horse outfits that had ponies weighing 700 to 800 pounds who could carry an 180 lb man and a 40 pound saddle for ten hours a day, day in and day out. In same outfits I've seen big 1,000-1,200 horses that couldn't stand the work and could be used only 2 or 3 times a week. You can't tell much by size or looks. Sometimes the most likely lookers will prove to be the most useless, while a horse that doesn't look like ten cents will win honors. My only rule in selecting a horse is to make sure he has the right bone and muscle and is put together in the right way.

Of course I have ideals - all horsemen have. My ideal is a horse that weights not over 950 pounds. I want him short in the back, well ribbed out to the hips, with long muscles that cover the kidneys. I want him fairly long in the hip, with fairly straight hind legs, closely linked between joints. I want him with deep shoulders and well muscled forearm. I don't care a rap for his color, but insist that he have strong bones and close linked joints. If I have a horse of this kind, I have all the horse I want or any man needs. And if there's a long distance race in prospect, a race anywhere from 500 to 2,500 miles in length I'd be most willing to wager that when the judges come into the roadway to meet the winner it will be this horse with me on his back.

Editor's Note: The above information may have been edited by Charles B. Roth or Gertrude Hopkins. At this point, the article shifts to Frank's natural style.

I read with interest of a number of endurance races that have been held lately. All the horses were of thoroughbred blood - either 1/2 bred or 3/4 bred. One of these races was held by the cavalry. The horses entered were bred by the Remount Society. Riders were officers of the Cavalry and I notice all used a type of English flat saddle. The article also had pictures of the horses. I must say they were a good-looking lot so far as looks go - but since I've spent a long time as an endurance rider I rode against every type of horse in the world. I wouldn't pick one of those horses for long, hard ride. **It's true, our Cavalry of today does not need a hardy horse as it did years ago and I can recall when there was real hard work for the horse of the Cavalry on the Western Plains. Often, there were rides of 250 miles and those horses carried their riders and a number of extra pounds of equipment. On those rides the horses got their feed by grazing and sometimes they were out of the forts 2-3 weeks at time with very little care. Still, they made good or better time than the long-legged horses of today, they were fine horses of the Vermont Morgan blood in those days - the rest were just horses of no particular breeding, most of the hardiest ones mustang, or old Spanish as they were called.** Those actually did their work under the McCelland Saddle and made as good a time as the horse who is used and trained for an endurance race today and few of them walked back to camp for they were riding a saddle that was hard to put them out of. They also rode with a straight leg and if their mount went down they didn't go over his head and then walk miles behind the mount into camp.

It is all very nice to attend a horse show and watch the movements of a good performer, but that horse in the show ring is not in any way an endurance horse and there's no use in trying to make him one tho' for the past 30 years I've noticed horsemen in our country tried to make the thoroughbred or horses of that blood endurance horses. It can't be done -- no more now than it could years ago. I spent a lot of money and time trying to make them long distance horses and it just can't be done -- they are too high off the ground for one thing; their necks are too long; most of them use up their energy with their action and style. If they are in a distance race and there are no other horses allowed it except those of their own breed, well, there is bound to be one horse that is a little better than the others - but let one rider in that race be mounted on one of those old Spanish or Indian ponies -- a yellow pony of any shade of that color from copper to cream, or one of those spotted ponies - give the rider time to train that pony for the race then stake the trail so every rider will be compelled to cover every foot of it, say nothing about the "style" of riding. (That is show ring stuff) don't mention anything about the weight any of the horses carry or about a horse being tired (if a horse travels many miles a day, he'll surely be tired at the end of it). It's a real endurance horse than can start out the next day as fresh as he was in the beginning. A horse that requires bandaging of the tendons is not worth fooling with as an endurance horse. If his legs can't carry him and remain in normal condition, that hoss would get no more training from me but someone else would own him as soon as I could find a buyer.

The thoroughbred is a grand horse in his place and that place is in a mile race track: he has been bred for that purpose from the beginning of his race (blood). There isn't any horse any other class of horse that can take his place a fast running racer. There are many horses that can do better work in rough country and who can stand more real hard work.

I rode my first endurance race back in 1877 -- a ride of 350 miles on rough trails which had been marked so every rider had to cover the ground; I rode a dun colored Indian pony who weighed less than 800 pounds. General Alfred Terry was the judge. All of the other nine riders were mounted on Army horses weighing from 1000 to 1200 pounds. My pony came in eight hours ahead of the rest. From that ride until my years ruled me from the saddle, **I've ridden endurance races and a lot of them and my mounts have always been the Indian pony or old Spanish.** They were the 1st horses on this continent brought here by the Spanish and have more endurance than any other horse in the world. In my many long races not one of these little yellow horses ever failed me: they are also the most sure-footed horses alive; they can share real hardship with the riders and still carry them. **They are game until they draw their last breath**. I never saw one with a shaky forward leg (knee sprung) or a curby hind leg; they are too close to the ground and muscled as no other is yet they have been overlooked and almost forgotten. Most horsemen today might call a man a liar if he told them that he rode one of those 100 miles a day for several days and all the food the horse got was from grazing and that only when the rider stopped to rest and the grazing was not of the best at that, yet there are men still living today who can back up that statement. I know of several. King Stanley rode 700 miles on one of my own horses. I doubt if this can be said of any other horse. This horse has several different Spanish names for different types of this horse yet they are much the same only different in color: some are spotted with odd marking about the head and face: the yellow ones run in many shades as I said before - from copper to buckskin and cream color even pure white (albino) there are a few men who have preserved his blood and I hope breeders don't get the idea that crossing that blood with thoroughbred will improve that hardy little horse.

I often read of crossing heavy breeds with thoroughbred, such as Percherons, Clydesdales and Belgians. Those horses are bred for heavy work -- draft horses. They should not be driven out of a walk. That sort of breeding looks to me like a violent [bad] cross; it surely is too violent [ridiculous] and to horse breeders it appears so, for I notice they breed the first cross back to the thoroughbred, and before this breeding is done the raisers have nothing but a thoroughbred in the end --- a tender, thin skinned animal who requires a lot of care, also a hoss that doesn't have "brains". You can teach him, but it takes a long time to learn him anything for he's been bred up for centuries only as a fast running horse and he was not required learn anything only to run between two fences in a circle (fence outside and inside, race track). There isn't another strain of horse living who can take the place of a thoroughbred on the race track and I say leave him at his job - that's what he was bred for - breeding him into a saddle horse of today is nothing more or less than a "style" that is floating over the country.

On the Bridle Path I saw a 90 lb girl on a big long-legged horse - the larger the hoss the better they like 'um but they look out of place. It amuses me to see a man or woman sitting back in the middle of tall rangy hoss with knees bent as though sitting in a chair and at every step taken by the mount the rider goes up out of the saddle (if it can be called one). In their hands most riders hold lines enough to rein in a four-horse team. These riders are taught by a riding master, but is this great horsemanship? It's a good thing for those horses that bridle paths are not many miles long. A rider who can sit tight in his seat as though he were part of the horse can ride the same horse day after day without wearing his mount out, but the few who can ride in this style are not on the bridle path nor did they learn from riding masters - they learned from years of experience riding in rough country and those riders could not ride that smooth level style on long-legged top heavy horses.

To return to endurance races:

Editor's Note: The rest of this article was published on the Hopkins website under the title of "Training Endurance Horses". It is article 26, but it was never published in the Vermont Horse and Bridle Trail Bulletin. This fact was confirmed by the Vermont Historical Society.

There are things to remember in training an endurance horse. First of all, don't let anyone give you advice - if you are not a horseman enough to know your mount, don't enter a distance race. Remember, all horses cannot be put in condition on the same amount of weighed feed. It is better to forget weighing - watch your horses' condition and feed him accordingly.

It's the duty of any good endurance rider to care for his horse himself, also his duty to bring his horse in well cooled at the end of each day, so the rider don't have to spend time cooling the horse when his mount should be resting. **One of the things an endurance horse needs most is - rest.** A horse who requires false courage, such as giving him stimulants of whiskey or anything of the sort is not a fit horse to ride in an endurance race.

Stopping a horse for 2 or 3 hours to rest is a very bad thing on a long ride. You will find after a rest of any length of time your mount will lag and get weary. If your horse has been well trained and put in condition for such a ride, it is the duty of the rider to dry his horse out on the last week or few days of the training, so the horse will not crave too much water when he is put to the hard work of the long travel of the race. Don't speak to your horse unless it is necessary or shift about in the saddle, for those simple things really fret your horse more than anything else.

Be sure you have the right agreement before you start to train - that the road you are to cover is marked so every rider must cover every foot of the ground: leave the compass and foolish things at home - they're only extra weight. If the road is marked every mile or two and at the parting of tracks or where roads cross or turn off; then each rider can go along without delay. Bright red paint daubed on trees, stones or fences, makes good marking. If the land is clear of these things, then stick a small stake on the ground and paint the top red. If you don't have this agreement signed, some riders may cut across country and make miles on you.

If your horse seems tired at night, get him to rest as soon as possible: don't keep him on his feet, rubbing and fooling with him. I always taught my horses to lie down by the command "lay down". Once they were down they would not get on their feet again but would rest.

One more thing I always had signed - that is if I rode in a race and my horse came in first, there was no way of "gyping" me out of the money by claiming my horse was not sound at the time he finished the race or the next day. This thing of a horses' soundness is indeed queer. I've seen horses declared not sound by one veterinary and in just three hours afterward declared perfectly sound by another vet.

There is this question of points in a long ride. Now this is the only point that I would sign on and pay my entrance for. Here it is: if I cross the line first, I have won, if not, I have lost, this thing of barring a rider continuing in the ride because his horse appears tired, is all foolish. *If a horse is not in condition to carry his rider, the quirt or spur will not keep the horse going. Your mount will slow up - that is, if he has not the ability to push on rider will soon see he is not making any time and he is playing a loser's hand. Rider will give it up and pull out of the race without being told by the judge.* I've ridden many an endurance ride and must say my horses were tired at the end of each day - I was tired too. Any man who rides for ten hours will get tired, but with a good night's rest, both man and horse will feel fresh in the morning - that is, if both of the have been put in condition for the ride.

If there were two or three endurance rides held every year and they'd allow anyone to enter with a reasonable entrance fee to make it a worth while purse and have these rides run thru without so much red tape; there'd be a lot of riders and horsemen interested and a great chance to find out the best type of horse for endurance. Let every entrant train his own horse to suit himself alone, allow the entrant to ride in any style he chose, and allow rider to ride any size horse he brings along. The only rules he must live up to are that every rider must ride one horse all the way and that the horse should not be ridden over 10 out of 24. Each rider must ride these 10 hours at the same time, for if the day is warm some of the riders may want to ride at night and in order to be fair to the other riders, let 'em all ride at the same time. Here is a tip from an old timer - train your horse away from the other contestants - don't let anyone know you are training for a race, always be a lone wolf, watch your horse as you train him, it's most likely that the horse you think will win for you will be the first to go to pieces, but don't let your courage go with him.

Try one in your string who is lazy and sleepy but close to the ground. **A horse who has no style or extra action, who only puts one foot before the other, a horse that will go along all day without worry,** it's likely no one likes this type of horse: they'll tell you he's good for nothing but I'll tell you this describes a real endurance horse. There's a little yellow stallion lying beneath the soil of old Fort Laramie, Wyoming who never weighted over 800 lbs - often less. I've seen many riders in many lands and many different classes of horses in these races; I've read of long rides that were within the law and outlaw rides, but that little stallion was the greatest endurance horse that ever lived and I was his proud owner. He was a horse I** caught wild in the Shoshone Valley; to me he was like his color - a golden hoss. Horsemen then and today would not give $25.00 for him: he was lazy, his back was short without the least rise up the withers. He was very meaty in the hind quarters. He won five hard long rides for me - one across country from Texas to Vermont, the others were not easy rides. Riders don't pick style and action in your endurance horse, choose one who after he is trained can carry you fifty miles every day for two weeks - then you need not fear any of those long-legged narrow built, top heavy horses of today.

If you have been successful in training one endurance horse, don't think you can use the same methods in putting the next horse in condition for the same hard riding for I have not found two horses that can be conditioned in the same way. You'll have to watch and correct the least mistake in time (not wait till too late) and you cannot depend on training one horse twice in the same way. Your horse might harden to his training the first time very easily, a year later you might try to put him in shape for a long ride and find it all different from the previous training, though the horse may have more ability than before after he has gotten into condition.

I've learned that most horses are better on endurances rides after they are seven years old. I recall a horse I raised out of proven endurance stock. When he was five years old I started to put him in shape for a 500 mile ride. Although I began easy with him, the horse could not stand up under the training. I noticed this in less than a week. The horse was turned over to his old rider who rode him nearly every day cutting cattle. When this horse was 15 years old I heard riders telling how tough this little stallion was, so I took him in hand and soon found he could pound the road from daybreak till dark. I rode him in one of the hardest rides of my career, this horse was as tough as they came, yet he could not stand easy training when he was five years old; the same horse won a 250 mile race when he was 20 years old. So you can't tell by looking at them what they can do; but if you pick one who hasn't too much daylight under his belly, a horse with a short neck well set back on his shoulders so his head hanging out there at the end of his neck will not tire him too much like it does those long slim-necked horses, then you're coming nearer to a horse who might be a real endurance horse; still, there's only one thing that will prove it, and that is the training. If the horse shows the least signs of weakening, don't fuss with him trying to patch him up by bandaging his tendons and other foolish things; for if the horse's running gear can't carry him, the horse is not sound nor fit for that kind of work. You are only putting in your time for nothing.

I've seen a lot of that kind of horsemanship but there's really nothing to it.

Editor's Comments:

*Given the number of races driven to their death in the early races, this statement is naive, but Frank is correct that tiredness alone should not disqualify a horse

**"I" may have been error. Frank did not catch Joe (see chapter 2).

2) Horses

Comment from Memoir:
Frank's Trip to Mongolia in 1906
Prewalski's Horse pp. 36-7

"Many wild ponies in the southwest - a different horse from those used by the herdsmen. The wild pony has a stub mane - much like the zebra - that grows about three inches long. The ponies are all of one color - a dark buckskin, or a blend of buckskins, and they are built all alike. Of all the species of the horse family, they are the most vicious - no way to gain their friendship and you can not subdue them under any conditions. I think I have as much patience as anyone, but I gave up the job of gentling them although I surely gave it a trial. The natives, afraid of these horses, will have nothing to do with them.

I heard how these horses could hold their own against wolves, etc., that they would gang together and kill large wolves and also men who bothered them. I came to believe it after I tried to catch a pony from a small band. I got the pony, but if my horse was not faster than the bunch I'd have been killed for these ponies tried to gang me. They swung in a circle and charged, striking with their forward feet.

I got a colt of about three years. I had learned if I stopped my horse and stood still, those ponies would stop their charging, so I roped this pony and set my horse at the end of the rope; they circled to charge, but when my horse stood, holding the pony, the band of ponies came to a stand. Some of them pawed and squealed, others whistled their defiance, but they didn't come closer. I had to drag that pony for he would not lead - choking made no difference and he tried to knock me out of the saddle. I roped nine of these ponies - every one was the same. The stories were true - they can't be handled."

3) Horsemanship

Comments from Answers to Letters:

Feed (pp. 8-9)

"Feeding good hay - say Timothy - and oats are best feeds I know for all kinds of horses. Some people feed other grain, but hay and oats are best.

When on hard rides, I fed chopped beefsteak with the oats when I could get the horse to eat it - about 1 1/2 pounds - at night, and a dozen fresh eggs mixed with the oats in the morning - some horses don't eat them. My Joe would eat both and all of the Whitey family would eat both eggs and meat. It is not good practice however to keep them on this diet - only when you put hard work to them. When my horses are not working hard I always give them a bran mash every Saturday night to loosen them up; this keeps their bones in good condition.

Some horses will eat more oats than others yet not keep in good condition. Such horses need attention - there's something wrong with them. The least thing wrong with your horse will show on his coat. He may appear in good spirits but if his hair looks dull there is something wrong. All the brushing, rubbing will not make it look right.

Any man who says a horse that works does not need grain and hay is too mean to give it to him. A horse can work on grass feed, but he will get thin and worn in a short time. The early grass in Spring is very weakening to the horse. After July, the grass gets harder and is better for the horse, but he should be fed hay and oats if he is to do any work.

Some years ago I wintered in Plainfield, N.J. A man visited my stable nearby and said "How good your horses look - mine are thin and rough looking - how do you keep um slick and fat all winter?" I said "I give um hay and oats, I don't show or promise them feed - I give it to um." If one feeds a horse right the horse tells the story - if not, the story is there just the same. In all my years being around a horse I never saw one who told a lie."

Grooming (p. 10)

"I always cleaned my horses - brushed them to keep their hides clean - but not as some who bother a horse by rubbing and fussing over him when the horse should rest. If my horse has worked hard, I clean his hide of dust, wash out his mouth, sponge his back with a moist sponge - not too wet so the water runs down his sides - give him a good bed and let him REST. Too much fussing is no good.

I once heard a horseman say that to give a horse an hour's cleaning was as good as two pounds of oats. I told him it was better to give the tired horse that hour to rest in and there would be no need to give the extra feed. If a horse is kept in good health his hide will look good without rubbing. Clean the dust from his hair - that's about 15 minutes work - and he will look just as good as if 3 hours were spent on him everyday. My experience with Arab horsemen showed me that they firmly believe in caring for their horses much as I do. They simply brush the dust from their hair and they never bandage or hood them."

Additional Comment from Miscellaneous Notes in Hopkins Collection: When Frank T. Hopkins was a guest at the Cavalry School in Vienna, he saw their horses. He was not too interested in the white gloves the men wore to stroke the horse's backs to show how clean they were. He asked them if they ever picked out the horses hoofs!

Sitting on a Horse (p. 4)

"I explained that in a previous letter I never grip my saddle in any way - just keep my balance and go with the horse. When a man rides long hours in rough country then beds down for the night and gets up the morning to face another day for a whole week at a time as I did, while a dispatch rider (for 8 years), he will learn the easiest way for himself and learn how to keep his horse under him. I can't explain it any plainer - it just came to me thru many hours of riding.

I started riding when I was very young and I recall riding without stirrups a little squaw pony my grandfather brought to me for my birthday. My father would not allow me to use stirrups for a long time until I had learned to keep balanced and "go with the horse" as he called it. It's true a rider can ride with his feet hanging but there is no way of bracing - that is if your horse turns short or if you wish to charge him short to stop suddenly* - it is best to have your feet in the stirrups. I always later rode with long stirrups - half of my weight in the seat and half in the stirrup - just so my feet got a grip. Many Mexicans ride in the old style today - they have more riding to do than the man in the States.

If I attempt to teach someone to ride I expect him to ride without stirrups until he has learned to keep perfect balance and that cannot be done with short stirrups. It is my habit to ride with my feet braced out away from the horse. This is a help in rough country where a horse might swing off short in order to pass something in the dark - maybe a rattlesnake - it has saved me from hitting the ground many times. The longer stirrup will not tire the rider as quickly and the rider cannot bounce around on his horse with a straight leg**. If a man rides long enough with a long stirrup to master the art he will not change.

I've had many great horsemen and women come to me on the quiet after one of my performances and offer to pay a good price if I'd teach um how to sit tight in the leather. Being know as a 'square shooter' I tell them the truth - it can be done maybe in 10 years of hard riding in rough country with rough horses."

*Editor's Definition 1: What this phrase would mean today is "setting the horse up for a quick stop."

**Editor's Definition 2: This phrase does not refer to posting, but to riding in a western saddle with a shorter stirrups.

Editor's Comment: Frank learned by experience. He knew what to do and how to do it, but not the principles on which an ergonomic seat is based. What he is advocating is similar to the classical dressage seat which is taught in the Spanish Riding School of Vienna. Learning to use it well requires years and a lot of riding without reins or stirrups, as well as special exercises.

Staying with a Twisting Bronc (pp. 13-14)

"First, the men in my day had to learn how to ride i.e. - to sit tight and have complete balance of themselves and horse. Once a man has mastered this he can ride any bucking horse until the jarring hurts him enough that the rider slides off of his own accord or someone picks him off the bronc. I've been unloaded often - anyone can get 'throwed' but if a man can ride in the old style it's just a matter of getting out of balance if he's thrown or if the hoss hurts him bad enough he will leave the leathers. It used to be a disgrace among horse breakers to leave the saddle before the horse quits. I'll tell anyone who asked me how to ride a bucker - to step up on a good-mannered horse and let me see him ride - then I could tell him if it were possible for him to stay with a rough one. I always rode buckers in the same way I rode the well mannered horse - got as close to the leather as I could and stayed there, placed my chin on my breast (the horse couldn't snap my neck) then left the rest of the work to the bronc - to buck till he was tired; I never made a noise hooten' and yellen' cause it only helps spoil the hoss and his 1st lesson he never forgets."

Riding over Jumps (pp. 14-15)

"I never took my horse's head away from him when jumping. You understand I never pulled on the lines to help my horse over a jump. I rode the same way always - the balance is the main thing at all times; to learn slightly forward when the horse raises himself to go over a jump helps him to balance; but to throw both feet forward and pull as hard as you can on a horse's mouth where he lights on his feet is far from helping your mount - it is at this state where most horses fall, if you've noticed a horse will not fall when jumping if there is no one on his back, so give him free rein and keep your balance when riding. Stay down in the saddle so not to make him top heavy, so you won't beat your horse over the jumps or throw him. Of course you'd not be classed as a stylish rider but you'll be saved from saying 'good morning nurse'. I never cared about jumping my horse unless it was necessary."

NB: [from Gertrude]: "He [Frank] said it was ruinous to the horse's kidneys."

Editor's Comment: Frank is correctly describing the old fashioned hunt seat. The modern jumping seat did not reach the United States until the 1930's when the cavalry began using it.

4) Endurance Riding

Comments from Answers to Letters

Long Rides Horsemanship (pp. 6-8)

"A man could ride any way he pleased, handle his horse as he likes.

Speaking of gaits a man must handle his horse to his gait - not try to change the horse from one gait to another. Any horseman can soon find out which gait suits his horse best. Some will trot if you start them up - others will swing into a rolling lope. Remember, there's a big difference between loping and running. If a horse runs he cannot stick to it long. Most big horses run. What I mean by running is a horse raises his feet high from the ground - too much work to cover the ground - the horse thus tires quickly no matter how tough he may be - for all 4 feet are off the ground at once - the hoss exerts himself too much to last very long. Any horse who tries to run will never make a long distance mount. It's better to trot such a horse - as for me, it's far better to get another horse and let one of those bouncing riders have the trotter.

My Joe could lope as slow as he could walk and he would swing into a lope just as soon as I picked up the rein. He didn't like to trot - it was same with him as any other horse I rode or owned - I let them travel the way they wished to - because trying to change their gait from their favorite way of traveling - it don't work out right. If I have a horse and don't like his way of traveling I change the horse, not his gait. I always rode a true loping horse - either he loped or walked. The true loping horse never has but two feet off the ground at one time, the same as where trotting. *There's no use trying to teach a horse a gait you like best - he will go back to his own style just as soon as you let him alone - you've got to keep reminding him of it all the time. I like to have my horses happy all the time and let them travel as they wish - they stand up better. I found that a true loping horse will carry me more miles in a day than any other by letting him lope along for a while, then let him walk up grade and down. Never hurry your horse down grade if you want him to last.

Of course, the mustangs are natural lopers. Just try to change them and you have no horse left.

I never start off in a hurry when on a long ride. In morning I allow the horse to lope along for 5 or 6 miles, then I start him into a fore spread**. If the roads are heavy, I allow for that; also for dry, dusty roads - they are bad for the wind of your horse. If the hoss does not feel good, don't scratch him with the spurs in order to get mileage out of him - the next day he may swing along and make up for what you lost. They seemed to know this as well as I do. If it very hot, rest your hoss in the middle of the day - it's better for both of you - then make it up after sunset or before the sun is too high. If in hilly country or mountainous, spare you horse - shorten the mileage, keep him feeling good, happy and don't speak a word to him while you are on his back unless you really have to for there is nothing that will weary him like talking to him while you're up there. I like to see my mount throw his ears forward and look at the road ahead and take in everything along the ride and not pay the least attention to me on his back - just as if I were not there - that's a 'happy' hoss - nothing worries him."

Editor's Comments:

*Like a canter, a lope is a three beat gait. On one of the beats, the horse has two feet on the ground, but not on the other two. This sequence was not well understood until movie cameras were invented. A lope somewhat slower than a canter, but softer and easier to sit.

**Once the horse has been warmed up, "fore spread" means the rider has asked him to lengthen his stride.

Horses for Distance Riding (pp. 10-12)

"The level-head or "lazy" horse as he's called, will do his work without worry.

I would not think of riding one of those crazy high-strung animals for any length of time - i.e. mileage. I got over that sort of business years ago. In the 1st place, they can't stand the training for a long race. They haven't brains enough to care for themselves. People who think these horses have so much stuff in um never gave that high strung animal a thousand or more miles to prove his ability. I've never seen one who be trained for a really long ride. To me, they're more yard horses. They'll tear around and sweat for a while, then their heads will begin to come down out of the clouds and soon their noses will be close to the ground. I've made a good living over that kind - they have so much life and are so tough they must be ridden every day or they'll carry their rider out of the stable and it takes 3 men and a boy to hold um while they're mounted.

I've always used a sensible horse for long rides, - one who would walk all day if I don't call on him to shake it up. I can't find any fault with a horse who has sense to care for himself - they never worry. That is one of the secrets in long distance riding - take care your mount don't worry. Never put him put at night where there's going to be noise or anything that will disturb his rest. I always like stallions best they seem to have more sense than mares or geldings.

As I said, the 'lazy' horse if he is in good shape, can do his stuff but you'll have to make him do it and he will pay for his oats. I never used one that I did not have to make him pound the road. I never failed to see that finishing goal ahead of the rest of them, and out of many long rides I've taken part in I have only lost once although I came in three days ahead. They claimed I fouled.

I never struck a horse with a quirt. I never mounted a saddle without spurs on my boots but I did not use them to cut up the horse - just so he'd feel it or straighten him up. Most of my horses were eager to mind when I spoke to them and if I spoke a little sharp they don't get over it for some time.

There was a horse I raised and called PARNDER. That horse would really feel bad and all marked up if I spoke sharply to him. I was usually careful not to hurt his feelings. One thing that seemed to hurt him the most was for me to take hold of his reins and lead him - that is, when I walked beside him. He was as near human as an animal could be. Sometimes I'd forget and take hold of the reins - he'd stop and look at me as if to say "let go that rein I've sense enough to walk with you." He seemed to understand every time I spoke and I never had to speak a second time when asking him to do anything."

Part III: Articles and Comments by Frank T. Hopkins
Section B: Published Articles

Editor's Notes:

All these articles were published in the Vermont Horse and Bridle Trail Bulletin. Complete citations are given in Appendix A of Chapter 10. The publication date for each one is given after the title. Minor errors in punctuation and spelling have been corrected. Boldface has been used to highlight key points. Unfortunately, some negative editing has been done in two of the articles. The errors are identified and corrected in the comments at the end of the article.

1) Horses

Mustangs (January, 1941)

With the coming of the automobile, some thirty odd years ago, it looked like the horse was nearing the end of his long trail. Many ranchers and small horse-raisers were stuck with a lot of horseflesh on their hands they didn't know what to do with; they turned their breeding stock loose in the foothills where the horses shifted for themselves until the war started in Europe, then there was a great demand for war horses - every stockyard near a seaport was filled with range horses - most of them were not broke even to lead. In three years' time our country was really short of horseflesh for farm work and pleasure stock.

Now the tide has turned and with many horse organizations springing up in all parts of the country, the horse still has a bright spot in the sun. Within a single year there have been a number of trail-ride clubs showing up in different states. All of this means more horse raising. It seems to me that if these breeders would stick to one class of horse, instead of crossing on different breeds, our saddle horses would be worth raising. **There are good qualities in all breeds** - some for one use, such as the running horse who has been bred for racing one mile or two at great speed, yet that horse has not the bone and cords [tendons] required for endurance racing. **There are many breeds of horses for different uses and each of those breeds should be kept in its separate class. If our breeders keep on as they are now, crossing**

on all breeds, the horses of this country in a few years will be nothing but a lot of scrubs.

Let us look at this breeding right; what is a scrub? Is it not a horse that has the blood mixture of different strains? Most of my life has been devoted to the practical study, training, and riding of the endurance horse and I have not lived years enough to complete that interesting study, but there is one thing that I have surely learned after spending much money for horseflesh, and that is - the hot blooded horse has no endurance. He may do very well in his own class - there are bound to be some better than others of course, but put the real hard work to him with a little hardship mixed in and you will find out that those horses are just not there.

[1]As a dispatch rider for nine years during the Indian troubles on the Western Plains, I tried out many different strains of horse. That kind of riding was hard on the horse and if he didn't have the stuff in him you'd soon find it out. Two or three hundred miles on a single trip was not unusual. The horse had to get his feed from the ground - all the care he got was to have his back rubbed off with a handful of buffalo grass. There were times when I had to race my horse for hours in order to save my life. Again, I would have a running fight with Indian scouts who were always lurking in the hills; the luckiest rider and best horse went on - the other generally stayed on the spot. Sometimes, there were rivers, good and bad, you had to swim your horse across. The winters back in those days were a good colder than they are now and the storms more severe - driving blizzards, cutting winds, deep snow and only a trail to follow - no shelter of any sort to put into. In the winter I broke the limbs from cottonwood to feed my mounts and dug down into the snow where I slept in the blankets. Plenty of that kind of work and hardship will surely test out a horse. During those nine years -1877 to 1886 - I had lots of time to find that comfortable spot on the old pigskin covered McClelland saddle and to learn which type of horse could best stand up under real hardship. I rode the best of the Kentucky Whips owned by the Army; the more life and style they had at the start the more miles I had carry messages on foot![1]

I remember one fine looking horse, weighing over eleven hundred pounds; he was bred in Kentucky but he died out there in Nebraska. I rode him out of Fort Robinson (Chief Red Cloud's old agency). After riding him about a hundred miles, all four of his legs were swollen, his ears lopped down the side of this head like a pack mules and that horse

202

actually started to die under the saddle. I could not leave a played out horse for the wolves to tear to pieces, so I hung the saddle up in a tree and told that horse that he was discharged from the Army with my "forty-five". I trotted along until I got tired, then lay down on the trail to rest and got up to run again and in that way I delivered that particular message. It was the last Kentucky horse I would ride. The Fort I rode out of carried a string of ten or more Mustangs for my own use and none of those horses failed to make their trips. One, a little blueskin stallion of eight hundred and fifty pounds, carried me one hundred and twenty-four miles in twenty hours. I had to shove him on, for I was being followed by Indian scouts. When I reached Fort Lincoln, that pony was pensioned off and sent to Fort Robinson to spend the rest of his years which were thirty-six - a ripe old age for a horse but not unusual for a Mustang caught wild.

At the time of Chief Crazy Horse's campaign I rode out of Fort Robinson covering other Forts. On the first day of December, 1880, I was sent with a message to Fort Bridger, a ride of about a hundred and eighty miles. *[2]When I started, the sun was shining, the sky was clear and there was about three inches of light snow that had fallen during the night. As I rode along, mule deer scampered among the scrub cedars. Farther along, I saw the fresh hoofprints made by a band of wild ponies who had probably fled before a prowling cougar. Coming from the high ridge about me, I heard the bugle call of an elk. As I rode along I noticed the dark moving forms of the bison as they browsed in the valley below. A spotted eagle screamed as he soared in graceful circles above me. It seemed a fine winter's day and even the hills belonged to the man who rode them. When I stopped to graze, the long, streaming shadow of my pony was no longer visible for the sun was directly overhead (it was mid-day). I loosened the saddle girths and my pony shoved the snow aside with his nose searching for buffalo peas, while I nibbled away at the dried beef I'd taken from my saddle bag. I could easily see Harney Peak in the Black Hills, and off to the west, the Laramie Mountains, the day was so clear. That afternoon, I rode into higher country and at sundown I made camp against the ledge of a yellow crag.*[2] After breaking cottonwood branches for my pony, I built a bush lean-to; with a small case axe, I cut wood for fire. While I rested a friendly coyote sang his evening notes from a pinnacle of rock above me. I dropped off to sleep with memories of the day thoughts of morrow before me. Throughout the night the pony would call and half awake, I'd say, "all-right boy", knowing that the mountain loin the pony smelled would not come close to human scent, but circle at a safe distance.

Morning broke clear with a high wind, the sun throwing long, red streamers across the sky. The pony was nervous. He knew as well as I did, that there was something coming on that gale of wind, and red in the morning is a warning to the plainsman. I was young in years but old in plains experience. *[2]At midday, it began to snow and the wind howled through the ledges. I turned off my course and made for a pine and cottonwood grove in a large gulch. There I worked with my axe in a blinding storm until I had finished the shelter for the pony and myself. I cut light poles and wove cedar boughs through them. With a pile of cottonwood at one end of the lean-to we were out of the worst storm I can recall. It snowed three days and nights. Every night, after the storm, the large grey wolves came. I kept a fire burning at the entrance of the lean-to and sat there with my rifle across my knee - now and then I shot one of those prowlers and then there was a fight. In the morning I could see where they had torn the wounded wolves apart, leaving only the bones and tufts of hair. During the day I could sleep safely, but at night I guarded my horse. On the fourth day the food ran out and I dared not eat wolf because of the rabies germs they carry. There was not even a rabbit to shoot -the snow was too deep. About the eight day, I was feeling mighty weak and my lips were parched. On the following morning, I was forced to shoot my pony, skin his hip and slice off a piece of meat and eat it - warm and raw - I was really hungry. I stayed there for five long weeks - the horse meat froze solid and kept, and I ate it again, but roasted on a stick. Right there I learned that money isn't everything in a man's life, for I had four hundred dollars of good American money in my pocket - and would have starved to death but for the horse!

The weather suddenly got warmer and then came a drizzling rain which froze, making a heavy crust on the snow. I made a pair of snowshoes out of the horse's hide, and with a number of extra rawhide strings and a chuck of horsemeat lashed to my back, I started out for Fort Bridger.*[1] I made holes in the snow at night to sleep in (If one digs down always in the snow and has good blankets there is no danger of suffering from snow. *[1] In six days I delivered my message.*[1]

I stayed in the Fort until April, then brought back the answer to that message. My Mustang shared with me these hardships which no other horse could. This is only one experience out of many in those nine years.

I could tell of Mustangs that carried me out when I had been badly wounded, even to swimming streams with me when I was too weak to sit up in the leather. Those little fellows have no "Style" but for me there is not another horse on earth for intelligence and endurance and I have been in many countries to find it so.

I **have often been asked why the Mustangs should be hardier than other horses. For many years they have run wild on the Western Plains having been brought there by the Spaniards.** History reads that these horses were of the best Arab blood lines*[3]; on the Plains they had to fight the mountain lions, wolves, and other enemies; man also was their greatest foe. Due to droughts, they were often without water and feed was scarce. In winter they dug through snow and frost for feed. Often they were forced to eat brush, or starve. **Only the hardiest of them survived. There were no weaklings for breeding-stock in the spring.** Year after year these horses were bred from the hardiest stock known to horseflesh. Inbreeding made them small, but of great endurance. Our great West was conquered by the Mustang for it was not "foot" man's country and other horses could not stand the hardships. **I once heard Gen. George Crook say that if the cavalry could not overtake a band of Indians in two hours, it was best to give up the chase, for those wiry ponies would wear out all the horses on our frontier.** Don't get the cowpony confused with the Mustang - they are different types.

After the Geronimo Campaign in Arizona, I was relieved from duty and rode my buckskin stallion from Fort Apache, Ariz. to Fort Laramie, Wyo. Three months later I rode the same horse from Galveston, Tex., to Rutland, Vt. *[4]This horse had been caught from a wild herd and like most of kind he was tough. Although I owned him until he died, I never knew the limit of his endurance.*[4]

When I returned from Vermont I joined Col. W. F. Cody's Wild West Show. In the spring of 1887 I went with the show to Earle's Court Exhibition, London, Eng. Two months later I entered one of my ponies in a long race from Earle's Court to Land's End, Cornwall, Eng. That pony weighed 850 pounds and he covered that ride of some 158 miles in twenty-eight hours of actual travel and finished nine hours ahead of the next best horse.*[5a] I rode a number of endurance rides throughout Europe.

Our next trip was to the World's Fair, Paris, France (1890*[5b]) There I learned of a World's Horsemanship Contest to take place on the military grounds at Marseilles, this contest to be hell from 9:00 AM to 11. a.m. every day for one year.*[5c] *[6]I signed up and rode with picked cavalrymen of all nations of the world besides riding in two performances daily with the Cody Show. At the end of the of the contest my Mustangs were judged the most active for footwork and all around supreme for endurance and courage.*[6] A month later I was informed that the Congress of Rough Riders of the World intended to pay my expenses to Arabia where I would take part in the 3,000 race.*[5d]

The following spring, I shipped out of Genoa, Italy, for Aden, Arabia,*[5e] taking three of my Mustangs, ponies that I had bred, and got them up to 950 pounds. They were strong and wiry, with the best of bone and muscle. I was worried about the strange country that my horses were to travel, but soon learned there was nothing to worry about - they took to the sand like ducks to water. They were sheltered under canopies like Arabian horses and fed vetches and barley which they also took to kindly. *[7]I soon learned that they were the best lot of horse thieves in Arabia that could be found anywhere and why shouldn't they steal a good horse from a despised Christian? I reported my loss to Ras Rasmussen and in less than an hour my horse and the two thieves were brought before me. Ras handed me a whip with three lashes branching out form the handle and told me to use it on the culprits, but I refused, preferring to remain on friendly terms with these strange people. When the thieves fell to their knees in the sand praising Allah, I did the same and told them it was Allah who had saved them from the lash and brought my horse back to me.*[7]

The 3,000 mile race is held every year since the domestication of the horse which dates to BC*[5f] and I was the only rider other than an Arab to take part in it. *[8]The long ride started from Aden: a hundred of the finest desert horses and many from the limestone sections entered the race, the most perfect group of horses I ever expect to see - those from the desert were gray or white, those from the high land chestnut, some sorrel and a few black. The route led along the Gulf of Aden where the air was not too dry for our mounts; then the trail went along the seashore to Syria. We then turned from the sea and rode up the border between Syria and Arabia; part of the way was limestone and the rest flaming fine desert sand. Water was scarce, the air dry and hot.

The Arabian horses could get along without water pretty well, but my Mustang began to gain ground once he got into the desert although he got water only once a day. At times there was no water for almost two days, still my "Hidalgo" went on and at no time did he appear weakening although he grew gaunt and lost flesh. There were days of sand storms and then it was impossible to go on. Horse and rider rested between the camels that carried our feed. When a rider got out in the lead, two camels were sent ahead with him and these camels were changed three times on the ride. Many horses dropped out; when we entered the desert only five finished*8 and I was in Aden*5g thirty-six hours before the next horse came in and that is where the ride ended. Every rider had to follow the same route - the time lost through sand storms did not count for all riders fared alike. It was the horse that came in first who won the race, any horse who got back to Aden surely deserved his title as winner.

I also won a 500-mile ride in the limestone country with a half-brother of "Hidalgo" and a 150-mile in the sand desert with the third pony; they were all from the same stud, but from different mares. I left my three stallions with the great horseman Ras Rasmussen who was an Arab by birth but of Lybian extraction. He was a fine man and remained a true friend of mine until he passed on in 1918. "Hidalgo" died the following year, a fine little horse with an iron heart. I have been luck to raise and ride those hardy ponies, and have given special performances with them before crowned heads of Europe, contested in three World Horsemen contents, and also spent thirty-two seasons with the great showman, Col. W. F. Cody, but all the credit of those performances I give to those little Mustangs of our Western Plains.

Bulletin Editor Comments:"

[I spent a day with Frank Hopkins a short time ago and want to tell you that it was one I will not forget for some time. I am sure that there is not another man in this country who has had as many horse experiences. His reminiscences would fill many books.

Starting as a dispatch rider, during the Indian war, at twelve years of age, joining Buffalo Bill and starring with him for over thirty-two years, competing in horse races and endurance rides all over the world, and giving riding exhibitions before all the crowned heads of the world, his has been no ordinary life. We hope to have other articles, from time to time, by Mr. Hopkins - E.E.J.]

Editor's Comments:

*[1]Quoted in Chapter 2.
*[2]Quoted in Chapter 11.
*[3]The Arab and Barb horses have often been confused. There is no Arab blood in the Spanish horse, but they are closely related to the Barb horses of North Africa.
*[4]Quoted in Chapter 3.

*[5]Misleading Information (Negative editing)

a) On the Land's End race, distance and time is more accurately stated in Chapter 4.

b) The Paris exposition was held in 1889, not 1890.

c) Given the distance between Paris and Marseilles, Frank could not have traveled back and forth daily to contest in both places. Since the Exposition ran from May to October, the contest could only have lasted six months.

d) This invitation was not given in Nov. of 1889, but in July of 1890.

e) This statement implies the race was held in the summer of 1890. As was discussed in Chapter 8, racing in the summer was not feasible and the only date when it could have been held was in the winter of 1892-3.

f) There are conflicting stories about how long this race had been run. This statement implies it has been run since were horses were first domesticated. Since the Arabs did not have horses in classical times, this date would not have been possible.

g) The race did not end at Aden, but on the shores of the Mediterranean Sea.

Editor's Comment*[5]: Frank's memory was not infallible, but the quantity of errors suggest Gertrude may have been editing this material without Frank's knowledge.

*[6]Quoted in Chapter 8.

*[7]The story about the horse thieves may or may not be true. It sounds like another one of Gertrude's attempts to present her husband as a romantic hero.

**[8]Quoted in Chapter 8.

The Mustang (Jan., 1944)

Editor's Comment: This article is the only place where Frank pleads for the preservation of the old Spanish mustangs.

A friend of mine, amateur historian of the West, asked me one day if I could name the most significant animal on the American continent.

"Think carefully before you speak," said he, "because there are many important animals - cattle, sheep, buffalo."

I replied: "I don't have to think before I reply to this question. I already know the answer."

"All right. Let me have it."

"The Mustang is the most important, most significant animal in America."

He replied: "I agree with you absolutely. I just wanted to see whether you agreed with me."

This statement of mine is absolutely true, as any one who will study Western history will discover. It sounds extravagant to say it, but I honestly believe that without the Mustang there would be no Western civilization. It was the sturdy legs of this game little native horse which carried our star of empire into the West.

As has been pointed out before, the country west of the Missouri River was not a footman's country. East of the Missouri the footman could make his way. He did. The early pioneers of the Mississippi Valley, the Ohio Valley, the Mohawk Valley, were footmen. They could travel through the woods, carrying their equipage on their backs, but when they set out across the desert plains, when they reached the towering fastnesses of the Rocky Mountains and beyond, they needed help. They needed some form of transportation beyond what they themselves provided.

The West was a horse country.

The Indians knew that. They had large herds of Mustangs. The first mountain men, Sublette, Ashley, Fitzpatrick, Bridger, knew it. The first gold seekers knew it. The first wave of farming pioneers knew it. The empire builders knew it.

And the horse which they used was the game little Mustang. He was not native to the country, for he was introduced by the Spanish conquistadors, but he had lived long enough in it to be thoroughly acclimated. **He was small, but hardy. He was tough. He could subsist on scanty faire. He was plentiful, in a wild state.** But the white settlers, taking what they thought was theirs by right, trapped him, trained him, and he became their principal help.

The Mustang served mankind well until a few years ago. Now, from the articles I have read in *The Horse*, he is facing his last stand. To let him go would, in my opinion, be a major American tragedy. In my day, I have watched the destruction of the buffalo, the antelope, the passenger pigeon. But we lay their destruction to a benighted, profligate generation. If we permit the Mustang to disappear we may be accused of these same qualities. And we will deserve the accusation.

But I don't want you to think that when I make a plea for the Mustang I am being sentimental. It isn't that. There's some sentiment attached to it, of course, and I don't like to see the bond between the old and the new destroyed. But the Mustang has a very practical value which it is good business not to throw away.

He has qualities which horsemen need. He had, indeed, all the qualities that go to make up an ideal saddle horse. What are they?

First, his **endurance.** I have spent sixty years in the saddle, taking part in more endurance races than any other man in history. I never rode another animal but a Mustang. Others were offered me. I rejected them. The reason is that I knew what the Mustang strain means: it means a horse that can keep going day in and day out, that doesn't need bandaging, fussing with and that can win endurance races whether the "rules" are made to its order or not.

Once when I was riding as a messenger for General George Crook, he told me:

"Frank, if troops can't overtake a band of Indians in two hours, it's better to give up the chase."

"Why, General?"

"Because they'll never in this green world catch them. Those wiry ponies of theirs can go ninety miles without food or water. They can wear out all the cavalry horses we have on the frontier."

The second Mustang quality it would pay us to have in our saddle animals is **intelligence.** You can't beat Mustang intelligence in the entire equine race. That's natural enough, too. These animals have had to shift for themselves for generations. They didn't have grooms keeping them out of trouble or trainers showing them what to do. They had to work out their own destiny or be destroyed. Some were destroyed in the working out of nature's survival law. Those that survived were animals of superior intelligence. It doesn't hurt any horse to have intelligence. The Mustang knows what intelligence means.

Third, **he's an economical little horse**. He can live where a stall-fed animal would starve. A friend of mine was telling me about accompanying a border patrolman in Texas. He was mounted on a fine big modern horse, this friend of mine was. The Texan, a grizzled old fellow, was riding a flea bitten little dun Mustang. They set out. They were riding through mesquite-covered hills. My friend, looking down on the little horse of his companion, thought: "I'll walk his legs off by nightfall. This will be good."

But when mid-afternoon came, so hard was the pace, it was the big horse that faltered. And by night-time my friend was afoot. But the little Texas Mustang was going as strong as ever. Next morning he was ready for another day of it. The bigger horse was so badly "stove up" he couldn't be used for five days.

Now, that little Mustang ridden by the Texan hadn't ever tasted grain. He was grass fed all his life. He picked his own food from the country, could live where even a cow would starve and knew how to take such good care of himself that he was always ready to go.

You have probably inferred from what I had to say on this subject that I'm heartily in favor of the Mustang Refuge in Arizona, that was once advocated by *The Horse*.

That project strikes a responsive chord in the heart of an old frontiersman like myself, and I know that there are thousands of other old timers who will feel as thrilled as I do about it. It seems to me that it is the opportunity to build up a typically American horse, something we do not a the present time have.

We have horses which we hail as typically American - the Morgan and the Standardbred. But they're merely replants of horses either from Arabia or from English Thoroughbred stock. But the Mustang is an American as George Washington, and Americas is a vast enough land, an important enough nation to have a horse of its very own. That means the Mustang.

In South America, in the Argentine, they had a native horse corresponding to the Mustang of the United States, the Criollo horse, you know. But they have always been more far-sighted than we. They took the Criollo, built up the breed, and now have a stud registry for the native horse, have important horse shows in the capitals every year, and in other ways have given their natural asset importance.

It is pretty late in the game for us to do the same thing here, for only a remnant of the Mustang herds remains. But it isn't too late. That is the point - it isn't too late for us to jump in now and save what we have of Mustangs and, if we choose, to build up the breed until we have a horse of which we can be proud - a staunch-legged , enduring, intelligent, easy-keeping, useful, all-around American saddle horse.

I know that the Mustang can be built up, because in past years I have many times experimented and bred endurance horses from Mustang strains. I do want to make it clear, however, that I do not mean we should cross the Mustang on larger breeds and produce a hybrid which is neither one nor the other. I mean we should take the Mustang, in this refuge, and weed out the inferior specimens, bred the superior ones and gradually evolve a top breed of genuine Mustangs. - *The Horse.*

I well remember some of the great rides make on mustangs. Fitzgerald, one of my friends of the old days, who, like the rest, left me standing guard alone (he passed on two years ago) was the last of the dispatch riders, excepting myself. One of his rides was on a small Mustang called "Fan Tan" not over 14 hands high. "Fitch" himself stood six feet three inches and weighed over 180 pounds. During the Moddox [Modoc] War, he rode this Mustang about 300 miles in thirty-seven hours with no rest for either horse or rider. Where would some of these large weight-carrying horses of today call a halt on such a ride as that? My rough guess is about forty miles from the starting line!

Our BULLETIN is not big enough for me to write of some of the real hard rides I remember even if I had the time to tell of them.

One of our members owns a Mustang who is known to most riders who have taken part in our 100-Mile Trail Ride. Although this mare, "Midnight," is thirty odd years old, she always holds her own on the trails and comes back in good spirit at the close of the day. This mare was caught wild from the Skull Creek band of Mustangs and shipped to a dealer her along with a number of other unhalter broke ponies. This horse dealer still handles a few carloads of these horses occasionally. "Midnight" was shipped here twenty-eight years ago and was sold on the halter to Mr. Charles Rankin, who took her to Connecticut after training her to the saddle. He sold her to play polo in Dedham, Mass. A few years later, her owner died, and the mare was purchased and returned to Connecticut. There she shifted hands three times before being bought by her present owner. The mare was now along in years but unbroken in spirit or endurance. "Midnight" must be about thirty-three years old now. They tell me that as a polo pony she was fast, very quick to turn and never seen to tire.

Many people do not like Mustangs because these horses will not take abuse - such as having their mouths full of iron bits, or riders constantly tugging at the reins. Mustangs will just tell anyone who rides them to "do it right, or get off and walk" - and most of them are capable of making you walk if they are not treated right! I have found them to be gentle, very friendly, and perfectly willing to share all kinds of hardships with me, and have never known one to quit or fail me in any way.

Trail Horses (Oct., 1946)

One hundred miles of trail in the beautiful green fills of Vermont are still marked with hoof-prints made by the horses who covered the recent Annual Trail Ride of the Green Mountain Horse Association; wind and rain may soon blot out those hoof-prints but the trails will be there for another year and the winter storms cannot erase the memory of the horses and riders who took part of it.

Many of them have been over the trails on former rides some were newcomers who had never been on a long ride before, all of them, including the children, seem to enjoy this experience. Some riders wondered if their mounts were bred right for trail horses - there is no such thing; it is the condition of the horse that counts for trail or endurance, and the trail or road is the place to give the horse work. A few miles every day for two months, before the ride, will put your horse in condition. It is bad to let the horse graze on grass for this will soften up his muscles. I have been on a few endurance rides and noticed there is not any special bred of horse for the trail; some horses are a little tougher than other because they have had more training; a good horse can be classed as "good" whether he has a pedigree or not. Some half-breeds, as they are called, do good work, they do not appear to tire or go bad in the legs. I saw one of them two years ago who had won four outlaw races, one after another, during a period of two months. The owner told me the sire of this particular horse was Standard-bred and the dam just "horse". I said it was the horse blood in his mount that counted on those hard rides. A few days later, I saw the mother of this horse; she bore the Pitchfork brand on her left shoulder. This indicated to me that she came from the Crow Indian Agency in Montana. Now, if we had a little more of that "horse" blood in our mounts today, they would have better bone and endurance. Showing how good a horse is - on paper - does not make him good on his feet or on the trail.

There is a horse used for cattle work in the far West and Southwest known as the quarter-horse. This is not a new breed - I remember them many years ago, but here in the East, most horsemen think these horses are bred for racing with a burst of speed for a quarter of a mile or so and therefore these horses are often entered in races. As a matter of fact, they are bred mainly for handling cattle; they have powerful hind quarters which enable them to throw their weight on their hind legs when coming to a square stop. Thy are also very cool headed and well-mannered; most of the have the best of bones and do not require a great deal care for are a horse of all outdoors and not the hot-house type; you will find them all "horse" and that horse-blood in your mount is what counts in the end - it is what is needed in trail horses.

Although there were horses of many breeds in this year's Ride I noticed no Arabians. They were a fine looking lot, most of them in good condition and not tired at the finish of the Ride. The cool weather, without rain, was in their favor. The judges must have had a hard time judging that lot of horses since so many of them looked good at the finish. The little seven-year-old girl on her spirited blue roan surely made a picture on the trails. Undoubtedly that Ride will always be bright in her memory no matter how many rides she takes part in through the years to come. We should encourage these children for they are to carry on in the future. Most of great horsemen throughout the country started handling horses as small children, some on ranches, others on farms and still others on the bridle paths of our cities. They usually grow up to be good citizens as their time is taken up with a favorite horse and they are not influenced by bad company.

There will be other rides over those beautiful green hills and trails of Vermont and it's likely everyone who attends will enjoy being there; to me this year's Ride was a little more interesting than the year before. I was out on the trails every day as well as up at 4:30 every morning milling around among the riders in the stable; everybody seemed to have a good time at the campfire supper out at Fergie's Farm singing around the burning logs and as the evening grew old many wandered away into the darkness bidding us good-byes and hoping to meet again.

There is something about a horse that appeals to most folks even if they have never handled one; they have amusing reasons sometimes for buying one. Right here I am reminded of the old hoss-trader trying to get rid of a horse with a bad trick. The trader, catching a certain look in your eye, thinks you like that particular horse. He might say, "Now, I don't know if I can let you have this horse - my wife thinks a lot of this mare - I'd better talk to her first - you know how it is, I want to keep peace in the family." As a matter of fact, the trader's wife is perhaps nowhere near the neighborhood at that time, has probably never seen this horse and doesn't care a hoot about the transaction anyway. Finally, after a lot of talk, the deal is closed, the trader gets his money and is rid of the horse and the buyer gets a runaway or balky horse on his hands - all because the trainer's wife loved that hoss.

I've loved horses as long as I can remember, but I do not fondle them or let them get too friendly with me; I do see to it that they get whatever is coming to them by way of good care and kind treatment and I always get their utmost confidence in return. *As a child, my mother encouraged me in caring for motherless colts that I brought in off the range. Every spring I had many to care for - some were chilled to the point of stiffness. Mother let me bring them right into the kitchen beside the old big cook stove and helped me rub them till they were able get on their feet. Many times I stayed up all night caring for them - seldom one died. I'd rob the milk from cows that had calves to feed these colts, and I'd milk gentle mares with colts by their sides. I got bowled over often by these old mares - some of them would chase me right out of the feed corral. I did not always escape without a few blood blisters where they nipped me in the seat of my pants as I crawled through the rails of the corral.* One new milk cow would give milk enough to feed four new-born colts; they they soon needed more milk than the cow gave so I had to figure close. Those baby horses learned to eat ground grain when a month old - that helped some, although the yonger ones needed milk. I was so busy there was no time to get into idle mischief. I do believe that any boy who grows up with horses is bound to make a good horseman - a horse is good compsany. A horse will not get you into trouble unless you teach him to jump - then he may jump into your neighbor's vegetable garden and leave you to foot the bill. It's all your own fault - don't teach your horse any foolish tricks!

Bulletin Editor's Notes:

Visitors at the Trail Ride have told me they would be well repaid for the time they had spent there, if they had seen and done nothing excepting talk to Frank Hopkins. There is no one in the country who had the experiences with horses that Frank has. We all hope that in spite of his eighty-two years, he will come for many Trail Rides to give us his expertise and help.

Editor's Comment:

*Quoted in Chapter 1.

2) Horsemanship

Gentling (Oct, 1940)

The breaking of colts has always been a great study among horsemen; some trainers tell that the well-bred colt will respond to training more quickly than one of unknown breeding - in fact there are scarcely two horsemen who will agree on the method of breaking or training. Now many times I have seen fine, high-bred mounts rear and shy and even try to run away when a small, harmless piece of paper flew in front of them. Yet these horses are trained by expert horsemen! Right here I wish to say than I consider such training poor horsemanship. It makes no difference whether your colt is highly bred, scrub, fuzztail, wild mustang or anything that is horseflesh, he will respond to proper training.

After more than sixty years of handling all kinds of horses I do not find any difference in their breeding; horses are much like humans - some are nervous, others quiet, and there is also the mean-tempered horse - all must be treated accordingly. The highly intelligent horse is the one who is hardest to train. He will try to put it over on you if you don't watch him.

In training colts, there are a few things that should be kept in mind - rules that should be followed at all times. If you cannot control your own temper, let some one else train your colt; you must always have patience. Do not take the advice of anyone or permit friends to stand around looking on while you are giving lessons to your colt and do not have anything around that will attract the colt's attention from where you want it. Remember, your colt cannot reason as you can, although he can remember of a long time. I recall one horse that remembered his stall over twenty years. I had taken this horse away from the C. H. Ranch, Wyoming, when he was two years old, twenty-one years later I brought him back to the Ranch and when I loosed him, he walked past thirty-four empty stalls to get to the one he had been kept in as a colt - so I must admit they remember.

Patting your colt only makes a fool out of him - don't fondle colts if you expect them to obey you. It is well to place a well-fitting halter on the colt when he is a few days old, do not fasten a lead or rope to the halter. Allow the colt to wear the halter at all times. If the mare does not object, you can take hold of the halter, but do not stand in front of the colt and pull on it, for he will sit back and most likely rear at the same time.

When your colt is about six weeks old, you should teach him to lead and stand tied. This must be done in the presence of the mare. Get a four-foot lead with a snap fastened at one end and snap this into the colt's halter; now, have a piece of sash cord about twelve feet long, tie a Bowline knot in the sash cord so it won't slip; the loop should be about three feet across. Take hold of the halter, lead with your left hand, facing the colt. Now, flip the loop ties in the sash cord over the colt's hips, allowing it to drop down nearly to the hocks, then jerk on the sash cord at the same time putting a little pressure on the lead rope. Your colt may kick - don't notice that - but jerk the cord again, keeping both ropes tight. Remember, do not have rope any longer than I have told you for you as well as the mare and colt might get tangled in the rope. If you halter break your colt in this way he will be a trailer; that is, he will never hang back. Anything I dislike in horsemanship is to see a man trying to drag a horse along behind him by the halter or bridle. Yet we see this every day with horse handlers. Train your colt to walk with you - not to be a trailer, you do not want the sash cord after the second lesson. Each of these lessons should not take more than fifteen minutes. Lead the colt a little each day.

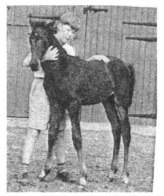

"EARLY GENTLING"
Paul Furnas, Jr., and "Paulenda."

Now, teach your colt to stand tied. Stand in front of him and hold the rope. Be sure you do not look straight into his eyes or stare at him. The colt may try to walk away, but you just the rope firmly in your hands and do this over many times. When he stands fairly well by holding the rope, put it around a fence post but do not tie it, stand back at the end of the rope and hold the end of it in your hand so you can give and take on it to avoid hurting the colt. As the colt moves about watch how he takes to it. After a few short lessons you will find that you can hold him without slacking the rope. Repeat this a number of times and your colt will be halter broke for life. Theses lessons take only fifteen to twenty minutes each for about a week.

After your colt stands tied, it is well to pick up his feet, first on the left, then on the right side, for you do not want your colt half broken. You must break both sides alike - if not, your colt will not be properly broken. Now you have a halter-broke colt and have raised his feet a number of times. The colt is about two months old and it is likely you want to turn the mare and colt out on pasture. That is the best for them. Let the colt have all the play and freedom he wishes. When the colt is eighteen months old, start giving him the real gentling. Do not be in a hurry to get on his back for there are many things he must learn before putting on the harness or saddle.

1. Build a training pen eighteen feet square - no larger. This must be high enough so the colt cannot put his nose or head over it. Have the bars close together so the colt can't poke his head through the fence. Now lead the colt into the pen, take off his halter. You get in there with a straight whip. Crack the whip a few times, but not loud. This will start the colt to milling around the pen. As he passes you, lower the whip close to the ground and snap him on the heels as he is going away from you. Make as little motion with the whip as possible and do not strike him hard - just sting him a little. After the colt has circled around you a few times he will turn his head to watch you as he passes. But do not look straight into his eyes or he will think there is something wrong. This is just the reverse from what some trainers advise, but after handling and breaking for many years I have found it the best not to stare into the colt's eyes. When the colt walks to one corner of the pen and faces you, reverse the whip, with the tip end behind you and walk right up to the colt and lay the flat of your hand on his shoulder. Do not pat him. The mere touch of your hand is caressing enough. The colt might try to get away. If he does, crack him low down on the heels; this time he may rush right back to you. If so, lay your hand on his shoulder again, then bring the whip down gently in front of his nose. He will reach out to smell the whip and he will see that it is harmless. Now, rub the whip down his neck and shoulder, then step to the other side and repeat the lesson, but do not go to his rear. Step in front of him, lower the whip gently and tap him lightly on the heel at the same time say "come here" and move back slowly. If the colt does not follow you, tap him again - a little harder this time. Step back as he follows you. Speak clearly when you give the command "come here", but not sharp or rough. When he follows you around the pen two or three times put the halter on lead him out to his stable or runway, for that is training enough for one day. Although it may seem to the reader that it has taken hours, this lesson has taken not over twenty-five minutes.

It is well to remember that the first lesson taught to the colt is the one he never forgets so be sure it is done right. Repeat this lesson for three days until the colt followers you at a trot around the pen, and be sure he follow you as freely from the left as from the right.

2. Now, you must break his hind quarters. Your colt not only has gained your confidence but has gained a lot himself. Without this, you won't get anywhere. When you take the colt into the pen for the second lesson he will look for the next act and take to it kindly. Get him to follow you, then lay your hand on his shoulder. He will stand. Rub the whip over his hips and down his legs. Slip behind him and reach forward with the whip and rub it along the sides - on both sides. Now, move slowly around the colt, leaning against him going under his neck and on both sides. Repeat these lessons for a day or two.

3. Who wants a horse that shies and bolts at the least thing that looks strange, or a horse that gets frightened at strange noises? Before you every harness or saddle him is the timee to break him of these faults. If he has confidence, he will trust you - that helps when breaking the colt from being scared of noises. Turn the colt into the training pen. Get a large can or pan and let the colt nose this before you start beating on it. Stand a few feet from the colt and tap the can or pan lightly at first, walking in a circle around the colt. Increase the beating as the colt gets used to it, then come closer and walk around still beating on the pan. Then give the command, "come here". He will follow you as you beat the can, caring not a hoot about it. Now, throw the pan on the ground - kick it around. Soon you can kick it around his feet or behind him without frightening him. Then, get an armful of newspapers. Walk up to the colt, let him nose them. Then rattle a sheet of the paper and watch how he takes it. Do not scare him at first and soon you can rattle the paper, throw it on the ground and he will follow you, walking on the paper. Throw sheets of paper above your head letting them fall around the colt, some of them falling on him or blowing in his face.

4. Put a light open bridle on the colt; use a straight rubber-covered bit, with three-inch leather washers against the bit rings. Allow the colt to wear this bridle one hour the first day then use it when going over the lessons, but do not attach lead or reins - just let the colt get used to the bit. Watch him, see how he takes to the bit. The leather washers will keep those iron bit rings from chafing his lips. When the colt gets used to the bit, place a three-inch leather band or surcingle around the body, back of the shoulders; have three rings sewed into the band one at the

center of the band to snap in the overhead check - one ring on either side about sixteen inches down from the center for the side lines. I use a piece of heavy elastic about eight inches long on the side lines that run from the bit to the belt. I bought this elastic from the makers of trusses for ruptures - there is just enough give in the side lines so the average colt won't fight the bit. The overhead check should not be tight, but it stops the colt from reaching down and pulling on the bit and rubbing the bit rings against his forward legs. You can turn your colt out in the pen without worrying about his getting his feet over the side lines - colts will bit themselves better than the trainer can do it. With the elastic sewed on the reins he will not fight the bit because the reins give. I had about sixty colts wearing these rigs in a large corral at one time and every one of them turned out in fine shape. The colt should wear this rig one hour a day for a week.

All lessons should be given in the training pen. Now, nail a two by four on two sides of the pen. They should be about ten feet high. Tie a line on these two by fours about the pen stretched across the center. Hang old clothes of different colors on this line. Then, lead the colt into the pen. He may appear nervous at first - stay with him until he quiets, then lower the line gradually each day until the clothes touch the colt as he moves around. Soon he will not pay any attention as he learns there is nothing to harm him.

5. Your colt should have a few driving lessons, no matter whether you intend to make a saddle horse out of him or not. Take the short lines off that run from the bit to the body band; replace them with long driving lines running them through the rings on the band, but be sure not to buckle or tie the lines at the ends, for you might get them caught around your foot. Tap the colt with the whip at the same time saying "get up". He may try to turn toward you. If so, drop the line down near the hock and pull. That will straighten him out. Be on the lookout for this. Soon, he will learn to go straight. Give a quick but light jerk on the lines and give the command "whoa" and slack the lines at once. If he does not respond, do it all over again. When the colt has started and stopped a few times at your command do not tax him further for that day, but slip up to his head and lay your hand on his shoulder as a reward. Repeat this lesson a few times. I have found it is very important to have a horse stop when asked. Train him to stop the very instant you speak - it may save your life - it has often saved mine.

6. Now, if you should slip when mounting your horse, or something else goes wrong, you surely would not want to get a flying hoof side of the head or anywhere about your body. Here is a way to prevent getting hurt. Your colt has worn the body band and knows it is harmless. Place a saddle on his back - it is best to use a stock saddle and a breast plate; do not cinch the saddle too tight. Allow the colt to wear the saddle for thirty minutes the first day. After four of these lessons in the pen, take a burlap bag about half full of fine hay packed lightly in the bag, rub it lightly around the colt's shoulders working it lower and lower as he gets used to it. Be sure you do this on both sides as in all lessons. Then work back to his rear with the sack of hay and rub gently around his hips and legs. This is enough for the first time. Repeat the next day carefully work the sack between his forward legs, then do the same thing on the hind legs. Repeat this for four days. Then, tie one bag of hay on either side of the breastplate so the bag will hang down in front of the forward leg clearing the ground about six inches. Tie two more bags to the horn of pummel of the saddle letting them hang just back of the forward legs. It is well to lead the colt around the pen a few times in case he gets scared at first, but stand away from him as soon as he quiets down. Do not tax him too long with this lesson -twenty minutes is plenty. Continue this for three days - 20 to 30 minutes a day, then attach the back strap with crupper to the saddle, hang one bag of fine hay on each side so the bags hang just a little in front of the hind legs and about eight inches from the ground. Lead the colt until you are sure it no longer frets him, then step a few paces in front of the colt, give the command, "come here". and make him follow you around the training pen. If your colt takes to this kindly, you should hang two more bags of hay from the back strap about ten inches from the roots of the tail, letting these bags hang around the hocks. Now you have eight bags filled with loose hay hanging around the colt's legs forward and behind - that is, four forward and four behind. Repeat the lesson with all the bags hanging around the colt's legs for a number of times. You will be well paid for your time used in this lesson for your colt has no fear now when anything touches his sides or legs and if the rider slips or falls off the colt will stop and look around at his rider.

I have broken many horses for trick riding and I rode them twice a day in Colonel Cody's Wild West Show and in all those years I was never hurt by my horse although I have had hanger straps break and saddles turned when I was hanging low on the side of the horse or going under his belly, and the horses always stopped stiff legged when I commanded them to by saying "whoa". I once had twenty-four horses follow me out of burning stable by just say "come here" and in spite of burning timbers following around them, they obeyed. Although some of them were badly hurt and had to be destroyed, still they remembered their early training.

How often do we hear of someone speak of the horse's mouth. Horsemen will ask, "has your horse got a good mouth?" Some will speak of a horse having a "cold" or "dead" mouth. There are still some strange things about horsemanship indeed. If a man trains his colt to obey the word of mouth instead of putting pressure on the bit he will never know whether his horse has a good mouth or a bad one. Some horses have tough mouths, others have shallow nerves and cannot stand the touch or iron on their jaws. Yet many horsemen will fill their horse's mouth with two large iron bits and besides they will fasten lines enough to those heavy bits to rein a four-horse tem. All of this looks stylish on the bridle path for most every park rider does it and every rider wants to be in "style" but I personally feel those rigs are uncalled for - they worry the horse and it surely is very bad horsemanship. Anyone acquainted with me knows I never used a bit of any kind in the mouth of my horses while riding in the ring in Cody's show although I rode at full speed and turned my horses end for end while on the run. Teach your horse to obey instead of tugging at his mouth. This must be done while he is a colt and before he has been saddled.

7. Stepping up in his middle is the last lesson of all and it don't amount to much so far as the colt is concerned. But it's a happy moment for the colt's owner, and why shouldn't it be when the owner has watched his colt grow from a clumsy, long-legged suckling to a slick, well-formed youngster and longs for the day when he can ride that horse he has raised. My memory has led me to drift away from the training lessons. The next step is to get your colt accustomed to the saddle he has worn while going through a few lessons.

8. Lead your colt out of the training pen with the riding reins fastened to the horn of the saddle so the colt will not turn his head. The lines should be even on both sides, but not tight. Walk around the fields with him; take hold of the saddle horn and put some pressure on it. Do this often - on both sides alike as you walk with him. Also pull at the stirrups and let them go, letting them swing against the colt's sides.

Take your colt out on these walks often. At times you should tuck your foot into the stirrup, but be sure the stirrup straps have been lengthened so you can tuck your foot in easily and be sure you have firm hold on the saddle horn, else your colt might learn a bad habit right here. I am not a lover of the flat saddle and will not use it under any conditions and I consider such a saddle not fit to train a colt with. I have seen many fine colts spoiled for life with the flat saddle. If the colt unloads his rider the first time he steps up on him, that colt will surely try it again - so get a Western stock saddle of three-quarter rig, not one of those make believe stock saddles. Get one with a sixteen-inch bulge at the fork, and the cantle should raise about six inches, with a four-inch woven hair girth that has a ring in either end. These girths are fastened with cinch straps; there are no buckle tongues to tear out or any chances of the buckle breaking. Lengthen out these latigo straps till the ball of foot fits in the stirrup. Half of your heft should be in the seat, the other half should be in the stirrup. Your knees should not be bent but straight as if you were standing. Throw your feet out away from the horse. Now you are braced in every way but do not stiffen in the saddle or brace back against the cantle - sit rather limp -forget about the forward seat. *Your colt is now nearing his second year. **You can ride him a few minutes but do not overdue it. Fifteen minutes twice a week is plenty at first. On these short rides teach your colt to turn, stop and start. Theses lessons should be given on the walk.** Do not excite your colt while doing it. When your colt turns fairly well at the touch of the rein against his neck then teach him to turn quickly. Increase the speed gradually, then you can start jogging the colt - but not fast or for long periods at a time.*

Your colt is perfectly gentled, not afraid of noises or anything he sees or hears. You are riding him. The colt has the best of manners. It is your duty to see to it that he does not develop any bad habits.

I do not approve of making a prisoner out of a colt. By tying him in a straight stall for any length of time he is liable to develop such habits as lip smacking, weaving, and later on, cribbing, and then wind sucking. The idleness from standing will often lead to those bad habits. Your colt's feet should be kept level from the time he is two months' old by using the rasp. It pays to hire good men to care for horses - they are the cheapest in the end. How often do we see grooms scratching horses' legs with iron curry combs and jabbing them in the ribs because they do not stand for the abuse! Any horse cared for in the proper way will enjoy the company of his keeper.

It might appear that my way of training will take a long time, but twenty to thirty minutes a day is all the time required. I have trained many colts in this way - some that had been spoiled by other handlers, still they came through all right. It takes more time and patience of course to train one that has been spoiled. If anyone follows my way of gentling and training he will own a horse worth being proud of.

I have learned these methods from some of the most expert horsemen in different parts of the world and have used them for years in my practical experience in handling range-raised horses and a number of wild mustangs that I have trapped myself. I have also handled a number of high-bred horses of all breeds - there is no difference in their handling.

Editor's Comment:

*Whether or not a two year old should be asked to carry weight is a controversial issue. Even with the light work Frank describes, it may be risking the colt's soundness. The temptation is always to start treating the colt more like a mature horse. Many experts recommend waiting until the horse is at least three years old. Sadly, over the years I have seen far too many horses broken down by too much work too soon.

Horses and Horsemen (July, 1943)

Horsemanship should begin with the raising of horses and successful raiser selecting only the best breeding stock, for even the best oft times proves not good enough.

The care of brood mares should not be neglected; keeping them in dark stalls should be avoided. My own experience has taught me that the mares who run outdoors the year 'round produce fine, husky colts. It is important that both mares and colts be sheltered from storms and bad weather, in a place where they can run in and out, at will. During cold weather, brood mares need more feed. Blankets are not necessary - in fact, the mares do better without covering, since Nature provides them with heavy coats of hair in Winter. Naturally enough, scientific horsemen will not agree with me on this, for the simple reason they have never tried it.

After weaning, the colts should run outdoors year 'round, if the desire is to raise hardy horses. When the colts are a month old, they should be halter broke, and this is the time to pick up their feet (on both sides) often. Personally, I do not sanction the practice of patting and fondling them as this encourages the colt to become unruly.

At eighteen months of age, the colt is ready for gentling, part of which consists in teaching him not to fear strange noises or unfamiliar objects. I prefer schooling colts in a training pen not over eighteen feet square; thus the colt can not get away and is also forced to obey his trainer. When giving the lessons in the pen, it is best to take off the halter; this gives the youngster more confidence than he would have if you pulled him around by the head. Most horsemen are in too much of a hurry to put on the harness or saddle, whereas it is wiser to have the colt perfectly gentled first. The bucking colt is not confined to the range type along. I have seen stable-raised colts that would buck for all points of the compass, but none of them will buck, kick, or get excited if properly gentled before saddling.

The colt should not have the bit in his mouth for the first year of working under the saddle; using a well rigged up hackamore will teach him not to go against the reins and it far better to pull him around and give him lessons in reining with the hackamore than it is to spoil his mouth with an iron bit.

No horse can be considered "handy" if it requires two hands to handle him under the saddle. Training colts at the end of a long line running them around in circles seems to me a foolish bit of horseplay though I am aware that this is practiced frequently by some of our most up-to-date horsemen. There is not a colt handled in this manner that obeys rightly, for he can do about everything he has a mind to, at the end of that line. Too often, we see "jaw crazed" horses - that means they were never gentled nor taught anything except to be pulled around by the bit. Such horses are also termed "high spirited"; most that "spirit" lies in that bruised jaw caused from too much tugging at the bit. Then too, such horses are called "mean" and condemned as "outlaws", when the fault really lies with the handler.

*[1]I recall a little stallion, the meanest bunch of muscles and bone ever wrapped in horse hide, who had been caught as a wild mustang and sold from the Trading Post at Fort Laramie, Wyo. The horse

breakers tried to take the rough edge off him by choking him down and throwing him every day. This game little horse fought without giving an inch of ground. He was finally classed as a 'killer' and outlaw. He was run into a small corral and left alone. I watched this little feller fight the burning ropes that choked him, but every time, the horse 'won the round'. I could not forebear telling those breakers they might learn something from that mustang if they hung 'round long enough. They said he was mine if I wanted to feed him in the corral, so every day I cut grass and fed the horse, by holding the feed in my hands. At first, he would not come near the bars. After a few days, he was hungry enough to make a grab at the grass and jump away. Later, learning there was nothing to harm him, he would poke his muzzle through the bars. Finally, I got him to eat grain from a wooden measure held in my hand. As I was only a boy then, it seemed to me I'd accomplished something and I ran over to Chief Sadheart's tepee to tell him about a wild horse eating out of my hand. 'Hi-w-in', he said, and started out for the corral with me in tow. There the old Chief told me of many wild horses he had tamed. He said to me, 'this horse is not bad - just afraid of man' and added that I should look though the skin and see the real horse who was all good, not mean. He then called my attention to the stallion's markings - a black roan, the white of his face spreading down the sides of the jaws. Both front legs were white nearly up to the chest. There was a white spot on the hips that reminded me of a bootjack and from this mark the pony got his name of Bootjack. Within a few months, under Sadheart's tuition, I trained the first wild horse which I owned and which was my true friend until he died - full of arrows - five years later. The remains of this brave little animal rest not far where he fought those burning ropes of the horse breakers. I always recall old Sadheart's words - 'when you can see through the skin, you will find the real horse.*[1]

Since the early days of horsemanship, there has been more or less superstition among horse handlers all over the world. The Indians thought of their buffalo horses as something sacred given them by the Great Spirit that they might run down the bison to feed their people. Those ponies, always faster than other horses, were not used battle, nor did the Indians ride them to the hunting grounds. It was a custom of these people to have the mother of a great warrior place a bison robe over the buffalo pony when he was being led to the hunting grounds - this was supposed to bring much meat. Suh beliefs do not end with these simple people - they are prevalent among highly educated folks in other places. I recall an instance while riding with the "Bill" Show, in Lexington, Ky., where I met a horse raiser who invited me to his farm and showed me some of the finest horse flesh I ever saw. He spoke of the mares and colts on pasture a mile or two down the road. The darky hitched a fine-looking mare to a light buggy and as we rode along I commented on the graceful action of the mare. The road was rough, with deep wheel ruts. Suddenly, the mare stumbled. Immediately my Kentucky friend laid the whip on to that mare, raising ugly welts on her slick hide. He sawed and jerked on the reins, finally getting the mare under control. He explained, "if I did not put the whip to her she would stumble again the next time she came to that spot." He may have been right - she did stumble when we returned - but disfiguring the horse seemed to me a cruel fancy.

Over in France, some years ago, all the horses were docked; roaching their manes and pulling the hair out of their docks leaves them the appearance of a mule. Aside from being a part of their beauty, Nature has given horses manes to fan themselves with while traveling fast, and has also given them tails to protect themselves from flies and other insects, but man is never satisfied - he thinks he can do a better job.

There is no horse living who naturally has more than three gaits - walking, trotting - (or if left-handed - pacing) and running. All other gaits are artificial and if such horses are not steadily schooled in these gaits, they will soon forget them; if fact, if turned loose, they will never use them. Show horses sometimes tire of this ill treatment and become real man haters.

Then there is another type of horseman - what I call the "paper and pencil" horseman, who can tell you to the ounce just how much feed a horse should have according to his weight. He gives fine talks on his research work and advises us how to sit in the saddle for perfect balance; he does not, however, consider that all horses are not built alike - some are heavier forward than others - so this sort of "balance" applies more to machinery than to the horse. If your horse is perfectly balanced in the shoeing, then step up in his middle and ride him - you'll have no further trouble.

As to the feeding - one horse may gain flesh on his rations, while another of the same weight might not only lose flesh but knock the stable down at night, looking for more feed. Such horsemen can tell you all these things - yet they lack the simple art of picking up a horse's feet or tying a halter rope correctly. I've seen them drum on a horse's tendons and pull on the fetlocks, which a thumb and forefinger pressed on the right spot will cause any horse to raise his foot readily.

With some horsemen, the quality of a horse is overlooked, so long as he stands over fifteen hands high and is a good color. The best horse I ever saw was less than fourteen hands high and many died trying to follow him after that sack of gold at the end of the rainbow.

You all know that fellow who shows up around auction sales and horse affairs, wearing a clumsy pair of riding boots, his heels decorated with plug spurs. He's looking for the super horse - one that will never exist. This horseman reads all the horse books and is well enlightened on horsemanship, so far as the *books* go. He can tell a breeding expert who has probably spent a lifetime on a certain breed, just how to improve it, and raise horses than can be used for any purpose - from a draft horse down to a shetland pony! His ideas are all right, but some of us get awful drowsy when he has the floor.

Then, there are horsemen who spend all their spare time riding on the bridle paths in our large cities. They usually are very kind to their mounts, carry cube sugar in their pockets and believe in having the most up-to-date tack, with an entire disregard of how the horse feels about it. Their riding master has taught them all about horsemanship (except what they really should know). Some of these riders pet and fondle their mounts when someone is looking on - often, though, these horses come into the stable with bleeding mouths from too much riding on the bit or having them "in hand". After a few summers the horse steps out a little proud forward. Yes, he is getting old. His owner thinks about getting a new horse, full of fire and life, to take his place. Any dealer is willing to take the old horse, proving he also gets a good amount of money in the trade for the new horse. The old horse finds a new home in some riding academy where he is jerked around by Tom, Josie, and Kate, for the remainder of his days, his former owner not caring a trooper's damn what becomes of his faithful old friend. But these horsemen are always in the latest "style".

Some of us recall the horse days before the coming of automobiles, when we often heard someone say his horse could *road* along ten miles an hour. Such a horse was worth owning then and now, if he could keep it up for any length of time. These horses were not plentiful - I've owned a few - some could travel ten miles an hour and stay out all day, and be ready to do it all over again the next day. You won't find them in pedigreed stock though. This sounds bad, but it's true enough. I've spent many years learning it and paid the price to know. There seems to be no record of a long, hard race being won in our country by a pedigreed horse. I am not condemning our fine-blooded horses - far from it - and it's because they have not had the opportunity, for many have been entered in such races and have been first to drop out. However, we are not all long distance racers and do not require such horses. Once you ride a real mustang however, you will probably agree with me as to his endurance.

It has been my privilege to visit most of the cavalry schools, including Vienna. All have their own ideas of schooling horses and most of them are good. I've long heard of the horsemanship of the Russian Cossacks and they are considered great. After spending four months with them, I did not approve of their methods of training.*2a

History dates the Arab on horseback for hundreds of years. **I have found some Arabs hard on their mounts, not taking the care that is usually attributed to them of their horses and racing them until they drop from exhaustion (when raiding other desert tribes).*2b** Arabs ride only mares - the stallions are used for breeding and spend most of their lives standing tied by the hind leg to a stake driven in the sand. When a horse colt is foaled, he is killed at birth (unless they want to raise him for breeding), the mare's milk being used for human consumption. There is better horseflesh and as good horsemen right here in our own country as can be found anywhere. If one starts early in life, grows up where there are a number of colts foaled each year to handle, there is no reason whey he should not make a first-class horseman, but it is well to overlook some of the nonsense that goes with horsemanship today.

I once heard a great horseman, O. R. Gleason say, "take your horse's head away from him and you take his feet away from him also." This is quite true, for more horses will fall on a tight rein than those allowed to have their head and see where they're putting their feet, especially in rough country. If you think I am mistaken, watch the sports sheets of your daily papers and take a look at the pictures of horses thrown with their riders on the ground about twenty feet ahead of their mounts. All of these riders had their horses "in hand" as they say, riding with a tight rein.

Now let's switch to a large cattle range in the far West and watch the horses cutting cattle. They can turn on a nickel and hand you some change while at full speed, and come to a square stop with a heavy steer at the end of that piece of "twine". And remember, they are not working on a lawn moved field - yet they very seldom fall. You will notice, every horse has his head free (with a loose rein) to balance himself and see where he is placing his feet. We should not scoff at this kind of horsemanship - it is a beautiful sight to watch a well-trained "cow hoss" work, and it takes a real horseman to train him. You will note also, they never use a martingale on a horse.

Our plains Indians are some of the best horsemen in the world. I have yet to see their equal elsewhere. I've watched them gentle wild horses and their method of doing varied according to the horse they handled. The wildest horses were herded into the river - where some of the breakers would swim with one arm over the horse's neck close to the shoulder. Others rode along the river bank on both sides, keeping the horse in the stream. After a time the wildest horse became gentle and seldom tried to buck when mounted. We can credit to these same plains Indians our oddly marked horses which our westerners are so proud of today, like the Overos, Tobianos and Appaloosa. The Palomino was also bred by these people, although there is nothing left now but the color. Such horses were bred for war mounts, every tribe having its own color or marking. They bred them true to this particular marking.

The best individual horseman I knew was a Gypsy - of the Stanley-Cooper band who have long been known to us as horse traders. "King Stanley" was happy when he was training colts and he spent a lot of time milling amongst them in the corral - sometimes he carried a saddle blanket on his arm - otherwise a bridle. He was never in a hurry to saddle a colt, but when he rode out of that pen it was surely gentle and broke! He could ride one horse more miles a day without playing out the horse than any other man I knew and as an all around horseman I'd like to see his equal. Although "King" spent thirty years of his life mostly in a wheel chair, he was a horseman to the end.

Professor O. R. Gleason was another expert. I met him through Mr. Dickerson (Whose son now has Travelers' Rest Arabian Horse Farms) before the coming of the automobile. At the time, I was riding with the Buffalo Bill Show and our setup was in Memphis, Tenn.*3 I put on an act which called for much horse training. *4When Cody with his cowboys, freed the Deadwood stage coach from a band of raiding Indians, I was shot off my horse in the ring and lay there until the sham battle was over and the ring cleared of all riders. My horse then lay down beside me, pushed himself over till his saddle touched me, then, pretending I was badly wounded I grasped the saddle with one hand and my pony rolled up on his haunches bringing me to a reclining position on the saddle, when he got to his feet, took a step ahead, turned back, picked up my hat and then started to carry me out of the ring, to the thunder of applause.*4 *3This was all done without my seeming to give the pony a signal of any kind and this is what interested Gleason. He wanted most to find out how I direct my horse through this act without a single motion or signal. He interested most in this - not in me - but when our season ended I joined him in his horse training exhibitions and traveled with him for three winters. I must say he was a real trainer. His books probably are still on the market and they are worth reading.*3

In mentioning the plains Indians, I neglected to say that Chief Gaal*5 did more in the line of breeding for color and endurance in war ponies than anyone. He was not only a horse raiser, but a great warrior who led the Cheyenne against Custer. I saw him riding with his band on to Standing Rock Reservation; he dismounted, took off his war bonnet and untied the knot in his horse's tail (to show his people they should not go on the war path again). Gaal died two years later, a spirit-broken man and I shall not forget his giving me his most prized possession - a spotted stallion. Following the Indian ceremony of surrender, Gaal place the reins of his horse in my hand and said, "H-is-teen" (for you). When I hesitated to accept what I knew to be his most prized possession, he added in his own language, "He is yours - to show my good friendship to you - keep him and his good blood, and may the evil spirit never be your friend." I am not ashamed to admit the lump in my throat and the thought that maybe the white man should stop trying to teach the Indian and let the "Redman" teach him a few things worth while.*5

Editor's Comments:

*1Quoted in Chapter 1.

*2aFrank's objection to the methods used by the Cossacks was not about their techniques, but the way they ruled their horses by fear.

*2bColonel T. A. Dodge spent a considerable about of time with the Syrian. Arabs in the 1890's. He noted and was upset about the same practice.

*3In the last part of the nineteenth century horse tamers put on many dramatic shows for naive audiences. Like Gleason, these men were a mixture of showman, charlatan, and expert. They impressed the general public, but not real horsemen, like Frank Hopkins. They knew how often their quick fixes either broke the horse's spirit or were not permanent solutions. There are several stories about how Gleason and Frank met. Like Bill's show, he could not have traveled in the winter. These stories probably were invented by Gertrude to enhance her husband's prestige.

*4Quoted in Chapter 4.

*5Given the errors in this story, it probably was invented by Gertrude to enhance her husband's prestige. Chief Gall was not a Cheyenne, but a Hunkpapa Lakota. After the Battle of the Big Horn, he fled to Canada, but returned and surrendered in 1890. He and his band were shipped by rail to the Pine Ridge Reservation. He died there in 1894.

Horsemen and Horsemanship (Jan. 1945).
As told to Charles B. Roth in The Horse

[Frank Hopkins has told us a great number things about Horsemanship in the past and we are happy to reprint this splendid article. - Ed.]

Every year many good tempers and horses are ruined by men who, new to it, take horseback trips. A man from the city goes on a Western hunting trip, say. Horsemanship is new to him, and his kind of horsemanship is certainly new to the horse. Both suffer. The tempers sometimes recover, but spoiling a horse is a more serious matter. Yet all any man needs to know about horsemanship, in order to get the most out of the horse and his trip, is a few simple rules and practices.

Ever since I was seven years old I have been a horseman; not an amateur with a couple of saddlers in a boarding-stable somewhere on the outskirts, but a professional horseman earning my living by the saddle. When I was 13, I was a full fledged dispatch rider out West. Later I went into endurance racing, and never was beaten. Three times I won international contests to determine the world's most expert horseman. So what I am going to tell you is the result of living with horses for more than sixty years.

The most important single thing in horsemanship is to adjust yourself to the horse. Here is where many men who profess expertness fall down. They try to make the horse over to their ideas, instead of adjusting themselves to the horse. I refer particularly to the matter of gaits. A man must handle a horse to his gait, not try to change the horse from one gait to another. So find out the gait best adapted to your horse. With some horses this will be the trot; with others it will be the gallop, or lope. The gait that the horse favors is the one he can follow with least fatigue. In all my years of horse handling I never tried to reform a horse's gaits. I changed horses if the gait of one did not suit me. It was the easier and more satisfactory way.

The kind of riding I am going to discuss in this article is not bridle path or show riding. In their places, I have no doubt, these forms of riding are estimable. But their place is not afield, where you ride day after day over mountain trails or pathless wide spaces. This is the kind of riding I want to discuss; the riding of the outdoor man. And it is as different from the other kinds I mentioned as day is from night.

The first requisite of a good outdoor rider is a tight seat. Now a tight seat depends on two things; a long stirrup and perfect balance. The long stirrup is necessary for balance, so we can say that the long stirrup is the first essential to correct riding. This form of riding is generally referred to now as the plains style, because we men of the Western plains, who rode hard, who rode far, who lived in the saddle, found it to be best for our use, mastered it, used it altogether. I realize that trying to teach the plains style to any one in so short an article is difficult, if not impossible. In fact, I doubt if any one, no matter how diligently he practices, can learn it after he has grown to maturity. It takes a lifetime to master. But there is no harm in learning it as well as you can, for it is by far the most effective way there is to ride. Also the safest.

Lengthen your stirrups until the ball of your foot rest snugly - in the stirrup and the leg is practically straight. You are now "sitting down in the leather," as we used to say. Stay right there. Don't go bobbing up and down; don't rise to the trot; don't stand in the stirrups. Sit tight, no matter what the gait. The position of the upper body, indeed, should not change one particle as long as you are in the saddle.

It's a pretty sight to see a man ride this style, if he can really ride. But few can. The old timers who learned to ride it are mostly gone; and the younger generations don't get enough riding practice to master the position. And that seat is the snuggest of all. Old time riders, cowboys, and cavalrymen, who rode this way could be separated from their mounts only by and end-over-end tumble. An ordinary fall or trip didn't dislodge them; when the horse got to his feet they were still on his back. Why, even a bullet didn't budge some of them from their saddles. I myself was shot seven times while on horseback - but I never lost my seat.

This way of riding is not only pretty to see, not only the tightest and snuggest of all ways, but it is also the only practical way on long rides.

When a man can ride for an hour, then put himself in the hands of a masseur and have the kinks and stiffness rubbed out, it doesn't matter much how comfortable he is while on the horse. But if he has to get into the saddle at sunup, ride all day over hot, rough, hard country, then get off the horse at sundown - and do it all over again for three months hand-running, he seeks the way that is easiest on himself and on his horse. And the way I just described is it.

Young riders often ask me what ability in a horseman I consider to be the most important. I always reply that it is the ability to keep the horse happy. I mean it. If a horseman can keep his horse from worrying, keep him in a happy, even mood all the time, he will get more out of the horse than he can in any other way. It's common sense that he should. Yet how little it is heeded! You've watched cowboys "haze" their horses, beat them with quirts, spur them up, then jerk them to their haunches, and in every other conceivable way persecute them. Pretty poor horsemanship this. "But the indictment doesn't stop with cowboys. I've seen polo players and fancy riders fret their horses even more." And then they wonder why the horse doesn't do more for them or why he doesn't stand up as well as some other fellow's on a long day's ride. **Treating the horse is like treating any other servitor. You can drive your help in home, office or factory and get some work out of them, of course. You can encourage your help, keep them happy, get twice as much. So with the horse. Take your choice.***

I like to see my mount throw his ears forward, look at the road ahead an take in everything that goes on, not paying the slightest attention to me up there on his back. This means a happy, carefree horse; a horse that I know will be under me at the end of a long day, because he has not a thing in the world to worry about.

You will notice that I say I don't want the horse to pay any attention to me. Does this mean that I don't speak to him? It does. Talking to a horse, diverting his attention from the job, wearies him more than any other single thing. I never speak to a horse when on his back except, of course, to give an order. Don't talk to your horse. And never pat him nor make over him. Fondling a horse spoils him.

If you ride on some outfits in the West, one thing that will strike you is the way they neglect the grooming of their horses; if you frequent polo stables or riding academies of the East, one thing that will strike you is the great care they give their horses. Cowboys look with disdain on curry comb and horse brush; stable grooms look on the cowboys as savages and on their horses as cow. Which are right?

Neither and both. By that I mean, they are both wrong and both right. To neglect a horse, as cowboys do, does the horse no good, while to over-coddle and over-care for him, as hired grooms do, is often more harmful than beneficial. I really believe that many fine horses, polo ponies and the like, are spoiled by too much care, too much bandaging of their tendons, to much fussing over.

My own practice, which always worked out 100 per cent, is to brush the horse thoroughly to keep his hide clean, but never to rub or to fuss with him when he should have rest. If my horse has worked hard, I clean his hide of dust, wash out his mouth and sponge off his back with a medium-wet sponge or rag. Then I give him a good bed and let him rest. One I heard a horseman say that an hour's cleaning was as good as two quarts of oats. I told that horseman that it was better to give a tired horse that one hour of rest; then he wouldn't need the extra feed. In Arabia, I observed the great Arab horsemen caring for their horses in almost the same way I cared for mine. There are no better horse handlers anywhere than those desert Arabs.

Now comes feeding. It is important, of course. Yet it is really a simple subject. Experience has taught me that there are only two foods for the horse - oats and timothy hay. Buy the best. Cheap food is dear food in the long run. Occasionally I have met men who do not feed their horses, but let them pick grass of a living. The only trouble with such men is that they are too stingy to buy feed. They may delude themselves that their horses will do as well unfed as when properly fed.

But they don't delude the horses. If anyone feeds a horse right, the horse tells the story. If not, the story is there. In all my years, I never saw a horse that told a lie.

I suppose that if you go on a trip, you will have to take the horse that is offered you, but if you can make a choice and want my honest advice, it is this: Pick out a lazy horse every time. This may sound strange. But the lazy horse, or level-headed horse as I prefer to call him, is one that will work without worry. I always selected them for my long rides, never one of those high strung devils so much praised by horsemen as having so much fire and life. I want a horse that will walk all day unless I call on him to shake it up. I never had a horse on any of my long rides that I didn't have to make pound the road.

When you start out on a long ride there is one cardinal rule: Take it easy in the beginning. That animal under you is the most remarkable thing of flesh and bones ever put together, capable of unbelievable endurance. But it can't be abused or pushed too hard at first. My own practice in my long rides was always to take it very easy the first day. Others passed me in the beginning; I passed them in the end, when passing was something important.

There's been a good deal of bunk passed out about what the horse is really capable of doing. You've heard tales of riding 150 miles a day, 200 miles, even farther. Horses vary in their ability to endure. So do humans. Some horses can carry you 50 miles in a day, others 100. And you can't tell from looking at a horse whether he's a 50-mile animal or a 100-mile. The farthest I ever rode a horse in a day was 124 miles; had to that time. I always thought too much of a horse to ride him till he dropped of exhaustion.

It's common among horse men now to praise big horses and look down on small ones. But I've never found any specifications, linear or avoirdupois, that could tell me what a horse could do under the saddle. A horse to me is no smaller than his ability and no longer. I have seen 700- and 800-pound horses carry 180-pound men in 40-pound saddles all day, day in and day out. In the same outfits, I've seen other horses, larger, weighing 1,000 pounds and over, that couldn't stand the gaff of every day use but had to be rested and used only on alternate days. There's no rule of size or appearance that will enable you to judge how hood a horse you have. Only the road will do that. Sometimes the most likely looker turns out to be the most useless performer - while one of those horses that doesn't look like ten cents will win honors.

I never put a measuring-stick on a horse nor put a horse on the scales. If he has the right bone and muscle and is put together right, he's what I'm looking for. My ideal horse is short in the back, well ribbed out to hips, with long muscles covering the kidneys. He has a fairly long hip, fairly straight hind legs closely linked between joints. His shoulder is deep, his fore or upper arm well muscled. His color doesn't make bit of difference to me. But the quality of his bone does. Beware of clean, thin limbs and long slim ankle joints. Pick a horse with strong bones and close-linked joints.

Now I want to give you a few words about mounting. That is important, especially if you have to ride a strange horse. About the worst thing that can happen to a horseman is to be dragged. Even expert riders dread it. If you learn how to mount properly, and dismount properly, you can avoid most of that danger.

The way to get on a horse that is strange to you or on a horse that you know will bolt or buck every you mount is to "check" him when you get on. Checking is easy. This is the way of it: Take hold of the left rein in your left hand and also take the cheek of the bridle in the same hand just above the bit. Put your other hand on the horn. Now pull the horse's head around toward you, at the same time springing into the saddle. He can't do anything until you get up on him, and then you don't care what he does. If he is inclined to jump around and be restive, your checking him around to you keeps him from getting out of control until you are seated in the leather and prevents your being dragged by a horse that bolts when you get only one foot in the stirrup and are helpless. When you dismount, use the same system: pull his head around, hold it here, and step off.

Chances are you're not going to ride many bucking horses, not if you can help it. But if you get on one that does buck you want to know what to do. Here is what. If you're entirely green and don't care about the embarrassment of jumping off, the best thing is to leave the horse as gracefully as you can. Take hold the horn with your right hand, swing your feet clear of both stirrups and slide of the left side. But with a little experience you can ride the ordinary straight bucker easily enough. The main thing to remember is to sit down in the leather and stay there. And keep your balance. I add one more rule: keep your chin pressed hard against the chest. There's a reason for that. If your chin is there you are in no danger of getting your neck snapped when your horse bucks viciously.

Give your horse a fair deal; treat him as considerately as you would treat a human assistant; see that he gets proper feed and decent place every night to rest; do not demand impossible things of him - and he will carry you with satisfaction wherever you choose to go.

Editor's Comment:

*When Frank compared managing humans to managing horses, he was ahead of his times. Modern management theories have been applied to horses in my book, *Human Views and Equine Behavior.*

Understanding Horses (July, 1946)

How well do you understand your horse? This noble animal has always been a friend to mankind, helping him till the soil, carrying him into battle, fighting bravely, and sharing his pleasures. Unfortunately, to many the horse is only a beast of burden to be used for work or pleasure and when no longer useful, is given no thought as to what become of him. To me, this powerful animal is also the most beautiful of all creatures that walk the earth.

Horses, though highly intelligent, are like children in that they must be taught. Science tells us that horses and dogs cannot tell colors, nor can they remember. I recall a statement once made to me by Professor Gleason that horses cannot tell color. I begged to differ with him and he asked me for proof. We were on a ranch in Wyoming there were at that time a large number of suckling colts; the brood mares varied in color - some were spotted. I cut out of the bunch six mares - a dark buckskin, a black, a white, a golden sorrel, a spotted mare, a dark mare with a white rump (an Appaloosa). Their colts were place in a corral, out of sight of the mares. Then I called the Professor. Here were the mares - with their colts all marked so there could be no mistake.

There was a man to lead every mare off to a distance of nearly a quarter of a mile the mares held about two hundred feet apart. The men made sure the mares didn't whinny to call their colts. The first colt led out belonged to the spotted mare. It ran in a straight line to its mother and every colt when let loose went straight to its dam. Not one made a mistake or varied from the straight line to its mother!

I recall one horse in particular, who after twenty-two years, remembered the stall where he had been kept as a colt, also the watering trough on the opposite side of the large barn. When this horse was turned loose, he walked past thirty-eight straight stalls to get to the one where he had been kept as a colt - and he walked around the tier of stall to get to the water trough.

In schooling the colt, be sure you give him his first lessons correctly - for it is the first few that he will always remember; those that follow won't mean so much. You can have a gentle, easily-handled colt if the first lessons are give properly, or you can have a head-tossing, rein-pulling, nervous mount. It depends altogether how your colt has been handled at the very start. Teach him then what you want him to do and you will have no more trouble.

If you are the nervous type, you have no business training colts; neither should mean-tempered, overbearing individuals train colts; the colts will be much like their handlers.

Don't get the idea into your head that you must show the colt you are his master and teach him to fear you - he will see right through this very quickly. Speaking sharply, jabbing with the bit, are sure signs that the handler is a mean-tempered individual with no feeling for the hurt to his horse's mouth.

The secret of handling horses is to get them to really like YOU not to merely like what you feed them from your hand. In my years of training I do not recall giving a horse anything from my hand in payment for what I got him to do - nor do I believe in fondling and pampering him and if anyone can get is horse to obey more correctly or quickly I'll be glad to meet him. I know there are many horse folks ready with that old salt shaker when they hear or read anything different from the usual method they have been taught in handling horses.

In the East, most handlers use the English way of training. They seem to think a horse is not much good unless he can jump. They run the horse around in a circle with a long lead line, cracking a whip. The horses are taught to jump on this lead line. Very few horses care about jumping and it surely is not good for them. Many a fine horse is spoiled in his first season of jumping. To those who are not acquainted with other kinds of horsemanship, this appears all right. It is, however, far from pleasant for the horse and it is quite noticeable to the experienced on looker.

I have ridden quite a bit in rough country where there was much fallen timber and have never seen a downed tree across my trail that I could not ride around and bring my horse back without his being lame. Any horse who has been jumped much will show the effects of such jumping, especially in the shoulders; after a few seasons he will go to pieces. Here on Long Island were there are fox hunts every year, the country is fenced with split rail fences for the purpose. Many good "jumping" horses are destroyed and their riders get pretty well smashed up. Horses resent being treated thus and become unruly.

I recall one horse owned by a friend of mine, Austin Spoffard. He bought this horse in Kentucky as a finished Hunter. After two seasons of hunting, this horse would start to run away when mounted, no matter what rig was on his head or who rode him. Finally, Spoffard called me by telephone and asked me to come down, although he doubted that anything could be done for the horse. I went down to look him over and when they led the horse out of the stall I noticed his ears were laid back and the look in his eyes anything but pleasant. There was nobody about this place that the horse liked. On looking him over I asked: "How much do you want for this horse?' Spoffard said, "How much will you give? He is real bad and might hurt you." The deal was closed when I offered $100 and said I would take my chances. I took my bill of sale and led the horse away. I did not try to ride him but got into the training pen with him for just fifteen minutes every day for a week. He soon was a changed horse, no longer laid his ears back and the look in his yes was pleasant. With a well-fitting hackamore on his head, I walked him around a large, corral, turning him into the fence when he tried to bolt, at the same time calmly giving the command "stop". He soon learned to obey and would not go against the rein. The rein was always slack; this was new to him as he had always been handled on a tight rein with a jaw-breaking curb. In less than a month that horse grew so quiet that it was necessary to call on him if I wanted to get him into a trot; he was really lazy. Well, I gentled the horse and lost a good friend; Spoffard was the maddest man on Long Island when he saw one of his neighbors riding that horse two months later on a fox hunt! I had made a neat-looking hackamore that looked much like a bridle and this rig went with the horse when I sold him, also the story that good horsemen do not hang onto their horse's head but ride in their saddles and not all over the horse, bobbing up and down and wearing out their mount. The man who bought this horse from me spent a few days with me before buying him and gave me was is considered a very good price for a first-class hunter. He also thought my training was well worth the price. This horse "Alex" has been used on many hunts since and came to be known as of the best horses at that game and still wears that "bridle" on a loose rein.

Don't think for a moment that I don't make some mistakes - I often do, even though they are corrected at once. Recently I made one while training a three-year-old Arabian in a training pen. He took to his training kindly and then I took him out into a larger enclosure where he ran and played. I watched him a while then walked to the far end of the corral and called "come here". At once the colt came running - he did not stop until his nose rested on my shoulder. That was all very fine. I then slipped his halter on and led him in to his stall where he was used to being kept. Now here was the mistake I made: this colt was eating; I stepped into the stall, unsnapped the rope from the halter, then walked back about twenty feet from the colt and gave the command "come here". At once the colt got all excited, threw his ears forward while his eyes took on a wild, scared look as he stared at me through the iron grating on top of the partition on his stall. His grain didn't mean a thing to him but my command did. He probably thought, "How can I come to you when I am tied?" Although the rope was unsnapped, he did not know it. There were some people talking nearby and I doubt if they noticed my mistake. I stepped back, got a long lead rope, fastened it to the colt's halter, took my stand in the same place and the command "come here" at the same time giving a light pull on the line then slackened it. The colt at once rushed out and put his nose on my shoulder; he was still a bit nervous but quieted when I talked to him in a low voice and returned him to his stall. A small mistake like that, if not corrected immediately will make a horse lose confidence in you. The owner standing by, did not notice this; I hope the colt overlooked it.

I have often been asked what "gentling" a horse means. **Although there are many things connected with "gentling," the first is to show your horse you are his friend in such a manner that he will have the confidence to come to you when in trouble and if he is frightened will look to you for protection instead of trying to run away.** My article on "Gentling" appeared in a previous issue of the Bulletin. Gentling in a training pen is not to put fear into your horse but to take the fear out of him and teach him that you are his friend. If the colt becomes real scared, he will crowd against you and it is hard to get him to move away while he is frightened. Horses that have not been gentled will rear and bolt and try to get away so "gentling" is really important.

Some years ago I gentled a range colt and trained him to being "ground tied" by giving him a few lesson on the stake rope. This colt had been run off the range only three weeks and still needed training under the saddle though he was doing very well. A friend came riding along while I was giving the colt a mile or so on the road, calling "You're just the man I want to look at a horse I want to buy." We rode along slowly to the Lazy D ranch, dismounted, leaving our horses ground tied - which means the reins are thrown on the ground. As we went over to the corral, a covered wagon came along the road with two mustangs running as if they smelled a panther; the cart's curtain was flapping out behind the wagon and this frightened my horse; he took off in high gear and my friend said; "There goes you colt." I got up on the fence and called: "Come here, Britt, come here." Although that colt was leaving that part of the country, he turned at once and came to me at full speed, still frightened and trembling. The "gentling" I had give him was remembered and he came to me for protection. I remember that horse for many years - that was the only time he ever tried to run away; I could hardly blame him for being frightened with all that noise and the curtain flapping out over him as the wagon passed him.

There is one more horse I'd like to mention - one that I understood. I was carrying an important message during a heavy thunderstorm. When the lighting stopped, it was so dark I could not see my horse's head. Suddenly my horse stopped at the old dirt road, turned around and got into his loping stride again. A few minutes later I heard water lapping against the horse's legs and then reaching my own feet; the Grand River had over-flown its banks and was rising fast. I then felt my horse going up hill where there was no water. To a man who could not see, this was something long to remember; had it not been for that horse's "sense" I would have been drowned with him. Had I tried to rein him, we would have been drifting down the trail to God-knows-where. I dismounted and stood there in the darkness soaked to the skin, waiting for daylight, muttering a prayer of thankfulness of a horse and rider safe out there in the bad lands of South Dakota.

The question has been asked, "Does the cold-blooded horse respond to training as readily as the well-bred horse?" to which I reply:

"Yes, they learn things more easily than those hot-headed horses." For many years I have had to have patience with horses as well as humans. I've noticed often a man will take advantage of your good nature and put you down as a simple fool when you are merely having patience with him, where the horse seems to have sense enough to appreciate your friendliness towards him. I have trained many wild horses that never came in contact with a man before; those horses were the easiest to train; at first, they might come at me striking out with their front feet because they were cornered in the training pen, but when they learned there was nothing to harm them, they became friendly and obeyed my command more readily that horses of highly-bred stock. You can't expect to have a wild horse friendly if you rope him and choke him down, then have a man get into the saddle and spur him until the horse is busted or winded. That kind of horsemanship is nearly as bad as the horse show method of training and about as cruel.

Now about the hackamore horse; it is a big mistake to think anyone can take his horse out on the road or trail and ride him with a hackamore. The colt or old horse should be trained in the corral and taught to stop and turn at your command - not to be pulled around by the reins. The hackamore horse should obey at all times on a loose line - in fact any horse should obey on a slack rein; whether in the bridle or hackamore; if not, it's plain to see that horse was never gentled or taught anything except to be pulled around by the head. Many horses will pull on the reins and fret when under saddle. If you take the pains to trace back to that horse's early training, you will find that the pulling habit started with a scratch of a spur or a sharp clip from the crop when the trainer out of patience while giving the first lessons. If your horse has some sort of fear when you are on his back, it will always remain with him through life unless corrected - and very few horsemen know how to correct had habits in the horse. Many try with the spur and jerking on the bit which makes matters worse. Horsemen, you cannot correct a fault in your horse while riding or driving him - the only place to correct these bad habits is in the gentling pen (which should be 18 feet square and high enough so your horse can't put his head over the fence). Treat him kindly, make him mind you; above all, don't give him anything to eat from your hand as a reward for minding you.

If our readers think this kind of horsemanship is just "talk" call around some day and watch old man Hopkins in the training pen!

3) Endurance Riding

Endurance Horses As I Know Them (July, 1941)

Of all the questions asked me during my years of horsemanship, the most frequent has been, "What breed or strain of horse do you consider best for endurance riding?" Although this is a hard question to answer, my reply has inevitably been, "the horse that can stand up under the hard training that is necessary to prepare him for such work."

In training my own horses for endurance rides, I soon learned that if the horse showed the least sign of weakness at the start, it was best to stop training that particular horse and begin with another; you cannot patch up a horse who hasn't legs strong enough to carry his body - all the rubbing and bandaging will not strengthen them - it may weaken them. If I noticed one of my ponies bracing when I stopped him, that horse also was out of the training string. What I mean by bracing is this: if he stretched out, as many high-class saddle horses are trained to do when standing. Experience has taught me if a horse braces all out from under him *naturally,* it's a sure thing his back is weak - then, to me, he is not worth feeding.

It does not take long to detect the courage in your horse when you start to train him; most horses with 'style' and over-action are lacking in heart and courage when given real hard training. For instance, when I expected to take part in a race of say a thousand miles, I did not intend to come in third or fourth at the end of the ride - it was my ambition always, to finish first. So I trained for it. I knew that a horse who could not stand up under fifty miles a day for the last two weeks of training would never carry me on a long ride. There are many riders however who believe if they ride a horse a mile or two each day and feed him well they have given him all the care and training they consider necessary; surely, the horse is in good flesh and spirit. Here let me say the endurance horse needs far more careful training than the one mile race horse. Of course, his training is different from that of the speed horse.

I never believed in being in a hurry at the start in training, rather preferred to go slow and watch how the horse hardened. Some horses harden quickly, others do not. I always taught my horses to lie down and rest after their work. It is well known that most horses will stand on their feet no matter how tired they are, but I've always thought it best to get my horses off their feet as soon as the saddle was taken off. If they are taught to lie down they will stay down and rest for hours.

When a horse gets hardened, he should be dried out gradually until he is satisfied with three twelve-quart pails of water daily. Most riders feed too much hay and overfeeding of grain does the horse more harm than good. Fussing over and rubbing a tired horse after a hard day's work is one of the biggest mistakes made by long distance riders. I always brought my horse in cooled out at the end of the day, brushed the dust from his hide, washed out his mouth, nostrils, eyes and his sheath and up between his hind legs, then gave him a slap on the breast and said "lie down" and he would drop to the straw while the words were in my mouth. I let him rest two hours before feeding. As it is natural for all horses to roll, I usually let him roll before brushing him. Many riders do not like the extra work of brushing. Personally, I prefer to see my horse happy, so at the end of the day I let him roll all he wants to and shake himself. I always loosen the saddle girths when stopping, if only for a short time.

In sixty years of long distance riding I never used a bit in my horse's mouth believing the bit will worry any horse a little - many of them pull on the bit and fret, some will hold their heads higher than is comfortable for them. All these little things help wear the horse out on a long trail. Talking friendly with your mount while up there is not a good practice either for he is paying attention to you instead of the trail ahead.

Often I have been asked, "What is the best weight and size for the endurance horse?" **In my opinion, the horse is no larger than his ability, and not a bit smaller**. *The best endurance horse I ever knew weighed eight hundred pounds and stood less than fourteen hands high and I was his proud owner. He never won any blue ribbons, neither did he take a silver cup, for pedigrees were unknown to my 'little yaller plug', but I want to say that little stallion earned his feed and a few thousand dollars to boot. He was one of those mutton-withered fuzztails that no one would care much about owning. ... He had the heavy, strong bone, cords [tendons], muscles, required for hardship, although I admit he did lack style and action. This pony seldom carried his head above the level of his back; his joints were short in the ankles [canon bones]; all four feet were placed well under his body. I never saw him rest a foot - he stood on all four. Often, I gave him three months of the hardest training a horse could stand, yet there was no sign of filling in of the tendons or bone trouble of any kind, neither do I recall a single day that he did not shake his head and let his heels fly when the saddle was taken off, but I do remember my many narrow escapes from being hit by those flying hoofs! On a long ride, that little horse could not be beaten.*

I do not wish to give our Bulletin readers the impression that I dislike those fine blooded horses - on the contrary, I have owned many of them in my day and admire them as much as any horseman, and often go quite a distance just to lay a hand on their slick hides. We should be fair-minded about our horsemanship; each breed of horse can be used for what it is bred for and no one breed can be used for ALL purposes. My sincere opinion is that mixing the blood of different strains is fast destroying the real good horseflesh throughout the world. The English Thoroughbred has been bred for speed for over four hundred years and there is not a horse living that can take his place on the running track; it is well to leave him his job on the race track course. Why waste that blood that has been carefully built up for so long on heavy work stock and raising scrubs which are neither running horses or draft animals? The Arabian horse has been crossed so often that there are truly few of the straight Arab horses in existence today; they have been crossed for the purpose of getting a larger horse; still, the quality of the true Arab is not there. **Our Arabian Horse Club of America has some of the finest straight blooded Arab horses in the world and there are still some in Egypt.**

To return to the endurance horse: In endurance riding, I have noticed it is the small horse close to the ground who wins on the long, hard rides. Size in the saddle horse does not mean much to me - some large horses do very well for three or four hundred miles and I've seen them miles ahead of the bunch at the start, then go to pieces in the next hundred miles. I noted that those horses who got out in front the first day or two and made a lot of mileage were the ones were out of the ride first. Always keep an eye on that lazy hoss who hangs back there in the trail drag, for he may pass you some day and you won't see him again until that ride is over. That's how I started out on my long distance rides - never in a hurry, for there were miles before me. A mistake most riders make is to shove the horse a certain number of miles in one day; some plan cover a stated number of miles every hour. A horse is not a machine. How does he feel about this? Although your mount cannot tell you in words, he will surely tell you by his condition at the end of every day. Many a real endurance horse has been ruled out of a ride because he was overtired from being shoved too hard for a few hours at the beginning of the ride. If the horse acts a little sluggish when starting out in the morning, let him loaf for that day. I've often stopped riding after a few hours when my horse was dull (probably due to change of country, feed and water). When the rules did not permit such layoffs, I would not sign to ride in that race. I always allowed my horse to travel as he wished with a loose line. Some prefer to hold their horses' heads up on a tight rein because it looks "stylish" but that foolishness only worries the horse and tires him. I rode all day without taking the rein in my hand, but when I wished to turn my mount on the trail I twisted slightly in the saddle.

It is well when training for a long ride to teach the horse to walk fast - that is the best gait for a long ride; too much trotting is out of the question. If you can get hold of a true loping horse, he is best for a long distance. However, such a horse is scarce amongst highly bred stock. The Mustangs are the true lopers and travel to that gait altogether in the herds. **I once rode one of these twenty miles at a lope without slacking back into a walk or trot. This was done to win a bet for our late President Theodore Roosevelt. The ride took place at Fort Russell, Wyo. The judges followed on bicycles, so there was no chance of changing gaits. Roosevelt won his bet. One thing about that ride may sound queer to some readers - at the start, there was a twenty-five cent piece placed under each of my feet on the wooden ox-bow stirrups, and one under me in the seat of the saddle. If they were not there at the end of those twenty miles Roosevelt would lose the bet. However, he "collected" when I raised in the saddle and the last of three quarters slid down the side of the saddle seat. I had rubbed knees with "Teddy" many times on narrow trails and he had seen me do the same trick often although not at a lope the whole distance. A rider must have years of "sitting tight" to accomplish this trick, but as it had been my business to perform all kinds of tricks in the saddle as a showman before the public of the world, that little trick was only a matter of sitting close to the leather, and sitting close is a mighty good thing to learn if one intends to ride for a long distance.** The style of riding might change from time to time but horses are the same as they were years ago, only they are more tender and cannot stand the hard knocks that those cold-blooded nags had to stand or die trying to.

My mustangs lost a lot of their hardiness if I stabled and blanketed them in the winter, so I gave them good dry sheds with large runways, and they were free to run in and outdoors as they pleased. They were as tough as pine knots.

Next to the Mustang for hardiness, I believe are those oldtime Morgans, so hard to find today. I well remember those shortlegged chunks - much like the small horse of Holland. My father was probably the first man to bring those horses into the Northwest. I can recall when he went East and bought a number of mares and stallions although I was only a small shaver at the time and recall it only as one waking from a pleasant dream. Father had been wounded at the wagon-box fight [in 1867] and laid up for a long time but when he got well enough he went to New England and brought those horses back with him. They came by rail to North Platte, then were driven overland to Laramie. The first winter, all of them lived on the range without housing which is unusual for stable raised stock. In a few years he had a large herd and every cowboy in that part of the country was proud to ride of those C.H. horses and would say 'this yere one is a Morgan and the best cow hoss in these parts.' And they were top stock horses; many of them had a great burst of speed from a standing start; they could handle those old moss-horned cattle that weighed twice as much as they did. It was a pretty sight to see one of those horses come to a square stop with sixteen hundred pounds of beef at the other end of the rope. Those horses weighed between nine and ten hundred pounds and they could bust any bull or steer on the range and do it right. Father liked the straight blood in all his stock so the Morgan blood remained clear as long as he lived. In thirty years time those horses were spread all over the North and Southwest. That blood at the present time can be found in every Western state today although the horse changed, for they have been crossed with other blood and are much larger.

Although I did not pet or fondle my horses nor allow anyone else to, it is likely I showed my appreciation by careful handling, kindness and care.

Recently I saw a great horsewoman of our country riding one of the finest saddle bred horses that could be found anywhere. The horse had the best of manners. I also saw this fair rider feeding the horse lump sugar from her pocket, petting and talking to her. Yet, when this woman mounted, she worried that horse every minute she was up in the saddle by the slightest movement of her arms, this making tension on the bit. I merely mention this, to show how unknowingly some riders can worry a horse. To a man who has had a horse between his knees most of his life, these little things are quite noticable.

Editor's Comments:

*Quoted in Chapter 3.
**This race probably did happen, but the involvement of Theodore Roosevelt is questionable. The trick with the quarters is an old vaquero way of testing the rider's skill.
***Quoted in Chapter 1.

A Judge's Impression of the Ride (Oct., 1941)

The Green Mountain Horse Association's Sixth Annual One Hundred-Mile Trail Ride was a colorful event this year. It would be hard to find a group of horses in better condition, so few of them showed signs of tiring. All actually finished in good spirit. The weather was cool and without rain during the whole period of the Ride. Taking part in this Ride were a splendid group of horsemen and horsewomen who would class as excellent riders in any horse event.

Some of the trails are quite severe, with many long, steep grades, nevertheless, the footing was good and not a single horse injured the entire one hundred miles.

On the second day, three very good horses and riders lost the trail losing two hours or more before they finally straightened out, thus putting them out of the contest.

I observed a spotted gelding on the Ride loping beside fast-walking horses, but he stuck to his gait which is the true gait of the Indian War Pony. This horse showed other signs of having such blood in his veins; for instance, he loped all the way, except when walking. Some horsemen not acquainted with that gait, expected to see this spotted horse out of the Ride the first day and remarked that it was poor horsemanship to ride the horse at that gait. Personally, I feel that it is better horsemanship to ride your horse at his *natural* gait than to try to force him to a gait that will wear him out in a few hours. It would be well nigh impossible to make that spotted horse trot under the saddle or any other place without actually abusing him. However, that spotted horse came in as fresh every day as he was going out - not even gaunted at the end of the 100 miles and he only lacked three points toward winning first place as the best endurance horse on the Ride! It is well for us to forget about show horses and the bridle path, for the 100-mile ride does not blend with that little trot in the park before breakfast. **On a real long, hard ride, the true loping horse will wear out six good horses who trot under the saddle.** I realize this is a very broad statement, but I have seen it proven many times and history repeats itself in that famous long, hard rides have always been won by the loping horse. So, trail riders, don't condemn the true loping horse nor doubt the horsemanship of his rider, for the rider is using good sense when he allows his horse to travel his natural gait.

There were so many fine horses and good riders of breeds and classes that the judges found it extremely difficult to arrive at their decisions. However, I can assure the riders that every horse and rider had the most careful attention of the judges. The rides were probably not aware that their judges and the recorder were up most of the night discussing and arguing the points of every individual rider and his or her mount, nor that these same judges even deprived themselves of viewing and enjoying the fine Morgan Horse Show in order that they might come to the final decision. Even then the judges were an hour and a half late with their lists, the competition was so close.

There were many large horses, also small ones, who did very well. Noticeable in the small horse group was Number 25 on the program on her little Indian "squaw" pony "Midnight". Although this pony is more than twenty years old and weighed but 790 pounds, she went all the way with the bunch and probably was in as good condition at the end of the ride as the others.

The Johnson twins made an attractive picture on the Trail. They rode all the way on their spirited mounts and showed remarkable horsemanship in carrying their horses along at an even, open gait.

The stable in Woodstock, with its high posts, is well equipped to care for a large number of horses. The excellent hotels, inns and lodging homes are close by to accommodate the riders and there is not a more convenient nor lovelier spot in our country to hold one of the rides. I really believe that any one who rides on these trails will gain more knowledge or riding than in any other way. Some of the riders were overheard to admit that they would be better acquainted with trail riding next year.

I have been asked to give our riders a few "pointers" such as I have through experience during my years in the "leather". Right here, let me say that you can not tell how good your horse is by just looking at him - only covering the trail and lots of it, will condition your horse for a long hard ride. Another thing - do not jump or nerve up your horse in any way while training for a long ride. Be careful about balancing your mount while in the saddle; **be sure to have your horse balanced as nearly as possible in his shoes.** Often a rider is unaware that his horse may not be naturally balanced; one horse might step with one forward foot an inch or more farther than the other, or it might be in one hind foot. Some horses travel too fast behind for their forr'd feet; it makes an awful lot of difference in his riding if a horse is balanced. If you wish to find out if your horse is properly balanced, take your horse by the halter and trot him over a stretch of soft ground - about fifty feet - then measure the horse's tracks, from the toe of the hind foot to the toe of the forward foot - be sure to measure five or six tracks on each side; if the horse steps a half inch or one inch or more shorter with one forward foot than he does with the other, that foot should carry a little more weight in the shoe. If it is a hind foot, the same method should be followed, *i.e.,* a little more weight in the shoe. If your horse travels a little faster behind than he does forward, there should be a little more weight put on both forward feet so he will throw them out. Of course, I can not tell you the amount of weight for an individual horse - you will learn that by having a little heavier shoe put on the foot. Keep trying it out until you have him stepping exactly the same length with one foot as he does the other. An unbalanced horse is quite noticeable, for he will have a little more knee action in one leg than in the other. There are some owners who will have a horse for years and not notice this. It will however make a vast difference in the riding if your horse is perfectly balanced. To keep your horse balanced, it is wise to make a chart showing the weight of the individual shoe for every foot and the size of the nails used, so your horse will be properly shod the next time and save you the trouble of balancing him again. If your horse is balanced when shod, wearing down his shoes will not unbalance him as he will probably wear down his four shoes alike.

Look at the feet often, if there are any sigs of thrush, treat at once, for thrush will lead to many foot ailments, even to low heels and dropped soles and pinched hoofs.

Remember, if the tree of the saddle does not fit our horse, he will not go right, no matter how the saddle is padded. Your saddle may fit many horses, but it may pinch the only horse that you choose to ride, or your weight may cause the saddle to bring pressure on the cantle end of the pads. These things are not easily detected on short rides, but you will soon notice them if your ride your over rough, hilly trails.

DR. EARLE JOHNSON AND FRANK HOPKINS
With the former's horses. - Neill-Hamilton Photo.

Some saddle-trees are not open enough at the withers for one horse, even though the saddle may fit another horse well. If the rider should come to a long, hard climb for his horse it is likely that the rider will let his mount take the hill slowly, while at the same time he (the rider) flops back in the saddle to rest himself, thus putting all his weight in one spot, digging the cantle into his horse's back - and there you have a sore back for the horse - even though you cannot understand how it came there. It is a sure thing, though, that the soreness came from the rider taking things a little too easy going up hill.

Padding your saddle too light will cause small skin corns. They don't appear sore when you feel of them, but when there are enough of them together, your horse will fret and worry.

Going down hill will sore the horse if the saddle does not fit properly. The English style or flat saddle, is rather hard on the horse's back regardless of how carefully you watch. It is not for long, hard riding. Many riders who have taken up long riding have changed to the moderate stock saddle, even though they could not be persuaded to use one until they learned of the comfort for both rider and horse.

Girth galls or pinches may be avoided by stretching your horse after saddling. This is done by taking the horse's toe in the right hand and placing the left hand against his shoulder, then pulling forward on the toe, thus pulling the skin wrinkles from under the girth.

Two or three small buckles on the girth will also dig into the horse and cause lumps on either side. It is far better to use cinch straps and do away with buckles entirely. Oh yes, they don't look stylish, but they are comfortable for any horse.

The head gear for your horse may suit you, but does it suit your horse? If not, he will have spells of fighting it. You have seen pulling horses and horses who seemed incurable. Riders, let me tell you there never was a horse who would get behind the bit and pull if that bit was hanging in the stable instead of being in that horse's mouth. I have broken some of the most vicious pullers that ever grabbed a bit and the cure was always effected by taking the bit out of the animal's mouth and gentling him with a choke cord, thereafter riding him with the old time hackamore bridle. No horse will pull without a good reason and in this instance it is the pain caused by the bit that does it, although there is no soreness visible. On the other hand, it may be shallow nerves or flattened bars on the under jaws; broken bars may lie under the skin in a horse's mouth all his life without giving him any trouble, but when coming in contact with the bit, your horse will pull and rave; some horses go stark mad from the sense of pain. Take this tip from an old timer, riders - put a little LePage's glue on the seat of your pants and stay close to the leather and keep your feet in the stirrups - don't ride on the bit. A fairly loose line makes a happy horse and contented rider. It makes no difference whether your horse is three years old or thirty, hot blood or cold - they all respond to proper gentling if rightly done. I have gentled wild horses twenty years old or more who never had come in contact with a man before, and they took to their training kindly; in

254

fact, I would rather gentle and break a horse who had never been handled than one raised in the stable fondled and patted from birth. During my years of handling all kinds in different parts of the world there is only one horse I recall that I could not gentle and there was a good reason for my failure to do so - the horse's brain was diseased.

While in Woodstock, some of the riders asked me for a few "tips" on long riding and I hope they understood me right. I was not talking merely to hear my own voice, but was passing on to those younger riders the benefits of my years of hard-earned experience. I have nothing to lose or gain by it and am always glad to give this experience to those who feel they may derive some profit form it, for my days of polishing saddle seats have about come to a close; but the lump in the throat and flush to the cheek when approaching a group of horsemen in the saddle is always there.

Good Fortune favored me for nine years in getting dispatches through for the Generals on the Western Frontier, likewise throughout the thirty-two seasons of my active horsemanship with that super showman, Col. W. F. Cody, and in successfully contesting against picked cavalrymen of all nations of the world. Meeting those riders in Vermont put a little more color in the dye. I enjoyed to the utmost being with them if only for a short while, and I hope to meet many new riders in addition to this friendly group in such splendid Association. I know of no better way of spending a vacation than on the bridle trails in the Green hills of Vermont.

Editor's Comment: More information on this ride is in Chapter 10.

Author Information:

For sixty-sixty years, Janice Ladendorf has been working with horses. Unlike most amateurs, she has trained her own hunters and dressage horses. One of her interests is the history of equitation and how its principles have been applied through the centuries in various equestrian disciplines.

The University of Minnesota awarded her a B.A. magna cum laude with a major in history and a M.A. in library science. Her further studies have focused on communication theories and animal behavior. They have helped her understand equine behavior, especially as relates to communication between humans and horses.

In her books and numerous articles, she has advocated using humane training methods to build a partnership with your horse. Currently she has four other books and a DVD in print. All of her books are available from Amazon and other on line retail outlets in both paperback and e-book formats.

A Marvelous Mustang is a nonfictional memoir told from the viewpoint of her Spanish Mustang. As a supplement to this memoir, she has recently produced a DVD from her video records.

Quest for the Silver Mustang is historical fiction. Set in 1832, it is the story of a girl's search for the horse of her dreams.

Human Views and Equine Behavior explains how new scientific ideas can be used to explain equine behavior and the interaction between humans and horses. All these ideas and the related training techniques have been evaluated as she worked with her own horses and observed others working with their horses.

Spanish Horsemen and Horses in the New World is volume 1 of Horses from History. It explains the contributions of the Mexican vaqueros to western horsemanship and the origin of the horses they rode. The horses brought here by the Conquistadors became the root stock for many new breeds both here and in Latin America. One of these breeds was what Frank T. Hopkins called American Mustangs or Indian ponies or Old Spanish.

Janice Ladendorf has been a research librarian, an inventory analyst, and an accountant. She lives in St. Paul, Minnesota. For more information about her published work, you may visit her website, www.jladendorf.com.

Acknowledgments:

Researching the material for her new book about Frank T. Hopkins book would not have been possible without the cooperation of the organizations and people listed below.

Library Services provided by Dakota County, Minnesota.

American Heritage Center, University of Wyoming. Their archives include the Frank Hopkins Papers. Mack Brislawn kindly copied them for me.

Paul Carnahan, Librarian, Leahy Library, Vermont Historical Society.

McCracken Research Library, Buffalo Bill Center of the West Cody, Wyoming.

Fort Laramie Historic Site Records, Wyoming.

Peter Shrake, Circus World, Baraboo, Wisconsin.

Wyoming Livestock Board, Brand History, Cokeville, Wyoming.

Executive Director, Green Mountain Horse Association for permission to use and reprint articles from the Vermont Horse and Bridle Trail Bulletin

Wyoming State Museum, Dept of State Parks and Cultural Resources, State of Wyoming, Cheyenne, Wyoming for permission to use their photograph of the Hopkins parade bridle held in their collection.

Made in the USA
Las Vegas, NV
14 June 2021